TENNESSEE PATRIOT

TENNESSEE PATRIOT

THE NAVAL CAREER OF **VICE ADMIRAL WILLIAM P. LAWRENCE**, U.S. NAVY

WILLIAM P. LAWRENCE AND ROSARIO RAUSA

NAVAL INSTITUTE PRESS
Annapolis, Maryland

Naval Institute Press
291 Wood Road
Annapolis, MD 21402

Library of Congress Cataloging-in-Publication Data

Lawrence, William P.
  Tennessee patriot: the naval career of Vice Admiral William P. Lawrence, U.S. Navy
/ William P. Lawrence with Rosario Rausa.
     p. cm.
  Includes index.
  ISBN 1-59114-700-X (alk. paper)
  1. Lawrence, William P. 2. Admirals—United States—Biography. 3. United States.
Navy—Biography. 4. United States—History, Naval--20th century. 5. United States
Naval Academy—Biography. 6. Fighter pilots—United States—Biography. 7. Viet-
nam War, 1961-1975—Prisoners and prisons, American. 8. Prisoners of war—
United States—Biography. 9. Prisoners of war—Vietnam—Biography. 10. Nashville
(Tenn.)—Biography. I. Rausa, Rosario. II. Title.
  E840.5.L39A3 2006
  359.0092--dc22
  [B]

                                                      2006019674

Printed in the United States of America on acid-free paper ∞

13 12 11 10 09 08 07 06   9 8 7 6 5 4 3 2
First printing

CONTENTS

FOREWORD

BILL LAWRENCE LAY ON HIS BACK on a concrete slab in a seven-foot-square prison cell. His ankles were secured to the slab by iron cuffs, severely limiting any motion. He had been caught tap-coding a message to fellow captives in the notorious Hanoi Hilton prison compound in North Vietnam and was committed to solitary confinement. Any form of conversation among prisoners of war (POWs) was a supreme violation of camp regulations, but Lawrence was a relentless advocate of communication as a way of sustaining positive morale within the growing cadre of captured American servicemen.

It was summer and the temperature had soared above 100 degrees, making the crude chamber unbearably hot. To avoid aggravating the blistering sores that covered Bill Lawrence's body, he remained motionless. He was in immense pain, not only from the harsh heat but also from injuries stemming from daily torture sessions.

He played mind games, hoping his imagination would serve as a buffer against pain. He built houses in his mind. He worked out math problems. He composed poetry in his mind. This helped, but only up to a point. He was on the threshold of despair, and despair under brutal conditions of incarceration that could lead to death.

A small, rectangular open space high up on the opposite wall allowed him to look out of his cell. Using every ounce of his waning strength, he began a crude sit-up. Bill remembered, "I stretched as far to my side as I could and I saw through the opening the top of the courtyard wall. Then, above the wall, I saw a patch of blue sky. In one beautiful instant, I felt cool water washing over every part of my body and God's hand on my head. At that moment I knew I would be able to prevail, that I would be OK."

Every day of his almost six-year confinement he lived the words of Winston Churchill: "NEVER GIVE IN. NEVER GIVE IN. NEVER, NEVER, NEVER!"

Bill Lawrence surely prevailed as he had his whole life, from boyhood in his beloved Nashville, through a remarkable military career and beyond. His is a great and enlightening American story, one of triumphs and tragedies, devotion to family, and dedication to the United States Navy. During his lifetime, he knew the highest of the highs and the lowest of the lows.

Bill and I were midshipmen two classes apart at the Naval Academy, and it was my privilege to work with him in developing the Academy's "Honor Concept," which is in force today at Annapolis. We were close friends ever since. Even in our student days it was clear to me that Bill was marked for success: he possessed all the necessary ingredients of intelligence, physical strength, compassion for others, a steady demeanor, and an unyielding desire to succeed and to do the right thing. Then, and throughout his remarkable thirty-seven-year career in uniform, he was a tougher-than-steel leader.

Not only was he ranked number eight academically out of his class of 724, but he also was Class President, was Commander of the Brigade of Midshipmen, and lettered in three varsity sports. After graduation he won his gold wings as a naval aviator. Following his first tour of duty, he attended the Naval Test Pilot School, graduating number one in his class.

He worked hard, married, and had three children along the way. He earned accolades for his performance as a naval officer whatever the assignment, whether it was as a junior officer flying jets from a carrier, Superintendent of the U. S. Naval Academy, Commander of the U. S. Third Fleet, or Chief of Naval Personnel.

Unfortunately, Bill Lawrence was forced to retire from active duty as a result of illness when he was about to earn the fourth star of a full admiral. In retirement he suffered from melancholia, a stroke, and other maladies. Thankfully, his wife, the marvelous Diane, continued her faithful vigil alongside this wonderful man. Her epilogue to this book provides a fascinating, if sometimes heartbreaking account of the sickness that drastically changed life for both Bill and Diane.

Happily, their children personify individual success stories: Bill Jr. is an Information Specialist Engineer and a published author on the subject. Frederick is a Specialist Engineer at Electric Boat Division, General Dynamics Corporation. Laurie is a highly regarded physician and assistant professor of emergency medicine at Vanderbilt University Medical Center.

Navy Captain Wendy Lawrence is a naval aviator and astronaut with over 1,200 hours in space.

Tennessee Patriot: The Naval Career of Vice Admiral William P. Lawrence, U.S. Navy gives exemplary lessons for all of us, young and old. They are not limited to the keys of a successful military career. Indeed, inherent in this volume is the portrayal of the stepping stones to a fully rewarding life with all of its downs and all of its ups.

I am honored to have been associated with Bill Lawrence, the embodiment of an AMERICAN HERO OF HEROES!

H. Ross Perot

PROLOGUE

I WAS AT 40,000 FEET in a cloudless blue sky over the sun-baked desert, traveling at .9 Mach number in a single-seat jet, sleek as a spear. I was twenty-eight years old, a Navy lieutenant, a fighter pilot flying from aircraft carriers, and now a test pilot, having graduated from the Navy's Test Pilot School at Patuxent River, Maryland. Streaming along, high over the earth, alone in the cockpit, feeling the immense power of the F8U-3, I thought, "It just can't get any better than this."

I lit the afterburner in the Crusader, executed a zero G pushover, and accelerated to transonic airspeed. I leveled at 35,000 feet, still accelerating, aimed at the dry lake bed at Edwards Air Force Base. I felt like I was speeding down a highway with no traffic in sight. I became transfixed, observing the airspeed indicator and fuel flow increasing at a prodigious rate. I was surprised by how hot it became in the cockpit because of the aerodynamic heating. I had to constantly reduce my temperature thermostat as the acceleration run progressed. I will never forget the feeling of seeing my airspeed indicator reading one thousand knots as I went through Mach 1, racing toward Mach 2.

There were no surprises as the aircraft and I rode through Mach 2 uneventfully. Nearing Mach 2.1, I remembered the admonition by Vought engineers to retard the throttle until an engine bleed valve opened before coming out of afterburner. Otherwise, the engine could encounter severe compressor stalls, which the Vought pilots told me sounded like artillery shells exploding next to the cockpit.

I brought the throttle back and shut down the afterburner with no adverse engine reaction. The immediate deceleration thrust me against my shoulder straps, similar to a carrier landing. With a feeling of exhilaration, I returned to base and made a couple of touch-and-go landings before returning to the flight line.

I derived heavy satisfaction from this successful test flight, but it was not until I was back at Pax River several months later, discussing the matter with other pilots, that it dawned on me that I realized I was the first naval aviator to fly Mach 2 in a Navy airplane. What a thrill to be a Navy test pilot during the 1950s!

This was but one of the many rewarding events I was so fortunate to experience as a U.S. naval officer. With this book I hope to share the multitude of experiences, good and bad, but mostly good, that life has provided.

William P. Lawrence
Crownsville, Maryland, 2005

ACKNOWLEDGMENTS

The authors wish to profoundly thank and acknowledge the following people for their invaluable assistance in writing this book: Paul Stillwell, historian, whose oral history of Vice Admiral William Lawrence was of immense value throughout the project and, alphabetically: Frank A. Aukofer; Lieutenant Tiffani E. Bell, United States Navy (USN); Captain Roland Brandquist, USN (Ret.); Daniel B. Bozung; Mr. and Mrs. Erwin T. Buckemaier; Diane L. Clingerman; Captain Raymond P. Donahue, USN (Ret.); Lieutenant Commander Harry Errington, USN (Ret.); Captain Jack Fellowes, USN (Ret.); Captain Barbara Ford, USNR; Guy Hanson; Katherine G. Jakobsen; Laurie M. Lawrence, MD; Captain Wendy B. Lawrence, USN; Captain John P. Leahy, USN (Ret.); Ray Madona; Rear Admiral Kathleen L. Martin, USN (Ret.); William C. Miller, PhD; Fleet Master Chief James R. Mitchell, USN (Ret.); Captain Kathleen D. Morrison, USN (Ret.); H. Ross Perot; Peter V. Rabins, MD; Esther N. Rauch; Frederick W. Rauch; Marguerite C. Rauch; Lieutenant David A. Schwind, USN; Captain E. A. Shuman, III, USN (Ret.); William L. Stine; Colonel David A. Vetter, USMC (Ret.); and Captain Edward C. Wallace, USN (Ret.); Mrs. Lynne T. Waters.

ACRONYMS

AAA	(triple A) antiaircraft artillery
ANA	Association of Naval Aviation
AOC	Aviation Officer Candidate
ASW	antisubmarine warfare
AT	aviation electronic technician
BDA	bomb damage assessment
CAG	carrier air group commander
CBU	cluster bomb units
COD	Carrier On-board Delivery
CNO	chief of naval operations
CNP	chief of naval personnel
CO	commanding officer
CVL	light cruiser
DACOWITS	Defense Advisory Committee on Women in the Service
DME	distance-measuring equipment
DMZ	demilitarized zone
EMC	electronic countermeasures
FRS	Fleet Replacement Squadron
GAO	Government Accounting Office
HARM	High Speed Anti-Radiation Missile
JAG	Judge Advocate General
LDO	limited-duty officer
LSO	landing signal officer
MIA	missing in action
NAMI	Naval Aviation Medical Institute
NASA	National Aeronautics and Space Administration

NATOPS	Naval Air Training and Operating Procedures
NFO	naval flight officer
NIS	Naval Investigative Service
NROTC	Naval Reserve Officer Training Corps
OD	officer of the day
OOD	officer of the deck
POW	prisoner of war
PAO	public affairs officer
PPBS	Planning, Programming, and Budgeting System
PRF	pulse rate frequency
RAG	Replacement Air Group
RIMPAC	Rim of the Pacific
RIO	radar intercept officer
ROTC	Reserve Officers Training Corps
RPM	revolutions per minute
SAM	surface-to-air missile
SDO	squadron duty officer
SERE	survival, escape, resistance, and evasion
SOA	speed of advance
SSBN	ballistic missile submarine
TACAN	Tactical Air Navigation
TLAM	Tactical Land Attack Missile
TOT	time on target
TPS	Test Pilot School
UHF	ultrahigh frequency
USN	United States Navy
USNA	United States Naval Academy
VAST	Versatile Avionics Systems Test
VSTOL	vertical, short takeoff and landing aircraft
XO	executive officer

TENNESSEE PATRIOT

Chapter One

NASHVILLE

"Young man, you never ask to be removed from a game.
The only time you come out of a game is on a stretcher!"

I WAS BORN DURING THE DEPRESSION to a stern taskmaster of a father and a compassionate and charming mother. They were loving parents, and I had a magical youth. My father, Robert Lawrence, was gainfully employed, our schoolteachers were tough but fair, I had three great brothers, and we played sports year round—football, basketball, and baseball. I was the youngest until Tommy came along thirteen years after me. Bobby was the oldest and Eddie was the next before yours truly. Our mother, Tennessee Brewer, who was known as Tennie, was the embodiment of southern gentility.

Our family even had a car, relatively uncommon at the time. Segregation was fully entrenched long before my birth date, January 13, 1930, but in my youthful innocence I was unaware of any segregation problems.

In those days just about every school in the south posted two pictures on the wall—one of Robert E. Lee, the other of George Washington. There was no sign of Abraham Lincoln. It wasn't until I reached my adult years that I realized Lincoln was a great American. He just wasn't discussed in my southern school.

I've always had an appreciation of history, and I like knowing about my ancestors. They hailed primarily from the British Isles and were various combinations of Scots, Irish, English, and Welsh. My maternal great-great-grandfather served in the Revolutionary War, following which he was awarded land in what was then known as the new territories. He settled in an area now known as Tennessee (which became a state in 1796), was a farmer and a politician, ultimately becoming speaker of the state senate. Sterling Brewer Junior, my great-grandfather, was a Methodist minister and educator. My grandfather, another Sterling Brewer, was a schoolteacher and writer.

On my father's side, my great-great-grandfather also was a Revolutionary War veteran and received a land grant in the Tennessee region. He was a sheriff and a justice of the peace. His son, my paternal great-grandfather, was a successful traveling salesman of dry goods, did considerable public service work, and settled in Nashville in the early 1900s.

My father, Robert Lawrence, was the first of the Lawrence family to go to college, earning an engineering degree from Vanderbilt University in 1925. He excelled as a lineman on the school's nationally ranked football team and played varsity baseball as well.

In those days the goal posts were situated on the goal line. When Vanderbilt played Michigan, my dad, nicknamed "Fatty," placed his feet against the posts for leverage and was instrumental in preventing Michigan from scoring from the one-yard line. Both teams were undefeated that year and tied for what was then the "national championship."

For forty-five years, Dad was the director of water and sewage services for the city of Nashville. He was the first to fluoridate public water. We lived in a large home in Nashville, which had a basement apartment for my grandfather, who had been widowed at thirty-six when his wife died in the influenza epidemic of 1918. His father, who was a teenager during the Civil War, passed on fascinating stories about his experiences. In turn, my grandfather captivated me with these tales, particularly those about the federal troops under Ulysses Grant and their devastating occupation of Nashville and other parts of Tennessee during the war.

My grandfather also introduced me to the legend of Sam Davis from Smyrna, Tennessee, a Confederate soldier who, as a scout, was tasked with contacting spies behind enemy lines and passing on critical intelligence. Davis worked in civilian clothes, which, under the articles of war, meant that, if caught, he was subject to execution rather than imprisonment. Davis was soon captured but refused to divulge the names of his contacts. Before the rope encircled his neck, he told the surrounding onlookers, "If I had a thousand lives to live, I would give them all before I would betray a friend." Sam Davis became one of my early heroes.

I remember seeing the Confederate flag flying alongside the American and Tennessee state flags. The war produced such hostility against the North that my great-grandfather Lawrence refused until his dying day to speak to a neighbor whose family, he believed, consorted with the Yankees (federals as they were called). A bit of prejudiced stubbornness that pervaded many southern minds.

We had a wonderful African-American lady named Mary Watkins, a single mother, who cleaned house and baby-sat for us. She earned a seemingly pitiful dollar a day plus bus fare, but she was invariably cheerful and I liked her a great deal. I certainly realized that prejudice against blacks existed in full force back then, but I was young and not inclined to challenge it, because, to me, the blacks seemed like a contented group of fine people. My brothers used to get angry with me when we rode the bus because I usually moved to the back where the blacks sat. I played often with black boys and had no real sense of the intrinsic evils of segregation.

Mary occasionally took me to the ghetto shanties on the northern side of town where she lived. Despite the blatant poverty of her neighborhood, I didn't witness anger or bitterness among the blacks who resided there. Instead, I remember laughter and a kind of resignation to the way they were required to live.

Another African-American who later came into my life was Frank Roberts. He did yard work for us, and every time we met he greeted me with a hearty, "Great to see you, Bill!" Toes showed through his shoes, his clothes were often ragged, money he earned for the day was folded and tucked into his socks. I always drove him into town, where he would ask me to stop for cigarettes and beer, which he would take as a gift to a friend, where, in exchange, he would spend the night, usually on the floor. Frank was constantly whistling. He was an enigma to me. He was unmarried, homeless, and came across as a man with no complaints.

Dad was a strong willed man. He respected blacks, made a concerted effort to employ them, and headed food-basket programs at holiday times.

We were Methodists and for more than forty years occupied the same pew in the Belmont Methodist Church. My parents were strongly religious, and I never saw either my mother or father consume an alcoholic drink. Church and Sunday school were mandatory, and I learned all the major Bible stories by heart.

Dad was an avid reader and subscribed to many magazines. I enjoyed *Life* and read it cover to cover, especially during the World War II years. I savored stories of land, sea, and sky battles.

Though his duties kept him busy, Dad managed to attend most of our football, basketball, and baseball games, whether played at home or away. He did miss one away football game, however. During the game, I suffered a painful deep thigh bruise and asked to be removed from the game. That evening when I returned home and gave Dad a report on the contest and my injury, he glowered and said, "Young man, the only time you come out of game is on a stretcher."

While at bat during a baseball game, I was hit on the head by an erratically pitched ball and temporarily knocked unconscious. When I awoke, I felt pretty normal and went home with my parents, who carefully observed me until the next morning. While lying in bed with my father at my side, Dad said, "When that ball struck you on the head, it bounced well into left field. That was the longest ball you hit all day." Vintage Dad.

My mother was as compassionate as she was strong. She was not vocal or strident in any way and had a natural facility for attracting friends. She had a wonderful sense of calm, was very popular, served several terms as president of the Parent Teacher Association, and was president of the popular woman's club. She led by example, a contrasting style to my father, who was usually inclined to declare, "Listen to me. This is the way it's going to be!" He could be bellicose, that's for sure. Menial chores around the house weren't included in his list of responsibilities. As the head of household, he expected his wife to act in a relatively subservient fashion. I remember my Dad in his seventies making coffee, considering that small chore quite an accomplishment.

Dad could be rough on Mom. One day, when I was sixteen and he had spoken harshly to my mother, I confronted him and said, "You shouldn't treat Mom like that." He shot me an imperious look, which clearly told me I was out of line.

Yet, Dad demonstrated great respect for my mother. Each knew their roles and carried them out with style and conviction. They also had an unwavering love for each other despite Dad's often-overbearing manner.

For three years at West End High School I was in the Army Reserve Officers Training Corps (ROTC) program and was our unit's commanding officer in my senior year. The war was under way, and this early training would help us adjust to military life should we go into one of the services. We had a wonderful old sergeant as an instructor who regaled us with tales from his combat days. His stories served to perpetuate my growing fascination with military duty, not necessarily as a career, but at least for a limited period during which I expected to have adventures and an opportunity to prove my mettle. Most of my schoolmates said they felt the same way.

With respect to my brothers, I revered Bobby, but Eddie and I battled each other with regularity. When I was able to land a punch on his nose, it bled easily. He would wrestle me onto my back so that his blood purposely fell into my face. Take that, Billy!

Eddie could sleep like a baby. We went to a movie one night and Eddie fell asleep. I couldn't wake him after the film, so I went home and informed my parents. My father ordered me to return to the theater and retrieve my brother, who was still asleep in his seat. I pounded on him until he finally awoke. He was groggy when I finally got him home, and I vowed right then I'd never go to the movies with Eddie again.

I loved to read history and became a fledgling student of the Civil War, developing deep admiration for Abraham Lincoln. I was especially intrigued by Ulysses S. Grant, because of his early campaign in the West during the war.

Later on in life I concluded that few things have been more valuable to me during my military career than knowledge of history, particularly military history. I still have a paper I wrote when I was in the eighth grade of my version of the history of the United States, recounting what I thought were the key events that formed our nation. One chapter was entitled, "The Contribution of Women." The lead sentence read, "Women have never received the recognition that they deserve for their contribution to U.S. history." At the time I certainly didn't consider this a visionary statement.

Years later, as superintendent of the Naval Academy and as chief of naval personnel, some opponents of women serving in the military, particularly in combat roles, believed I was an advocate for women primarily because my daughter, Wendy, was an Academy graduate (1981) and a naval aviator. Truth is, I was an advocate for women in the military, in whatever capacity, long before that.

With respect to history, I didn't realize it in eighth grade, but years later I became convinced there was no profession where the lessons of the past are as relevant as they are in the military. I called on my knowledge of history many times during my career to help me make vital, often rapid decisions. As commander of the Third Fleet, to which I refer later in this story, my longtime knowledge of the actions of Admiral "Bull" Halsey convinced me (against the advice of my staff) to sortie ships and aircraft from Ford Island in the questionable threat of the typhoon of November 1982.

Merging with my early interest in military history was a compelling inclination toward pursuing the technical field, particularly engineering. This probably derived from my wanting to imitate Dad, himself an engineer. He talked to me about West Point and Annapolis, both schools with outstanding engineering curricula—and great athletic programs. The price was right as well. If I could make it, my education would be paid for by the federal government in exchange for a few years of active duty. Although I took a long look at West Point, the Navy seemed to be a better fit.

It was also ingrained in me, however subtly, that public service promised to be a gratifying, productive way to spend my life. My dad and most family members from both the Brewer and Lawrence households agreed.

While such inclinations worked their way around the edges of my mind, I must admit my most acute interest in my youth was sports. I followed the college teams around the country and especially remember the excitement of listening to the annual Army versus Navy football game on the radio. I also attended most home games at Vanderbilt.

My time playing football, basketball, and baseball remains priceless to me, but young ladies were also of notable interest. Although I didn't have a lot of time between Army ROTC, athletics, and studies, I dated some wonderful girls during my high school years.

I made the all-state team in basketball and was all-city in football. At five feet nine and 170 pounds, I was a less than imposing figure when it came to athletics. However, I was strong, quick, and competitive. I worked hard at becoming mentally tough, and I tried to compensate for my lack of size with a never-quit attitude and an ability to think fast under pressure.

Not only did we have terrific teachers in the classroom, but our coaches also were exceptional. One who had extraordinary influence in my development as a youth was Emmett T. Strickland. He coached football, basketball, and baseball and embodied fully all those qualities of leadership, knowledge, and skill that drew unyielding respect. We really looked up to him. Our basketball team was so grateful for his guidance and instructional skills that years later we presented him a citation expressing appreciation for all he did for us. All living members of the basketball teams he coached signed the document.

It read, "You placed a key block in that wonderful foundation of qualities and values that we formed growing up in Nashville, Tennessee. You inspired us more than you coached us. You always led us and never pushed us. You taught us that mutual love and respect among team members would win more games than our playing ability. We also learned from you the famous maxim from Napoleon that in contests between human beings, the mental is to the physical as three is to one. Most importantly, you were a role model who provided us a daily example as to how we should strive to conduct our own lives." Wouldn't anyone cherish having those words said about them?

Emmett, my teachers, my parents, the sergeant in our ROTC unit—
these were heroes, people I personally knew and revered as I grew up. Beyond
measure, they influenced my development. The heroes I didn't know were
the great athletes who I read about or listened to as they played their games
"over the radio." But more important than all of these were the men—and
women—who were fighting the war on the high seas, in the skies of combat,
and on the dangerous ground of distant lands. I was blessed with the knowledge of great human beings to try to emulate.

I count my fortune every day for having grown up under the positive
influence of teachers, coaches, and family. All cared deeply about me as well
as about the multitude of young people entrusted to their care.

Chapter Two

ANNAPOLIS

*Unfortunately, an unfurled roll of toilet paper scored
a direct hit on the head of the Governor's wife.*

ONCE I GOT TO THINKING about the Naval Academy or West Point, the
notion of becoming a military officer slowly but surely eclipsed interest in
any other advanced-learning institutions. Fortunately, I had good grades in
West End High School, was valedictorian, and showed promise of an athlete capable of competing at the next level. Affiliation with the ROTC unit
also served me well in the immensely competitive arena that is the prelude
to acceptance at one of the military academies. By the time I was a senior, I
had been offered an academic scholarship at Yale. This presented a dilemma,
because I knew of Yale's outstanding reputation, but I continued to have
service academy aspirations.

A prominent Yale graduate in Nashville who encouraged qualified young
people to consider attending this prestigious Ivy League school had sent
information on me to Yale. I was offered an academic scholarship, with the
understanding that I would try out for the football team, then coached by
the legendary Herman Hickman.

Still, I had the sense that the family tradition of public service, my
affiliation with West End's Army ROTC program, and the patriotic fervor
engendered by World War II, as well as the chance to participate in athletics
beyond high school, continued to channel my interests toward the service
academies.

Unfortunately, Congressman Percy Priest of our district did not have any
appointments to the academies available. My father had been in contact with
Rip Miller, the assistant athletic director at Annapolis, who also served as a
recruiter for the football team. Miller had been one of the legendary "Seven
Mules," the linemen on one of Knute Rockney's great football teams at Notre
Dame in the 1920s. In the 1940s he was interested in me and by a fortunate,

if sad, turn of fate was able to gain an appointment to the Academy for me. The government scholarship would cover education costs in exchange for my commitment to serve in the Navy for three years following graduation

Pres. Franklin Roosevelt died in April 1945—which was the sad turn of fate—and, with the elevation of Harry S. Truman to the presidency, Tennessee senator K. D. McKellar became president pro tem of the senate. Rip Miller learned that Senator McKellar had overlooked appointing a candidate to the Naval Academy. Miller made some phone calls for me, and luckily I was given the appointment. I was elated and charged with excitement at the prospects of attending this great school.

Annapolis is a lovely Maryland city, capital of the state, and enriched with a long history. Its quaint and narrow cobblestone streets and the wood-frame homes that parallel them have stood the test of time. St. John's College, which borders the Naval Academy, is America's third-oldest institution of higher learning, and among its illustrious graduates is Francis Scott Key, who penned "The Star Spangled Banner." City Dock in Annapolis is the site where Kunta Kinte, on board the slave ship, the *Lod Ligonier,* came to this land. Author Alex Haley, a former Coast Guard chief petty officer, took up the story of Kunta Kinte and wrote the best-seller, *Roots,* about this noble man and his descendants. The homes of all four of the men from Maryland who signed the Declaration of Independence are in Annapolis and are in various states of preservation.

I mention this only to note that for all we, the incoming plebes of U.S. Naval Academy Class of 1951, knew, Annapolis was on another planet. We did not see much of the town that first year. We were "contained" not by walls so much as by a regimen that dictated virtually every minute of our lives, twenty-four hours a day, seven days a week. We knew this would be the case before we arrived on the banks of the Severn River, bordering the school. Yet, it was still a shocking transformation from the generally relaxed ambiance of Nashville to the sit-up-straight world of a military school.

In those days there were about two hundred midshipmen in each of twenty-four companies. I was in Company Three. Although I plunged into the disciplined routine with great enthusiasm, I realized right off the bat that the Academy was no West End High. I might have been a big fish in a small pond in Nashville, but at Annapolis as a plebe, I was just another fish in one huge lake. Because just about every one of us felt the same, we all had something in common—a diminished image of ourselves that tended to suppress but not subdue our egos while intensifying our determination to succeed.

Because I played football, among my initial experiences at Annapolis were the tortuous "two-a-days." From 0900 to 1100 in the morning and from 1400 to 1600 in the afternoon for two straight weeks before classes commenced, we trained for the coming gridiron season. These sessions were conducted in the oppressive heat of summertime Maryland. They were exhausting and painful in a way only those who have experienced the sport can fully understand. We sprinted, we blocked, we sprinted some more, we did calisthenics, we tackled dummies, we tackled each other, we scrimmaged, we learned plays, we were pushed to our physical limits. Mealtimes were all-too-brief interludes, and taps couldn't come soon enough. At night, drained of energy and despite suffering from swollen feet and an assortment of bumps and bruises, we slept soundly.

Reveille came too early, but the routine continued, and by the end of the three weeks, as the youngsters (sophomores), second classmen (juniors), and first classmen (seniors) arrived from summer training deployments for the beginning of the new school year, we were elated, because it meant two-a-days were over and one-a-days would begin.

The experience of two-a-days, ironically, was to prove invaluable to me during my incarceration in North Vietnam twenty years later.

Classes commenced and I found myself enjoying them from the outset. I have been blessed with an excellent memory, which enhanced my ability to absorb knowledge, and I sought every morsel of it I could. We had quizzes regularly, and the key to passing them was memorization. There are those in the academic community who criticize this "memorize and quiz" process as inhibitive to genuine learning. They believe this concentration on answering quiz questions rather than absorbing the subject in a more all-encompassing manner is self-defeating. To me, preparing for the quizzes instilled an "intellectual discipline" in our routine, while at the same time compelling us to acquire the knowledge.

I liked the courses at the Academy for their variety. They included the humanities, a particularly enlightening course on the U.S. Constitution, another memorable one on the diplomatic history of the United States, and what I call the "trade-school" classes: ordnance, gunnery, and, especially, marine engineering, which included the basics of boiler design and function. Our teachers and professors were excellent. Most were civilians; the remainder were active-duty officers assigned to the Academy.

We had little time for frivolity or relaxing, elemental in the introduction to military life. We marched everywhere, had to keep our uniforms sharp and our shoes polished to a luster, and were required to hit the books at designated study times as well as during every spare moment we could contrive during the day.

I was lucky, because I had athletics to break the tedium. Midshipmen spent plenty of time on physical fitness through intramural sports. But as a member of the football, basketball, and baseball teams, I got to travel, usually by train or bus, to other universities and colleges for our games. We also had our own training table, where we consumed a hefty forty-four hundred calories a day per man. Apart from this, athletes were totally integrated into the student body, except for my sophomore year, when the new football coach, George Sauer, got approval to bunk us in a separate section of Bancroft Hall. This practice was abolished the next year when senior officials saw little benefit to the arrangement.

The food at the Academy was marvelous. The Academy had its own dairy, which produced the milk we drank and the ice cream we devoured. The ice cream was frozen hard in large stainless steel bowls, which were placed in the middle of the rectangular dining tables. It had softened just right by the time we were ready to eat and was richer and creamier than any I ever had in Nashville.

Playing on the football team earned me no favors. The marine engineering course required us to make detailed drawings of boiler construction, and I was pretty good at this until I broke my left wrist during practice. Although I'm right-handed, this injury impaired my ability to work a T-square and to draw straight lines. This didn't seem to matter to my instructor, and my grades in this course plummeted. I never did learn whether or not that professor was a football fan.

I'll never forget the Army-Navy game of 1948. Army was an overwhelming favorite, but we played them to a stunning 21-21 tie. We celebrated at a postgame dinner with guests at the Bellevue-Stratford Hotel in Philadelphia, where the game was played. A teammate, Bob Rennaman, had arranged a blind date for me. As my date and I walked in, we were greeted by waiters with trays of drinks on them, drinks that I later learned were old-fashioneds. Obviously more experienced at this sort of thing than I, my date plucked one off the tray and sipped away.

Before this evening, I had never consumed an ounce of alcohol. The euphoria of our performance in the game prompted me to follow her lead, so I took a glass as well, sipped the drink, and hated the taste. We sat down to a steak dinner, and after twenty minutes I became ill, never having felt so sick in my life. I abandoned this lovely lady as Bob Rennaman escorted me to my room, where I spent the next hour throwing up. Our evening did not blossom into a romance.

The superintendent of the Naval Academy my first three years was Adm. James Holloway Jr., a highly respected and well-liked leader. His principal claim to fame was authorship of the "Holloway Program," which rapidly expanded the Naval Reserve Officer Training Corps (NROTC) in colleges and universities across the land. He brought a liberal mind-set to the school. He allowed first classmen every other weekend off, they could store civilian clothes in their rooms and wear them on the free weekends, they didn't have to march to class, and taps was at 2300 (11 PM), an hour later than for the rest of the brigade.

In those days, varsity athletes, especially football players, were respected to a degree you're unlikely to find at the Academy today. They came to be recognized as leaders, in part because of their prowess on the playing fields and their visibility on campus. In most cases these were academically sharp and dedicated midshipmen, deserving of the respect accorded them. Although I was not a star like our great quarterback, Reaves Baysinger, I was his backup (and later played halfback), and my participation on the basketball and baseball teams gave me visibility I might not have had otherwise.

My ROTC training at West End High contributed to my ability to adapt to life at the Academy. I gained a certain degree of popularity and was elected president of my class in both my junior and senior years.

The Academy occasionally held social activities. Although we didn't need to be reminded that members of the opposite sex existed, there was a heightened awareness of them when they graced the campus for dances and football weekends. I had dated in Nashville, had a sweetheart now and then, and was no stranger to tuxedoes and pretty girls in long gowns. But at Annapolis, thoughts of romance were held in abeyance as we traveled the hurdles and mazes of the educational process at a military institution, especially in the first two years.

In my junior year, I invited a girlfriend from Nashville, Betty Jones, to the June Week graduation festivities. She stayed with the family of an Academy officer, Cdr. Dusty Dornin. We had a terrific time and have remained friends through the years.

Time passed rapidly because of our round-the-clock schedules, and when Christmas came, the two-week's leave we were accorded was exceedingly welcome. During the summer, we also earned a month off. The balance of the summer nonacademic interlude was spent on a variety of duty assignments in the fleet.

On my first summer "temporary-duty assignment," I traveled with the football team when we were assigned as a unit to the USS *Coral Sea* (CVB-43) in the Mediterranean. The ship was commanded by Capt. A. P. Storrs (USNA 1925). Storrs, a legend in naval aviation, had been one of the pilots on a stunt team called the Sea Hawks, predecessor to the Blue Angels, the Navy's Flight Demonstration Squadron. Coach Sauer wanted us to work together as much as possible, knowing our nonfootball commitments were considerable and left little time for extra training. We conducted drills on the flight deck between flight operations, and at every port call, we found a soccer field or stadium and trained under the tutelage of Assistant Coach Vic Bradford, who had starred on the 1938 Alabama team that went to the Rose Bowl.

Playing football in the sunny Med was wonderful, as was shore leave in the south of France. It gave us a chance to spend our lofty pay of three dollars a month. I was inspired by watching the pilots launch and recover on the flattop and by talking to the flight crews in the ready rooms. I had read much about the exploits of naval aviators during the war and held these men in awe, especially those who flew from the carriers. I was also interested in submarine duty, one of the three prongs of the Navy triad, the other two being surface ships and aviation. This interest was rooted in the influence of two World War II submarine heroes, Cdr. Dusty Dornin and Cdr. K. G. Schacht, who were members of the athletic department and who endeavored to steer me in the direction of the subsurface Navy. Schacht had been a prisoner of war for three years in World War II.

In my youngster summer, we spent three weeks on a light cruiser (CVL), or light carrier, and in my senior year I deployed aboard the battleship USS *Missouri*. These "cruises" were rewarding, because we gained hands-on experience standing watches, observing the operational Navy at work, and whetting our appetites for the adventures that awaited us upon graduation.

Sports and studies were my life at the Academy. I played on the plebe football team the first year and then went up to the varsity. I joined the varsity basketball and baseball teams in my sophomore year and played under two terrific coaches, Ben Carnavale and Max Bishop, respectively. We had a colorful trainer named "Doc" Snyder, a retired chief corpsman.

I wasn't a star at Navy, but I never missed a practice regardless of injuries, and I considered myself a solid competitor. I was exhilarated just to be able to play at a level of competition that included games against not only Army, but also Notre Dame, California, Southern California, Missouri, and Duke.

I was relatively short but pretty fast and at one point led the basketball team in field goal percentage with a 35 percent average. That figure would bring laughter nowadays, because to be really on the mark, you've got to shoot closer to 50 percent today. However, back in the 1950s, our tallest player was only six foot three.

During my second year at Annapolis, I got to know the assistant athletic director, Commander Dornin, a bona fide war hero. He was from the Class of 1935 and had played end on the football team. He had commanded the submarine USS *Trigger*, which sank more enemy tonnage in the Pacific than any other U.S. submarine. He and his family lived in quarters at the Academy, and I spent much of what free time I had at their home.

Dornin was but one of many impressive combat veterans who were in our midst on the Academy staff either as professors or in some administrative capacity.

We had a company officer, Marine Major Antonelli, who was among several Marine Corps heroes on campus. He was one tough cookie. The story goes that he had jumped into a foxhole on one of the Pacific islands, grabbed two Japanese soldiers, banged their heads together, and captured them. When we'd see him walking down the hall, a palpable sense of trepidation came over us as we visualized the major in that foxhole.

For the most part, these heroic men were approachable, modest officers who had measured up to the extremes of combat and prevailed. We revered them for their valor and knew, in our hearts, that there was a good chance we might have to replicate them in the inevitable armed conflicts to come, such as the one brewing in Korea in 1950. They were role models and icons of the highest order, just as my teachers and coaches at West End High were. I was grateful for having been exposed to them at a relatively young age.

Capt. John L. "Jack" Chew was the executive officer of Bancroft Hall, a position that was the precursor to the deputy commandant billet today.

His predecessor was Capt. Frank Ward. Bancroft Hall, the largest dormitory in the United States, is where all midshipmen lived. Chew was an accomplished surface warfare officer, destined for three-star rank, who repeatedly tried to persuade me that destroyer or battleship duty was the way to go. But my enthusiasm just wasn't in surface training.

Chew nevertheless played an instrumental role in my young life. His close friend was Capt. MacPherson Williams, Class of 1930, an aviator who had been shot down in the Philippines and who, with the help of Filipino guerillas, evaded capture for several months while in the jungle before being rescued. In my senior year Chew introduced me to Captain Williams, who at that time was commanding USS *Greenwich Bay*, a transport ship and flagship of the Middle East Force. Mrs. Williams, who resided in Annapolis while her husband was deployed, had been pressuring Chew to find a date for their nineteen-year-old daughter. The cross hairs of their site scope fixed on me. Consequently, in February 1951, I was introduced to intelligent and attractive Anne Williams, who would later become my wife.

Captain Williams fascinated me with sea stories illuminating the carrier war in the Pacific. His love of flying and operating from the carrier was contagious, and it intensified my interest in aviation. Meanwhile, Anne and I began dating frequently my senior year.

The commandant of midshipmen in 1950 was a feisty and colorful naval aviator, Capt. Robert Pirie, U.S. Naval Academy Class of 1926. He won the Silver Star as a carrier pilot during the war and later commanded the escort carrier, the USS *Sicily* (CVE-118). He eventually became a three-star admiral and, at the apex of his career, was deputy chief of naval operations for air. Years after his Academy tour of duty, he was nicknamed "The Beard." His hair had turned gray, almost white, and reportedly because of a skin condition, he was allowed to wear facial hair, accentuated by a distinctive Vandyke triangle around the chin. He was a well-built, distinguished looking man and, with the beard, could have posed for whisky advertisements. He had a fiery temper; it was best not to rile him up.

Pirie had been ordered to the Naval Academy to establish an aviation department. I took some of the aviation courses and found them rudimentary, mostly nuts and bolts stuff, and I felt the courses needed to teach the strategic aspects of naval aviation—how it was used in the past, how it would be employed in the future. But, it seemed to me, the course was a good start for aviation aspirants.

One day in my senior year we held a pep rally at Tecumseh Court, which is adjacent to Bancroft Hall, before one of the football games. The new superintendent, Adm. Harry Hill, had invited Gov. and Mrs. Theodore McKeldin of Maryland to observe the exuberant pre-football game festivities. While the crowd of midshipmen cheered for the home team, some midshipmen who had remained in the building, hoping to enliven the event, heaved rolls of toilet paper from the upper floors of Bancroft Hall. Unfortunately, an unfurled roll of toilet paper scored a direct hit on the head of the governor's wife. That soured the moment and infuriated Captain Pirie. The rally ended when an enraged Pirie mustered the entire brigade onto the grounds, directing them to clean up the mess, which was rather mild punishment actually.

Because I played three sports on top of academic responsibilities, I felt as if I were running on a perpetual motion machine. I remember years later trying to catch up on events that occurred from 1947 to 1951. I hardly ever touched a newspaper or listened to news while I was at the Academy.

Meanwhile, in the quest to succeed in the classroom, a phenomenon called the "dope system" had evolved at the Academy. Essentially, it entailed cheating on exams, one class passing on questions to another that took the tests at a later time. As class president in my junior year, I became embroiled in this major issue of discussion among the leaders of all the classes. A group of first classmen had detected the practice in 1949 and began to express concern among themselves. This practice had probably begun on a small scale with a suggestion from one midshipman to another but then increased in size slowly until there was a large number involved. I didn't know it at the time, but the dope system led to what one might call my "defining moment" at the Academy.

We had a "lock-step" curriculum in those days. All midshipmen took certain basic courses. One of the two regiments would attend classes in the morning, the other in the afternoon. Those who took quizzes in the morning began passing on the questions and answers to counterparts in the other regiment, knowing the identical questions would appear on the quizzes in the afternoon. This worked well for the afternoon group but was of no benefit to the morning unit.

All were fundamentally honest students, but in the zeal to get good grades in the competitive environment of the Academy, they succumbed to "passing the dope." It reached a point where midshipmen were telephoning with regularity from regiment to regiment to acquire answers to the quizzes.

During my first year, little was said about honor and integrity. The leadership at the school, from the superintendent on down, probably figured these qualities were so thoroughly ingrained in the ethic of the naval service that there was really no great need to discuss them. Perhaps, through a kind of osmosis, midshipmen in their daily observation of senior officers would automatically acquire what the father of the U.S. Navy, John Paul Jones, called "that nicest sense of personal honor."

Passing the dope was flagrant at the athlete's training tables as well, so there was absolutely no doubt it was a pervasive practice. It bothered me that basically honest midshipmen were engaging in an unethical practice without fully realizing the seriousness of their actions. I did not consider myself a "do-gooder," but to me the dope system was bound to detract from the trust and confidence we needed to have in each other as warriors in the years ahead.

I, as the president of the Class of 1951, and the leaders of the Class of 1950, Chuck Dobony, the president, and Wayne Smith, Ames Smith, Don Fraasa, and Tom Ross, agreed that doping was a problem. During the first semester of the 1949–50 academic year, an ad hoc committee was formed to study ways of improving honor standards. As a result, Dobony and second class president (1952) Jim Sagerholm and I decided to assemble our respective classes and to seek their pledge to eradicate the dope system.

I was a bit nervous when my 725 classmates filled the auditorium at Memorial Hall. I stood at a podium, gaveled the men to silence, and got right to the point.

"I've asked you here to talk to you about the doping system," I began. There was silence in the ranks, all eyes leveled directly at me. The phrase, "dope system," conveyed a sudden sense of dread. "Simply put," I went on, "it's got to stop. Leaders of the other classes are making the same pitch to their groups. We're all under constant pressure to pass the tests. But that's part of the challenge we asked for when we came to Annapolis. All of you know what I'm talking about, and I won't waste any more of your time. Therefore, I seek your pledge to eradicate the system."

After a pause there was a resounding "Yes!" from the class. It overwhelmingly vowed that the dope system would die forever. Not surprisingly, the other classes responded likewise.

We reported our action to Captain Chew, and he passed it on to officials up the chain of command. They were impressed that we had taken this problem upon ourselves to resolve. This resulted in a heightened interest by Academy officials and led to the establishment of the brigade executive committee composed of selected first classmen and popularly elected class and company representatives. We were tasked with recommending ways of improving the standard of honor within the brigade.

During the 1950–51 academic year, Jim Sagerholm and I (I had been elected class president for our senior year as well and was chosen the brigade commander, the highest position in the brigade, authorizing six stripes on my uniform sleeves) joined with committee members and the president of the Class of 1953, a nineteen-year-old midshipman of extraordinary intellect and incredible enthusiasm, H. Ross Perot.

Ross and I hit it off right away, beginning one of the most profound and enduring friendships of my life. Ross's enormous success, in and after his Navy duty, and his unwavering patriotism, have never been a surprise to me. His actions on behalf of me, my family, and the other POWs during our captivity in North Vietnam are the stuff of legend. More on that later.

Ross had a very strong sense of right and wrong and a tell-it-like-it-is brashness about him. He had a Texas drawl to go along with his sound insights. Because we were plowing new ground, his contributions were essential and fundamental to our goals.

The committee laid the foundation that led to the establishment of honor standards. The term "honor code" was not used at Annapolis. That is a West Point term. For a full year, we spent two to three evenings a week developing the standards.

As class president and brigade commander, my plate was really full. This was an enormous plus for me, but it also spelled the end of my athletic career at the Academy. I simply would not have time for varsity sports in light of the responsibilities these two positions required. I had lettered in three sports for three years, and that would have to be enough. I knew I would miss the unparalleled excitement of running through traffic on the gridiron, driving to the hoop in basketball, or lacing a double to right center in baseball, but my other obligations, not to mention studies, had to take precedence. The coaches were, without exception, understanding and endorsed my decision. Had I been a superstar, they might have felt otherwise, but at this point in my life, it was more important to focus on my duties as a leader and on my studies, with varsity athletics set aside.

Early in the semester, Captain Chew began referring class "A" disciplinary reports to the committee for recommendations of punishment. Then, right after the Army-Navy game in December 1950, superintendent Hill, who had relieved Admiral Holloway, presented a challenge to all midshipmen.

In an address to the brigade in Dahlgren Hall, he said, "I will give full support and cooperation to all classes if you unanimously accept the responsibility for maintaining a high degree of personal honor within the brigade. I will not require professors to be in the classroom during examinations."

He made particular reference to conduct in recitation rooms and to the importance that must be accorded an individual's signature. If such obligations were accepted by the classes, he vowed that proctors would be removed from examination rooms. The committee enthusiastically viewed the admiral's proposals, and based on subsequent class and battalion meetings, the entire student body accepted the challenge. As a result, our committee was elevated on campus to a position of increasing prominence.

Admiral Hill was a surface warfare officer and definitely from the traditional, or old school, of the Navy. He was an amphibious commander and during World War II spearheaded the invasion of Okinawa and other Pacific islands. He was an avid baseball fan, he came to our games whenever he could, and I got to know him fairly well. In fact, we had met in the dugout, of all places, during a baseball game before he became superintendent. Now, as brigade commander, I and the brigade staff met with him after parades to be introduced to the dignitaries who were often on hand at such events. As superintendent, though, he managed to infuriate the entire Class of 1951, now seniors.

He reversed the "liberties" Admiral Holloway had extended to first classmen. Civilian clothes were prohibited from dormitory rooms; the off-duty alternate weekends were now limited to two per semester; and only three-stripers (company commanders) and above were excused from marching to class. The only privilege retained was the extension of taps from 2200 to 2300 for seniors.

The gripes these new rules ignited were automatically routed through me. I conveyed them to the hierarchy, but my efforts at getting the privileges restored failed. Consequently, we had some very unhappy campers in the Class of 1951, and it took a good part of the year for their collective anger to subside, if it ever did.

All moral turpitude offenses were to be reported to the executive committee for investigation and consideration, and if found to be well grounded, were to be reported further to Captain Chew, with recommendations. As could be expected, midshipmen took some frivolous actions mixed in with more serious ones. I remember one from my youngster year.

My roommate, John Leahy, and I lived next door to a cocky, mischievous plebe, Ray Bright, Class of 1953, who was an ex-Marine. One day he came into our room obviously dejected.

"What's wrong," I asked.

Shaking his head, he said, "Our company officer (an active-duty lieutenant) put me on report and gave me twenty-five demerits." That's a considerable hit. When a midshipman reached fifty demerits, he was toying with serious trouble with respect to his longevity at the Academy.

"What did you do?" I asked.

"Well," he said, regretfully, "I put a rather disrespectful, typewritten—but *anonymous*—note on his desk."

He'd been mad at something that happened to him and sought satisfaction through the written word.

"How did the lieutenant know it was you who wrote it?" I asked.

The plebe answered, "Apparently, while the company was at morning classes, he went through our rooms and checked everybody's typewriter. He checked the type with all the typewriters, and mine matched up with the note."

My roommate and I held back a chuckle. "You should have printed the note by hand," I said, trying to sound serious. "But there's no way the company officer could have checked all two hundred typewriters. He must have had other sources of information."

The ex-Marine pondered this and said, "OK, next time I write a note to the lieutenant, I'll do it by hand." He still wasn't going to let the matter go. This matter never came before the committee, and I don't think there were any more clandestine letters to the company officer.

Conversely, a serious case came before the committee involving the behavior of a classmate who had missed a mandatory church party muster. On a board in the battalion officer's office the muster officer would pencil in your name as you checked in. If you missed muster, an "A," for absent, was written after your name. This midshipman, who had a considerable number of infractions on his record already, was caught in the act of erasing the A after his name.

Outwardly, this may not seem catastrophic. But because of his past record, the negative trend of his behavior, and the dishonesty of this last act, we recommended expulsion from the Academy. Superintendent Hill agreed, and the man was separated.

We had taken a long look at the honor code at West Point. Instituted by Gen. Douglas MacArthur when he was the superintendent in 1921, this code stated a cadet "would not lie, cheat, steal or tolerate anyone who did."

The first part of this order was fine, but I took exception to the last phrase, which made it mandatory to "squeal" on a fellow cadet. I had discussed this during exchange visits with Army cadets. The committee agreed the West Point honor code went too far for us at Annapolis. We also thought that non-toleration, or mandatory reporting of an infraction, would lead to grouping together smaller offenses with larger ones.

Cadets at West Point were being separated for relatively minor offenses, which we considered a waste of a young person's life. I knew it would be hard to require midshipmen to report other midshipmen, especially their own classmates, because it was counter to all we did to develop mutual bonds of loyalty, trust, and friendship. And when it comes to combat, those three commodities can be as essential to victory as weapons.

I also knew that some basically honorable midshipmen, particularly during their early years at Annapolis, would mistakenly commit minor honor violations just through inexperience. Why subject them to public embarrassment, demoralization, and possible separation when the matter could be handled by firm counseling by other midshipmen? Finally, I believed a counseling option would send a strong message to others that the Academy officials trusted in the midshipmen's judgment and reliability. This would enhance the brigade's sense of ownership, pride, and responsibility for any honor standard.

Moreover, I disliked a codified set of rules or "thou shalt nots," as existed in the West Point code. These relegated an honor standard into another "conduct" system. We had one of those, and that was enough. We needed an honor standard that became a way of life, a philosophy that midshipmen adhered to because they believed in it, not because they feared punishment if they deviated from it.

The committee was keenly aware of the hefty responsibility that had been placed in its lap. We had a rigid obligation to our classmates. Each case submitted to us had to be investigated and reviewed thoroughly. Utmost fairness was mandatory. Personal feelings had to be set aside completely. Any action taken by the committee had to be in the genuine pursuit of justice.

Near the end of the academic year, we decided the committee must establish a formal procedure for conducting meetings. These would embrace summoning of witnesses, voting for punishments, and so forth. A special committee within the group was designated to work on this project and to have the procedure in readiness for the 1951–52 academic year.

This led to the formation of class and brigade honor boards with the responsibilities and procedures as we know them at the Academy today.

In the last paragraph of my report to the commandant, I wrote, "I feel the codification of the committee's operations in cases of moral turpitude should be stringently avoided. Honor is a personal quality, and as individuals differ, so do violations of honor. Efforts to standardize punishment recommendations after placing an offense in a specific category would render the committee a useless, mechanical body. Each case should be reviewed and considered on its merits alone. I recommend that the only systemization should be applied to the manner in which we conducted executive committee meetings."

The superintendent bought on to this, and the honor standard we established in the 1950 is still in effect at this writing.

However you looked at it, we were being trained as warriors and leaders of warriors. It boiled down to a simple question: Can you imagine going into a life and death situation in combat with shipmates who did not share your convictions of trust, loyalty, and friendship?

In my senior year, the relationship between Anne and me had grown, and I asked her to marry me. I was truly elated both by her consent and by being accepted for flight training beginning in September. Her father was now chief of staff of the Naval Air Reserve Training Command at Naval Air Station Glenview, in Chicago. Anne and I decided to marry in December in the chapel at that base.

With Anne at my side much of the time, June Week was delightful. I felt flattered, because the superintendent invited my parents to stay with him at his mansion-like quarters on campus. Obviously, Mom and Dad were honored by the kindness of Admiral and Mrs. Hill and were proud that I finished eighth, academically, in my class. It was a memorable week for all of us.

I was detailed to the commandant's office for the summer, welcoming on board the new plebes and tending to many administrative matters, one of which was preparing a report on the honor concept.

Admiral Hill had directed the midshipmen to purchase new, full-dress uniforms. These had been deleted from the inventory during the war years as a cost-saving measure. Midshipmen would now have to pony up $150 of their own funds for the uniform. The uniform would be worn for special parades and dances, maybe only two to three times a year. Considerable disgruntlement accompanied this directive.

A well-known tailor, Jacob Reed, had produced our regular uniforms for years. As I was available, and as the former brigade commander, I was selected to model this new full-dress uniform.

I was summoned to Captain Pirie's office and told to don a prototype set of the new uniform. I was immediately descended upon by a battery of Jacob Reed tailors, who encircled me and with pins, tape measures, and chalk; they probed and pinched, adjusting the fit.

Finally, I stood alone at the center of the room, embarrassed and uncomfortable at all the attention, with Captain Pirie frowning at me.

"Boy, that doesn't fit very well," he said. He put his hand under the buttons of the blouse at chest level. He tugged at the fabric and looking at the dismayed tailors, said, "Look at this. Look how badly this thing fits!"

What seemed like hours later the tailors had satisfied Pirie and I was dismissed. I admired Pirie, cantankerous as he could be, because despite his incendiary style, he was a great leader.

I cherished my time at Annapolis. I loved the discipline, the camaraderie, the challenges, and the unity of purpose. I was ready for new horizons and couldn't wait for my release in September.

Jet planes were replacing the piston-powered machines, and Navy pilots were flying these planes in combat missions over Korea. Thoughts of gold wings had long since superseded those of a submariner's dolphins. I wore the single gold stripe of an ensign on my shoulder boards, was fully prepared to enter a huge new lake as a small fish, and had absolutely no doubt flight training in Pensacola was the place I wanted to be.

Chapter Three

TRAINING COMMAND

Without warning and with the dreaded finality every pilot hopes
will never happen, the engine quit.

I WAS UNDER THE "BAG" over the raw, flat Texas countryside, blind to the outside world. My attention was totally focused on the attitude gyro, the turn and bank indicator, and the airspeed and altitude gages in the SNJ Texan. The bag was a canvas shield that opened, accordion-like, from behind the rear seat in the Texan two-seater and was pulled like a hood over my head and down to the top edge of my instrument panel. This simulated flying "in the glue," or bad weather when a pilot had no reference to the ground or his surroundings and had to depend on the information gleaned from the gages to control the aircraft and motor on through to the destination.

I was on an instrument training flight with my instructor in the front seat of the propeller-driven SNJ *without* a bag over his head. He took off and landed but was otherwise along for the ride. I flew while he graded me on my ability to scan the instruments and "fly the gages," keeping the trainer on its proscribed path of flight. We had launched from the advanced training base in Kingsville, Texas, about an hour's drive south of Corpus Christi.

The SNJ was a reliable bird and had been around since the 1930s. The Pratt and Whitney engine, rated at 500 horsepower, had more than enough power for fledgling aviators and was propelling us along smoothly as we cruised at four thousand feet and one hundred and forty knots of airspeed.

Without warning and with the dreaded finality every pilot hopes will never happen, the engine quit. I instinctively popped the hood back out of the way. The instructor called, "I've got it!" wresting the controls from me, which I instantly released, raising both hands free of the stick. I was not terrified. We were still flying. But I was unnerved by the unexpected silence, convincing evidence that our SNJ was now a glider.

The instructor made a Mayday call, which we hoped was heard back at Kingsville, and announced over the intercom, "I'm gonna spiral down to that field just ahead. Looks flat enough, and there's a road nearby."

"Roger," I answered.

"Tighten your harness."

"Wilco," I said.

We had practiced precautionary emergency landings in the event of engine failure, and my instructor was going by the book, keeping the gear up and locked, using the flaps as necessary, and hitting the downwind and upwind checkpoints in the descent at the right speed and altitude. Powerless, the SNJ creaked and groaned a bit as it glided downward, swiftly but under control. The instructor had secured the fuel pump and closed the fuel mixture lever to help prevent a fire on impact.

We hit the ground in a nearly level attitude and were thrown roughly against our restraints, sending a fine rooster tail of dirt and scrub brush into the air, and came to a stop within several hundred feet. Thankfully, there was no fire. We sat there quietly for a moment as the dust settled and our heartbeats decelerated; then we expeditiously disembarked.

"You OK?" asked the instructor.

"Yes sir," I said. And I was. I had felt no panic, because I believed the situation was under control, which it was. But that sudden silence was unnerving, and the impact was like tackling a fullback straight on.

We climbed out, and the instructor said, "I'll stay with the airplane. You go get help." I reached the road and started walking. He loitered around the yellow, stricken Texan in the quiet Texas wilderness. I was wondering what I would tell Anne when a battered pickup truck came by. I flagged it down and looked into the open driver's side window. An old-timer with a leathery face and a twinkle in his eye looked curiously at me in my soiled orange coveralls and said, "What's happened to you, Son?"

"Little trouble with the engine in our SNJ," I explained. "Had to land wheels up in a field back there."

"That's Kennedy Ranch land," he said, adding that, "You're one of the Navy boys from Kingsville, I bet."

"Yes sir," I said.

"Used to be a balloon pilot myself," he said, "in World War I. Hop in and we'll get you to a phone."

He drove me to a small roadside café full of ranch hands having their morning coffee, where I telephoned the duty officer at Kingsville and explained our predicament. A Navy van was soon on the way to pick us up. I thanked the gentleman to whose day my instructor and I had brought a little excitement. I also learned that across the road was the legendary King Ranch, the inspirational source for Edna Ferber's book, *Giant.*

On the van ride to the air station, I knew Anne would be shaken up by what happened. As a young girl, she and her mother went through a similar hell when Mac Williams was shot down in the Philippines and evaded capture for several weeks. Anne and her mother were in agonizing limbo, not knowing whether Mac was alive or dead. Still, I was alive and well and none the worse for wear.

Anne and I lived in an apartment in Corpus Christi, and I was commuting an hour each way to the base at Kingsville. That was bad enough. Now I'd have to tell her I was in a crash—crash, in this case, being perhaps too harsh a word.

Several months before the mishap I had driven alone to Pensacola, while Anne stayed with her parents in Glenview, with the understanding we would marry in December. The "Cradle of Aviation" is the descriptive phrase attached to Pensacola, a quiet town on the panhandle of Florida, several driving hours east of New Orleans.

Nine officers, twenty-three enlisted men, and seven seaplanes arrived at Pensacola to set up a flying school in January 1914. This unit had been operating in Annapolis. Its arrival in Florida began an enduring relationship between the community of Pensacola and naval aviation that prevails today. Pensacola is at the heart of naval aviation training. Plus, there's another side to that heart, because Pensacola has also been referred to as "The Mother of Naval Aviation" because of the large number of aspiring naval aviators who married girls from there. Indeed, Anne was the first baby born in 1932 in Pensacola while her father had duty there.

I actually was assigned to Whiting Field in Milton, Florida, a few miles north of Pensacola for basic instruction in the SNJ. The field, which consisted of two separate sets of runways—North Field and South Field, adjacent to each other—was named after Capt. Ken Whiting, a legendary flyer and the Navy's first landing signal officer (LSO)—the guy who stands on a platform at the aft edge of the flight deck helping guide pilots to landings on the ship. In those days it took extraordinary courage to be an LSO.

Whiting was the executive officer on the USS *Langley,* the Navy's first aircraft carrier, which was really a collier, or coal ship, with a wooden deck built over it. One day at sea, when a squadron of biplanes was making landings on the ship and having a miserable time getting aboard, Whiting became impatient with the airmanship on display by the pilots. Frustrated, he grabbed the white hats of two nearby sailors and climbed up onto the stern of the flight deck. Executing impromptu, but common-sense signals, he waved his arms, with the hats in his hands, and tilted his body this way and that, visually signaling the oncoming pilots to turn steeper or shallower, to climb or to descend, accordingly. It worked, and the precedent was set for the introduction of LSOs to the fleet. Early on, LSOs used tennis racket-sized paddles to "wave" aircraft aboard. Nowadays, a sophisticated lens system and other computerized aids help the flyers land safely on the flattops. But expertly trained LSOs remain on the platform at the edge of the stern deck, radio telephone in hand, talking pilots down when necessary.

I was amazed at the free time I had going through the training command compared to the feverish pace of the days and nights at Annapolis. There was an abundance of lectures and briefings in addition to the flights, but compared to the Academy, I felt that there was plenty of time left over to do my own thing. Every weekend we hit the white sandy beaches of Pensacola.

I readily took to flying. I made mistakes like everyone else but got the hang of basic air work rather quickly and absorbed the systematic procedures inherent in flying the Navy way. Basic air work consisted of controlling airspeed, altitude, and attitude, banking without losing or gaining height, trimming the aircraft smoothly, and staying ahead of the SNJ so that you flew it rather than having the aircraft fly you. I won't say I was a "natural," one of those rare types who is born to the cockpit. At the same time, I was never uncomfortable or anxious in the aircraft. It was an aerial classroom in which I thrived. When I soloed at Whiting's South Field in December 1951, I felt the same exhilarating self-satisfaction as my shipmates, but I knew primary training was only a start. I enjoyed flying, because it required a precise coordination of mental and physical skills, two areas where I thrived.

In December I left the relative warmth of northern Florida and motored to Glenview for the wedding. My family joined us, and Anne and I were married three days after Christmas, with both families present. We elected to honeymoon on the return trip south, and when we left the Chicago area, thirty-six inches of snow lay on the ground. Florida here we come.

We lived in a rented apartment in Pensacola at Navy Point, and I drove in a car pool to Whiting Field, completing the basic course with minimum problems. I was moving along through the syllabus quicker than the others in my class of twenty-five; I wanted to get my wings as soon as possible, hoping for assignment to a squadron fighting in Korea.

After I completed the basic course, Anne and I loaded the car and drove west to Corpus Christi, Texas, for advanced flight training at Naval Air Auxiliary Air Station Kingsville. We set up camp in Corpus Christi, and I was once again a commuter, driving an hour south to Kingsville and returning home each evening in the company of fellow students.

A young married couple going through flight training knew a marvelous experience in large part because of the friendships and social activities accompanying our collective pursuit of gold wings. Compared to later generations, my group tended to marry in their early twenties, so married men far outnumbered bachelors. The work was challenging and the hours long, but the tedium was erased by many joyous parties. Invariably, the men exchanged sea, or should I say, air stories, complete with hands waving through the air imitating airplanes, accompanied by narratives of aerial adventures, often of questionable veracity. The women listened for a while before, bored by the magnificent tales of flying, they circled their own wagons to discuss the challenges of being married to prospective Navy pilots and rearing their children. Those were memorable days.

I must admit flying came easy to me. I was not a "natural" in the sense that I jumped into the cockpit, flipped a switch, and roared off into the wild blue as if born to fly. I prepared for the flights with considerable study, tried to fly the sortie in my mind before even trudging out to the flight line and running through adverse contingencies, rehearsing the actions I would need to take in order to resolve them.

I could handle basic maneuvers without difficulty, actually excelling in instrument flying, and when I made my first carrier landing in the SNJ on the USS *Cabot* on July 3, 1952, without a single wave off, I felt I was well on track.

I was transferred to Naval Auxiliary Air Station Kingsville to fly the F8F Bearcat, a powerful machine that was the successor to the Grumman-built F4F Wildcat and F6F Hellcat, heroic performers in World War II. I flew part of the syllabus in the Bearcat, but some maneuvers in it were restricted because of structural problems that were then being corrected. As a result, I flew the F6F for bombing and air-to-air gunnery, which entailed high-g pull-ups and turns.

During basic flight training many of our instructors were reservists who had served during World War II and who had been recalled to active duty. They did this without complaint. One of my F8F instructors was Gordon

Smith, a colorful aviator, who commanded a squadron of Skyraiders in the Vietnam War and eventually reached flag rank. Gordon had to bail out of his bomber at night in an unusual attitude after being hit by enemy fire. He survived the bailout, even though he glanced off the tail of his out-of-control aircraft before his parachute opened. He was badly injured but was rescued by helicopter from the sea.

I completed my advanced carrier qualifications on the USS *Wright* in November 1952 in the Wildcat, again without a wave off, and shortly thereafter I became the first member of our twenty-five-man class to get wings. The ceremony was a straightforward affair without bells and whistles. Anne pinned on my wings, with Admiral Whiney, who was second in command to Vice Adm. John Dale Price, chief of naval air training, presiding.

Being first was not a goal, but I admit I put pressure on myself to get through the course as reasonably quickly as I could. From the outset, I "hawked" the training officers for unexpected openings or cancellations on the flight schedule, and instead of taking a few days off between phases of instruction, I proceeded directly to the next unit and tried to start right away. The war was still going on in Korea, and I believed I had a shot at duty with a squadron heading that way.

Luck followed me, and a dream came true, because I was one of a small number of newly designated aviators assigned to transition to jets. We didn't have to pack up the car, because the jet-training unit was at Kingsville.

I remember a British film about the advent of jet flight. A test pilot has started the engine of his potential fighter plane. The engine produces the distinctive din of a spinning turbine, conveying the sense of immense power, like the sustained prelude of a thunderclap. "The most exciting sound in the world," says one of the characters. I believe he was right.

I flew the straight-wing TV Seastar, which came in the single- and two-seat versions. It was a derivative of the Air Force's P-80 Shooting Star. Although quicker reaction time on the part of a pilot is required in a jet compared to a piston-powered plane, a jet is easier to fly. In a prop, the pilot has to manipulate a fuel mixture control, a revolutions per minute (RPM) lever, and the throttle. When adding power, particularly on takeoff, engine torque, which pulls the nose to the left, has to be countered with a significant dose of right rudder to stay on the runway's centerline. In a jet engine, there is no torque. You push the throttle forward and go.

Part of the jet syllabus included all-weather training in the Beech-built SNB, which was powered by a pair of Pratt and Whitney 450 horsepower engines. The pilot sat in the left seat, the student in the right. There was room for a couple more passengers in the cabin aft, one of whom might be another student waiting his turn at the controls.

We had to master the basics of descending and ascending at proscribed rates measured in feet per minute. We executed what were called standard-rate turns at a constant angle of bank while in those climbs, descents, and related maneuvers, all designed to exercise our scan patterns. Scan patterns are critical to anyone who flies, especially in weather conditions that force reliance on the instruments. A pilot must incessantly shift eyes from one gage to another and respond accordingly to the information each presented. The trick is, if you can detect an excessive turn rate or airspeed deceleration early and you reduce the turn or add power accordingly, you stay ahead of the airplane.

We learned to fly on designated airways, the network of strictly defined corridors in the sky used by aircraft traveling from one point to another. We had to discern audio signals based on Morse code transmitted from ground facilities through aircraft radios to our earphones. We learned to stay on the beam—the highway in the sky—or when we unintentionally deviated from it, how to return to the proper track in the sky using such tactics as the "fade 90," a difficult procedure involving a ninety-degree turn from the proscribed course, intense listening for the proper audio signal, identifying your position based on it, and resuming the right heading.

Nowadays, with global position satellites, Tactical Air Navigation (TACAN), and other gadgets, I can say without equivocation that pilots have it easier.

One of my all-weather instructors was Lt. Cdr. Tom Hudner, an excellent pilot and an exceptionally mild-mannered guy. I told a fellow student one day that I really liked flying with Hudner and how quiet and gentlemanly he was.

The student said, "You know what he did in Korea, don't you?"

"I knew he flew Corsairs over there," I said.

"He's the guy who crash-landed in the snow and tried to rescue Jesse Brown. He was awarded the Medal of Honor."

I was stunned. I was vaguely aware of that mission but didn't equate my instructor with it. Jesse Brown was in Hudner's F4U Corsair squadron, was hit by enemy fire, and was forced to land on the frozen turf of North Korea. Hudner, circling above, saw that Brown, the Navy's first black combat aviator, was trapped in the cockpit. In one of those perilous moments that separates a select few men from all the rest of us, Hudner made a decision to save another life that could have cost him his own. He landed his Corsair wheels up along-side Brown's stricken plane, unstrapped, made his way over the hard-packed snow to Brown's F4U, and tried to free him from the cockpit.

Tragically, the impact had compressed the front end of the F4U cockpit area, in effect clamping Brown's legs in place. Exacerbating this, the skin of the aircraft was so slippery from the icy cold; Hudner could not gain a firm foothold. After a time, a lone helicopter pilot arrived with an ax to try and cut Brown loose. But Hudner and the helo pilot simply could not cut through the metal.

Despite their valiant efforts, they failed to free Brown. Nightfall was coming, and the helo had to return to its home base and the enemy had to be near. There was no choice but to abandon Brown, who asked his attempted rescuers to pass on his love to his wife. This was one of naval aviation's most dramatic and heartbreaking episodes.

Now, here I was, a young pup, flying in sun-baked Corpus Christi a world away from the frigid landscape of North Korea, in southern Texas, with a man who had earned the highest military honor in the land.

Jet training went well, and I was one of a small handful of newly designated pilots rewarded with orders to a jet unit, the Ghostriders of Fighter Squadron 193, based at Naval Air Station Moffett Field, a few miles south of San Francisco. I would be flying the McDonnell straight-wing F2H Banshee, the most advanced jet fighter in the inventory. For me, this was naval aviator's heaven. VF-193 was the Navy's only jet night fighter squadron, the key word here being "night."

In 1952 the Navy and Marine Corps had logged three and three-quarter million flight hours. During that time, 399 pilots and aircrew members were killed and we lost 708 aircraft as a result of accidents. That translates to a rate of fifty-four major mishaps every one hundred thousand hours in the air, an astounding figure by today's standards, where the rate has been around two major accidents for every one hundred thousand flight hours and fatalities commensurately less.

I mention this because the advent of jet-propelled fighters and bomb-ers, particularly those that operated from the existing straight-deck aircraft carriers, created a steep learning curve that was bound to result in accidents. This is not to say airplanes were falling out of the skies like leaves in autumn. However, it *is* to say naval aviation was considerably more hazardous in the early 1950s than it is today.

Many a career naval aviator will tell you his or her first tour of duty in a squadron was the most memorable, if not the best of all that followed. All of a sudden you are out from under the "I'm-looking-over-your-shoulder-to-make-sure-you-do-it-right" syndrome so pervasive in the training command to the world of "you're a fleet pilot now!"

This does not preclude close scrutiny of a new pilot's performance by seniors, especially the skipper. You are welcomed into a cadre of twenty or so fellow pilots with its own jets, its own complement of two hundred or so sailors who maintained the aircraft and the squadron records, and its own exclusive identity, manifest in our insignia, which we sewed onto our flight jackets and which appeared on the bulkheads in our hangar and on the Banshees themselves. Best of all, VF-193 had a true warrior's mission, which was to shoot down the bad guys, and we were on our aircraft carrier, the USS *Oriskany*, headed for Korea, where the bad guys were. It doesn't get much more macho than that.

Cdr. Deke Carr was our skipper, a stern and capable aviator with an aeronautical engineering degree but not much charisma. He was the antithesis of the individual who was our most blithe spirit and the absolute best pilot I ever knew, the irrepressible Alan Shepard. Shepard stuck in Carr's craw, because Alan loved to exercise the Banshee to its extremes and did it well, but on occasion went too far.

As Skipper Carr once proclaimed, "Alan Shepard is an excellent aviator, but he occasionally exceeds the bounds of good flight discipline."

Al was a graduate of the Navy's Test Pilot School (TPS) in Patuxent River, Maryland. I lucked out and became his wingman, and even though our personalities were poles apart, we blended well and became close and lifelong friends. Where I was inclined to be temperate, Alan was venturesome. He liked the ladies and they liked him. More than anything else, he wanted to become a Blue Angel and was terribly disappointed that at that time only naval aviation cadets could qualify. Cadets were flight students, often without college degrees, who were in an enlisted status going through training and who became ensigns upon pinning on the gold wings. This policy eventually changed, but not in time for Alan, Naval Academy Class of 1945.

I was assigned as the line division officer, responsible for aircraft activities on the flight line. With the able assistance of a chief petty officer and other senior enlisted personnel, who had served in World War II and really knew their stuff, I supervised a wonderful group of young sailors who had the strenuous duty of preparing the jets for flight, fueling them, keeping them clean, sending us off, and meeting us when we returned to start the whole cycle again. It was one of the best jobs I ever had.

I took immense delight in working with the eighteen-, nineteen-, and twenty-year-olds, many of them from farms and impoverished areas, who were acclimating themselves, not without difficulty, to the disciplined life of the Navy.

I was later assigned as the personnel officer, and not long after became the administration officer with department head status. But my heart stayed with the sailors in the line division.

On board the USS *Oriskany* (CV-34) en route to East Asia on my first official Navy deployment, we were operating about forty miles south of Barbers Point. We were flying practice bombing missions using a target on the island of Kahoolawe to hone our bombing and strafing skills. The Banshee was considered a fighter bomber. We could carry two five hundred-pound bombs and twenty-millimeter shells, which fired through four cannons configured in the nose. The war in Korea was winding down, but we needed to be ready, just in case it continued. I was on the bow catapult with two five hundred pounders suspended from the pylons under the wings.

With my Banshee cinched firmly to the catapult, I ran the engine to full power, booted feet firmly planted on the brakes. It was a typically bright blue day in this part of the world, and I was looking forward to the dive bombing. I checked my instruments and gave a sharp salute to the yellow-jerseyed flight deck officer, signaling I was ready to go. The hydraulic-powered sling shot fired, and I instantly knew that something was wrong.

I did not get that exhilarating boot in the behind that would send me a couple of hundred feet down the catapult track and heave me into the sky at over one hundred knots. I was experiencing what every carrier pilot dreads but only a few, fortunately, undergo: a cold catapult shot. It was impossible to stop the Banshee, but it wasn't going to fly either because of insufficient speed off the end of the bow. The aircraft rolled down the deck and after a short toss, dribbled, wings level, into the sea.

This was a potential catastrophe, but two things worked in my favor. The straight-wing F2H plummeted, wings level, into the water. A swept-wing jet would tend to fall off on a wing, complicating impact. Also, the aircraft floated long enough for me to unbuckle my seat harness and to step out onto the wing and into the warm Hawaiian waters.

The crash alarm sounded on the ship. On the bridge, the skipper, the colorful Capt. Charles D. Griffin, who occasionally wore a railroad engineer's hat and a silk ascot around his neck, swung the ship away from me in a manner that kept the huge screws at the stern safely distant. Within minutes, the ship's helicopter was hovering overhead and sending a hoist cable down.

I worked myself into the horseshoe collar and was pulled slowly out of the water. I sensed the helicopter was straining, but happily the crew hoisted me up, hauled me inside the fuselage, and within minutes delivered me back to the flight deck, less one U.S. Navy jet fighter bomber.

I was no sooner checked by the flight surgeon and deemed fit for duty when the ship's amplifier boomed, "Lieutenant Lawrence, report to the bridge immediately." Wet flight suit and all I hustled up to the bridge, figuring I must have done something wrong and was about to get chewed out.

Captain Griffin was seated in his upraised chair, not unlike a Lazy Boy on a pedestal, at the far left corner of the glassed-in bridge overlooking the flight deck.

"Lieutenant Lawrence reporting as ordered, sir!" I said.

Griffin eyed me seriously, but there was the beginning of a smile on his lips. "Good job, Bill!" he proclaimed. "Good job!"

I sighed inwardly with relief, chatted a bit with the skipper, and then retreated to the ready room. Along the way, I ran into the helo pilot and thanked him profusely for saving me and for the professionalism of his crew.

He said, "You know, you could have made things easier for both of us had you abandoned your parachute."

I turned red with embarrassment. One of the cardinal rules before pickup at sea is to get rid of the chute. Keeping it attached adds immensely to the helo's burden, because of the drag it crates. In the hurry to save my skin, I forgot a basic procedure. Live and learn.

Through the wives' pipeline of communications, Anne would certainly hear of my cold shot, so I explained it all in a letter, emphasizing that I was unhurt and how I was expeditiously plucked from the sea by the pros in the helicopter. She was happy I was OK, but like any wife, it was no small matter of concern to her. She neither complained about the distress nor expressed any misgivings about my continuing to fly.

Chapter Four

ALAN SHEPARD AND THE MANGY ANGELS

"This is Ghost Rider," Alan began, "all aircraft go to max conserve."

ALAN SHEPARD WORE THE F2H LIKE A GLOVE. Flying on his wing was a dream. He was smooth as satin at the controls and had an acute sense of what is now described as "situational awareness." He was a newly minted lieutenant commander and reported to the squadron following a tour of duty that included matriculation at the Navy's Test Pilot School and engineering test pilot assignments at Naval Air Station Patuxent River, Maryland.

One night at sea aboard the USS *Oriskany,* a "gaggle," a large group of aircraft, was airborne awaiting clearance to land. One of the air group's planes had a mechanical problem and had to "take the barrier," that is, land and be snared to a stop by an upraised "fence," not unlike a tennis net but taller and strong enough to halt a fast-moving jet.

Suddenly, there was chaos in the dark skies over the Pacific. This had never happened before to most of us, including the air traffic controllers on board the *Oriskany.* In effect, they lost positive control of the situation. We were directed to land on our sister ship, the USS *Midway* (CV-41), a short distance away.

Alan Shepard was not the most senior pilot in the air that night. Yet, it was he who had an innate sense of the present disarray and danger. Our planes were hardly more than separate patterns of lights crisscrossing in the sky. While some were paralyzed into inaction, Alan was mentally working out a solution. He calmly transmitted a cautionary message to the airplanes.

"This is Ghost Rider," Alan began, "all aircraft go to max conserve." This meant reducing power to save fuel, which is expended at a much greater rate in a jet than in a prop. He then calmly began sorting out the various flights from the different squadrons. He assigned them altitudes and headings, and like a Spanish shepherd (no pun intended), he gathered his sheep and got them funneled toward the backup carrier, the USS *Midway*.

Following an anxiety-saturated hour or so, all hands made it down safely, and there was no doubt that Alan Shepard was the man of the hour.

Alan and I took advantage of the opportunity to qualify as officers of the deck (OOD). As part of the air wing, we did not stand watches on the bridge because of the necessary time-consuming instruction required to do so. Still, it wouldn't hurt our résumés to qualify as OOD. The price we had to pay was that we stood the watches on our own time. Squadron responsibilities prevailed. The watches were four hours long, so we traded sleep, the evening movie, acey-ducey games (Al was an expert acey-ducey player), and other leisure activities for learning how to operate the ship. We both got our qualifications, but it was drudgery.

One night, Al and I were both on the bridge, the carrier steaming along quietly. He looked at me for a long moment in the dim red lighting of the bridge, clearly exhausted, and said, "Why are we doing this? Why aren't we down below sleeping like everybody else?"

Good question. But we both knew the answer. The experience would be career enhancing.

I was once asked if my athletic inclinations enhanced my ability to fly airplanes. Hand-to-eye coordination and motor skills are critical whether a flyer was a quarterback, a clarinet player, or an Elizabethan scholar. But the competitive mind-set of athletes does give you an edge. I used to get butterflies before a game identical to those that flutter in the stomach when you're at full power awaiting a catapult shot on an aircraft carrier. When the action starts, though, the butterflies disappear, replaced by a "go get 'em" charge that makes you want to be as good as the next guy, if not better.

At the same time, you can take aggression too far. One day during aerial gunnery practice, I thought I was making good runs on the target banner being towed on a long length of cable by another plane. We dove in from a "perch" several thousand feet above the banner, which was white, with a bright orange ball in its middle. The trick was to keep the aircraft in trim and to track the banner through the gun sight in the dive, leading the target à la Sergeant York so that upon reaching a specified altitude and airspeed, you could depress the trigger on the control stick and, with reasonable certainty, expect the 20-millimeter cannon shells to burst through the strip of cloth.

After several runs, I was hitless, which is extremely embarrassing for a fighter pilot, one of whose priorities was shooting down enemy aircraft. This just wouldn't do.

With renewed determination and a grimace on my face, I rolled in for another run. I established a nice lead through the sight, and as the banner tracked across my line of vision, I fired. Out of my peripheral vision, I saw the red of the bull's-eye as I whizzed by the banner and felt a dull thud.

I pulled up as per procedure and, with sickening realization, noted what looked like a metal rod imbedded in the leading edge of the tip of my right wing. Fortunately, it didn't affect the flying characteristics of the Banshee. I knew I'd be dressed down for this and dreaded the return to the ready room. I knew I was in line for a chewing out by Commander Carr.

The rod, it turns out, was part of the support apparatus for the banner. I scored a hit all right, but not with any bullets. To my surprise, Commander Carr actually praised me for my aggressiveness, but he made it absolutely clear that what I did was verboten, unsafe not only to me but to the tow plane as well.

I learned my lesson and eventually acquired the knack for air-to-air gunnery competence. I was able to hit the target without flying through it.

Alan Shepard may not have been able to become a Blue Angel, but this did not prevent him from forming his own personal acrobatic team. He worked his extraordinary magic with Lt. Wendell Smith, the flight schedules officer, and persuaded him to post Al and three others on the same flight as often as feasible. I was one of the three chosen by Al to be the slot man in what was to become his personal rendition of the Blue Angels. John Mitchell flew the left wing, Preston Luke the right. We would complete the assigned portion of the mission according to the schedule and then use the remaining time for acrobatics. We flew in stair-step port and starboard echelon formations but spent considerable time in the diamond. From my slot position in the diamond, slightly below and right behind Shepard, who led from its apex, I had an excellent perspective and could coach Mitchell and Luke to close in or loosen up and to polish the geometry of our maneuvers.

What a marvelous experience, flying with Alan Shepard. We executed loops, wingovers, and aileron rolls and got pretty good at it.

In the ready room one day Al sat us down and said, "We've got to have a name for our group."

I'm not sure what we needed a name for, and I don't know who came up with it, but the "Mangy Angels" became our appellation, and it stuck.

"Mangy" was in deference to our sweat-soaked, infrequently laundered orange flight suits, which gained a kind of character with age. "Angels," I think, assuaged Al's disappointment at not becoming a genuine Blue Angel.

In Korea, the armistice had been signed before we reached the Sea of Japan. I admit I was disappointed, wanting to experience combat first hand. But that was self-serving, and I was pleased just to be this close to the action. In fact, we made periodic flights overland in Korea. At one point I was part of an exchange party that went ashore for several days to see how the grunts—our ground troops—were handling matters. Some of them, in turn, came aboard the *Oriskany*. I visited soldiers of the 2nd Infantry Division in their trenches south of the Chorwon Valley.

From a raised platform, we gazed through binoculars at the North Korean soldiers moving about in their padded uniforms. It was bitterly cold in Korea, and while our soldiers manned their positions on the frozen tundra, I thought of our warm accommodations aboard ship. The only time we got the chills is when manning or debarking from our Banshees. We slept under clean sheets, while our Army counterparts made do with tents and layered clothing. Compared to them, we ate like kings. I thanked God for my life aboard ship, and the U.S. Navy, of course.

We wore cumbersome "poopy," or exposure, suits in cold weather, a single-piece costume from neck to boots, like the one William Holden wore in the film *The Bridges at Toko-Ri*. If a pilot had to bail out over water, the suit would prevent him from instantly turning into a Popsicle. It was hoped that a rescue helo would reach him within a few minutes. I was blessed never to have to go through that experience. The rubber neck of the suit, by the way, was almost air tight. Turning your head frequently goes with the territory of being a wingman. There was a time or two that I nearly blacked out from diminishing blood flow to my brain caused by the taut fit of the suit around my neck.

We were at sea conducting a fleet exercise and briefing for a routine flight when Al told us, "The guys on the flight deck deserve a treat. They bust their tails for us all day and half the night. Today, we're gonna salute 'em with a diamond break."

A normal break occurs at the culmination of a flight. In right echelon, the formation parallels the ship's course, passes by it on the starboard side, proceeds a set distance beyond it, and then, individually and in timed sequence, each pilot turns sharply 180 degrees back toward the flattop, completing the oval circuit by landing on deck.

The Blue Angels sometimes performed their break from the diamond formation, which is a bit more dramatic and difficult to do. Al wanted ours to serve as a tribute to the hardworking plane captains; flight deck directors; mechanics; chock bearers; ordnancemen; metalsmiths; electricians; safety officers; and fuel, crash, and salvage crews, who are the true creators of the bizarre ballet of motion called flight deck operations. They were important to us, and we loved them for it. In return, they held us in very high esteem.

Following our next mission, Al led us back to the ship, and when we were cleared in, I slipped into the slot forming the diamond. We descended to five hundred feet and rifled through the sky at three hundred knots. All eyes were on us as we whistled by the ship. A half-mile beyond it, John Mitchell, from his left wing position, broke, whipping his Banshee into a sixty-degree angle of bank turn toward the downwind leg. Fifteen seconds later, Al stood his Banshee on its wing and pulled. I was next, followed by Preston Luke. Our neatly spaced quartet completed the circuit, much to the delight of the audience topside, except for the commanding officer of the VF-193 fighter squadron. Infuriated, he ordered Shepard into his presence and let him have it. "You know that's an improper procedure. I won't have you hotdogging out there. You're in hack for a week."

"In hack" was a form of punishment for officers that restricted the miscreant to his stateroom except for meals. Good thing Al wasn't claustrophobic. A stateroom on a Navy ship has a lofty sounding title, but in reality it's an all-gray, cramped space that is usually shared by two or more people. Al had his own stateroom, so he was alone during his period of restriction. I felt sorry for our Mangy Angel leader and visited him whenever I could, sometimes sharing a meal with him.

Al had a vision of the Mangy Angels photographed against the background of majestic Mount Fujiyama, a revered Japanese landmark. Not flying straight and level across the mountain—that had been done before—but going straight up, paralleling the upward thrust of the mountain's snow-capped peak.

"We'll make the cover of *Life* magazine," he declared. When the *Oriskany* went into port at Yokosuka, Japan, some of the air group's aircraft deployed to Naval Air Station Atsugi, west of Tokyo, to keep our flying skills honed. This afforded Shepard the photo opportunity of his dreams.

Sharing our ready room was the F2HP photoreconnaissance detachment, about a fifth of the size of a normal squadron in terms of aircraft and personnel. Photo pilots made high-speed, low-altitude, straight, and level runs over "enemy terrain" to film possible gun emplacements and the like. The pictures were immediately processed upon arrival back at the ship for analysis by the intelligence officers.

Al cornered Lt. John Romano, a "photo" pilot. John flew the F2HP version of the Banshee, which was equipped with an aerial camera for filming terrain where enemy installations might be deployed. In wartime the film would be developed on the ship and analyzed by intelligence personnel, and suspect areas would be targeted.

"The Mangy Angels have need of your services, John," Shepard said. Al's subtle, but nonetheless overpowering, personality gave Romano pause. "I want a photograph of the Mangy Angels by Fuji, and you're just the guy to do it," Shepard said. This request had the tone of a directive, even though Al had no purview over the photo detachment or its people.

Romano eyed Shepard suspiciously. "I don't know, Al . . ."

"We'll form into a diamond, go into an easy dive to gain airspeed, and then pull up into a loop," Shepard explained. "You fly alongside us from a comfortable distance and turn on the camera as we start up into a loop. We'll want the frame that captures us perfectly vertical with the mountain. Got that?"

We could tell Romano was reluctant to do this, but Al persisted. "Nothing to it," Al said. "You'll get a great picture."

Romano suspected he'd be the subject of ribbing from his fellow pilots if he didn't comply with Shepard's request, so he said "OK," without much enthusiasm.

Next day the Mangy Angels and John Romano, after completing our portion of the mission assigned on the flight schedule, flew to Mount Fujiyama. We did some steep turns and a couple of aileron rolls to get John acclimated. His photo mission seldom called for acrobatic flight, so wrestling his Banshee through high-g maneuvers was a departure from his routine. He flew well clear of our formation but turned and pulled and rolled over with us, as if connected by an invisible rod to our diamond. He then followed us through two practice loops and signaled he was ready for the live run. Mount Fujiyama waited patiently in the background.

Al positioned us for the ultimate loop, several miles abeam the slopes of the mountain. It was a bright cloudless day, the sky as blue as the waters of the Marianas Trench. In the loop, once we pulled up we would trade altitude for airspeed, all the while holding four and a half g's on the Banshees. The waist and leg pockets of our pressure suits would inflate, preventing blood from draining south from our brains and exposing us to blackouts. Technically, a pressure suit is designed to maintain pressure over all or part of the body under conditions of low ambient pressure.

The plan was for Romano to take sequential photographs shortly before and after we went through the vertical. Somewhere in the filmstrip would be the aerial image of the ages.

Al carefully analyzed our position relative to the sun and mountain and transmitted, "Mangy Angels stand by to descend." We had just pushed over, when Romano radioed something garbled and unintelligible. A second or two later, lucidly now, he frantically exclaimed "We've gotta go back to Atsugi. Right now! We've gotta return to base!"

"You got a problem, John?" Al asked calmly as he leveled off. There was no answer, but we saw Romano in a turn back toward the air station. Filled with equal measures of curiosity and disappointment, we loosened up and silently followed Romano home, wondering what the dilemma was.

After we landed, the Mangy Angels convened at John's jet, where he stood by the Banshee, pale as a zombie and looking as weak and bedraggled as someone who had just been mugged.

With sincerity, Al asked, "What happened, John? What went wrong?"

Sheepishly, Romano said, "I got sick. I threw up in my oxygen mask."

We held back the chuckles in deference to our shipmate.

John added, "Not used to doing acrobatics, I guess."

High-g flight was all in a day's work for us, but the photo pilots hauled their birds around in acrobatics less frequently. Perhaps we should have figured on that beforehand. Shepard was disconsolate as we strode back to the hangar, Romano reluctantly in trail. We commiserated with our leader. We were thoroughly convinced that the world had just been denied the greatest aerial photograph ever taken.

Our carrier air group commander, colloquially known as the "CAG," was a wonderful naval officer, the kind of man who symbolized not only the ferocity and skill of a combat pilot—he earned the Navy Cross flying the SBD Dauntless dive bomber in World War II—but also the flair and personality of the so-called type A personalities who populate U.S. naval aviation. At this writing, God bless him, Rear Adm. James D. "Jig Dog" Ramage still lights up a room when he enters and at the annual Tailhook Association conventions draws the attention of the young flyers like filings to a magnet.

Jig Dog is quick with a smile, is honest as the day is long, and was admired by seniors and juniors alike. It was Jig Dog who, in his later years, established the Enlisted Combat Aircrewmen Roll of Honor to recognize the unheralded contributions of that cadre of brave youngsters who shared the identical dangers in combat of their pilots in fixed- and rotary-wing aircraft.

In another example of Alan Shepard's acumen and solid airmanship, he was flying on Ramage's wing (while I was on Al's) during a flight over the Korean landscape. We were above twenty-five thousand feet, and Jig Dog's Banshee, in the lead, began to weave gently but erratically, as if he were inebriated. His Banshee rose slightly and then descended. This had a ripple effect throughout the formation as we worked to maintain position. Shepard, always thinking, always ahead of the situation, instinctively identified the problem.

"CAG," he radioed sharply, "plug in your oxygen mask. Plug it in now! Do you read? Over."

Ramage came back with a mumbled reply. There was a nervous silence. The oscillations of CAG's jet lessened, and then settled down completely.

"Roger," Ramage said, as if coming out of the ether. "I read you. My oxygen line came loose." Ramage had been on the threshold of hypoxia (lack of oxygen), which conveys with it a sense of well-being, like drunkenness along with loss of motor skills. In an airplane that's a recipe for disaster.

Later, on the *Oriskany*, Jig Dog went up to Shepard and told him, "Alan, you saved my life today!"

The *Oriskany's* commanding officer (CO), Captain Griffin, was a likeable guy, but he wasn't terribly happy with what our jets were doing to his flight deck. Our air group was the first to have three jet fighter squadrons on board. A squadron of prop-driven AD Skyraiders complemented our little air force.

The flight deck was constructed of mahogany over a base of Douglas fir, a combination that heretofore sufficiently withstood the beating imposed by propeller aircraft slamming down on it. We were still negotiating a learning curve with jet operations, and an element of that curve was landing technique.

We were flying the approach pattern like our piston-powered counterparts, turning in close to the ship and, when over the ramp, or stern edge of the mobile runway, taking a cut upon signal from the LSO. We would nose over and then ease back slightly, as the Banshee, now powerless, fell heavily from the sky. As a result, we were gouging up the wooden deck.

At the end of his rope because of the continuing damage, a furious Captain Griffin assembled the entire air group, including Jig Dog, at the touchdown area.

He pointed to the torn splinters of wood and patched holes. "You pilots are ruining my flight deck. It's got to stop." He then stormed off, knowing Jig Dog had a word or two for us. Jig Dog explained that the LSOs and the pilots had to do a better job of cushioning the landings, that we couldn't continue to just hack power and plunk down.

Thus chastened, Jig Dog added a final sentence, one that became our motto for the rest of the deployment. "From now on," he shouted, "Don't dive for the goddamn deck!"

Cdr. Mickey Weisner became CO of the Ghostriders in 1953. A tough task-master like Carr and a seasoned aviator, Mickey was one of the incredible band of pilots and aircrewmen known as the Black Cats. They flew PBY Catalina patrol planes on daring and largely successful night missions against the Japanese in the Pacific during World War II.

VF-193 was tasked with evaluating and developing tactics to be carried out in the dark. Night flying had been conducted from the flattops during the war with propeller planes. The advent of jets created special challenges, particularly with respect to recovery operations. The angled deck was in development, as was the Fresnel Lens, with its yellow meatball and green datum lights to help guide pilots to safe landings. But at night we were still depending on LSOs to help bring us down.

In a prop, throttle response was virtually instantaneous. In Banshees and other jets of my generation, spool-up time—that interlude between the pilot's pushing the throttle forward to increase power and the engines actual response—could be several seconds, a literal eternity when at certain points in the descending turn and final straightaway to touch down. Anticipation was the key—and concentration.

At night the LSOs wore coveralls with electrically illuminated strips on their arms and legs and likewise lit signal paddles. They were bright as Christmas trees as we sighted them about half way through our final approach turn.

Then and now, a night carrier landing is an exercise in maximum concentration, constant scan between the instruments and the ship, and as near perfect basic air work as is achievable by the individual pilot. It is the singular skill that distinguishes a carrier pilot from all others in the world of aviation.

Like most everyone else, I exhorted the Lord to provide a semblance of horizon when we conducted night landings. An overcast or moonless sky was the enemy, because, except for the minimally illuminated ships, the world above, below, and all around was black. The black of the sea blended perfectly with the black of the sky. Result: no horizon, no reference line, except what was available through the attitude gyro in the cockpit. A lapse in concentration meant an introduction to old man "vertigo." He would tap you on the shoulder and say, "You think you're upside down, but you're really right side up." The dictum all naval aviators are taught applied: BELIEVE YOUR INSTRUMENTS! Not your body.

I dreaded being the first one in the pattern, because the LSOs would be just "getting their eye." They tended to improve with each pass.

We developed a traffic pattern that included a breakup well ahead of the ship at five hundred feet. As I passed the carrier downwind from a horizontal distance of approximately two thousand feet, I eyeballed the yardarm rising from the island structure, its lighted tip two hundred feet above the flight deck. Trying to fly at the same level as the top of the yardarm, I adjusted my pressure altimeter to two hundred feet.

A destroyer or a cruiser was positioned at the proscribed 180-degree position. I commenced a half-standard rate turn over the ship, eased throttle, and began a gentle descent from my already-low two hundred feet toward the moving runway. Alternatively, and with a rapidity inspired by the fear of getting behind the aircraft, I scanned the instruments and glanced out at the ship, repeating the sequence continuously.

At the ninety-degree position, I sought one hundred-feet altitude, aiming for seventy feet at the ramp, the very end of the deck. The deck itself was sixty feet above the water. That left ten feet from the cut to touchdown. We were taught that it was important to look for the reflection of our belly light on the water as a clue to and confirmation of our height.

Once, during a briefing in the ready room a pilot asked, "What if your belly light is out?"

Someone in the back exclaimed, "Well, that's just tough shit!" This prompted a crescendo of laughter, typical of a naval aviator's inclination toward black humor.

There was a tendency to overshoot on final, but from about seventy-five degrees on in, the LSO was a big help, guiding us in his nicely visible electric suit with the illuminated paddles.

The LSOs weren't always perfect. One night I was in the groove, feeling pretty good about my approach, when the LSO called "Power," meaning add throttle. I did so, got too fast, and took the cut, but because of my excess speed, I floated over the wires and plowed into the barrier. I wasn't hurt, but the Banshee sustained minor wing damage.

Then there was the night John Mitchell put his F2H in the spud locker, the tail end of the carrier right below the flight deck. I had "trapped" and had taxied forward to the bow parking area. In the Banshee, we had to keep 70 percent rpm on the bird even when idling on deck. This was to generate air flow through the exhaust section to prevent pools of fuel from building up and creating a fire hazard.

People were moving about my aircraft, and I feared that my 70 percent power setting might blow someone over the side. So I came back on the throttle. Meanwhile, Mitchell, in his Banshee, was on final approach. Suddenly, a balloon of fire exploded from my tail section—a residual fire—visible for miles in the dark night, not to mention Mitchell in the final stage of recovering on the ship. Later, John told me that my bright fire did not cause him to crash. Nonetheless, his jet slammed into the back end of the *Oriskany,* the lower half breaking off and dropping into the water, while the forward portion containing John and the cockpit wedged into the ship and stuck there. Fuel from the Banshee sloshed onto the hangar deck, but thankfully there was no fire.

The crash and salvage crew rushed to the scene, their first priority being to save the pilot. A sailor wearing a silver asbestos suit worked his way to the cockpit. It was empty.

"Where the hell is the pilot?" he yelled. This was quickly reported to us in the ready room. Mitchell must have fallen into the sea. The ready room, normally a spirited chamber ripe with life, grew instantly somber. We hung our heads disconsolately, each fellow pilot mentally working his way through the loss of a shipmate.

Then the phone rang and the squadron duty officer (SDO), Lt. Wilmer Gilbert, answered. He listened for a moment then said, "Where are you calling from, John?"

For a crazy instant I thought, 'Maybe he's calling from heaven.' There was an anxious moment, all eyes fixed on the SDO, who held his hand over the transmission end of the phone. "Mitch is OK!" he said excitedly. "He's down in sick bay." Chins lifted from chests; there was a collective exchange of questioning expressions, then a burst of cheers.

Incredibly, following the crash no one had noticed Mitch safely egress from the cockpit, nor did anyone pay special attention to him as he proceeded belowdecks to sick bay. He later explained, "I figured the doc would want to check me over anyway. So I just went straight to Medical."

I've always wondered if anyone else in the annals of naval aviation ever pulled a disappearing act like John Mitchell's.

We also flew night intercepts guided by the controllers on the ship. These were relatively routine events, hardly different from daytime exercises when we practiced pursuing an "enemy" fighter. Still, in the dark, one had to be very careful, because our airplanes in the dark were hardly more than a pattern of fast-moving lights in the sky.

VF-193 also experimented with nuclear weapon delivery techniques. Pilots were split into two groups, one focusing on night work, the other on the nuclear aspects. I was primarily a night flyer. Al Shepard was the only pilot who flew both night missions and nuclear weapons delivery. The latter, incidentally, consisted of low-angle loft, high-angle loft, and over-the-shoulder maneuvers, all designed to toss a bomb toward a target while allowing the delivering plane to achieve a safe separation distance from the subsequent explosion.

My first squadron duty clearly exceeded all expectations. Moreover, all the Ghostriders survived our two deployments. Our sister squadron VF-191, flying F9F Cougars, had less luck.

Chapter Five

FAST AND FASTER

I'm not sure how many times I had to shut down the J65
because of excessive vibrations, but it was more than several. . . .

ED HEINEMANN, THE GREAT CHIEF ENGINEER of the Douglas Aircraft Company during the 1950s, once said, "If the jet engine had been invented first, there might never have been piston-powered engines for aircraft." Ed presided over the design of an impressive array of airplanes, especially the "Sky" series, which included the Skyhawk, Skyray, Skywarrior, Skyknight, and Skylancer. He knew his stuff. Another of his axioms was, "Acquire the engine, then build the aircraft around it." Which was his way of saying the obvious—the engine is the heart of any flying machine.

The Douglas Company's experimental Skystreak and Skyrocket clearly demonstrated we could go higher and faster. The former achieved two successive world speed records of 640 and 650 miles per hour (mph) respectively in 1947, well before the booming 1950s. The swept-wing Skyrocket reached 1,238 mph in level flight and peaked at 83,235 feet in a climb test in 1951.

Every new type of aircraft had to undergo extensive testing at Patuxent River before approval to enter full-scale production. Moreover, thanks to the British, whose innovative achievements included the angled deck, the mirror landing system, and the steam catapult for aircraft carriers, there was an escalating need for test work. Envisioning this, and not a little influenced by Alan Shepard, who had already done test flying, I applied for TPS.

It was with disappointment, then, when at the completion of my tour with the Ghostriders, I received orders to the training command as a flight instructor. I would be able to bag a lot of flight time teaching others how to fly the Navy way, but I desperately wanted to be a part of this fast-blossoming jet age. Turbine power was key to the technological boom that was propelling us into new regimes, the unknown some called it, and I wanted to be a part of it. Moreover, the Korean War had ended, but the malice engendered by America's troubles with the Soviet Union had created the Cold War and the consequent rush to arms.

Lieutenant Commander Al Shepard had been ordered to a unit involved in aviation training devices, a career step that held no appeal for him. Somehow, he was able to convince the powers that be to send him back to Patuxent and engineering test pilot duty instead. I was inclined to dutifully accept the cards I had been dealt. However, to my elated surprise, my application for test pilot training was approved by a board convened for that purpose, and my orders to the training command were rescinded.

Before checking into TPS, I was sent to the University of Southern California to attend its highly regarded Aviation Safety Course, an excellent prelude to test pilot duty, although it portended frequent assignments to accident investigations, of which there was a near abundance at Pax. Among the school's technical courses was one in aircraft investigation procedures. I was the first graduate of this school to matriculate at the TPS, so I was destined to serve on a number of the boards formed following flight mishaps. This was a dreaded endeavor, necessary but sometimes demoralizing, because there often were fatalities involving people I knew and had flown with. At the same time, these in-depth and incredibly detailed investigations served, to a degree, to prevent future accidents. Quite often the findings of these boards resulted in design changes to aircraft.

After my return from sunny California, Anne and I packed up our belongings, shipped what we could, and drove cross country to Maryland and a pastoral sixty-four hundred acres originally called Cedar Point but now commonly known as Patuxent River.

The air station at "Pax" had been established during World War II, and because of its remote location on the shores of Chesapeake Bay with the Atlantic Ocean to the east; it was an ideal site for testing the new birds developed by the Douglas, Grumman, Chance Vought, McDonnell, and other companies.

Anne and I couldn't have been happier, because we would be living in a recreational paradise, with water sports and rolling green landscape. I would also be reunited with irrepressible Commander Shepard.

We would also become friends with another illustrious pilot destined for glory, John Glenn, then a Marine Corps major. The sober-minded but affable Glenn is one of the most pleasant individuals I ever knew and was the equal of Shepard when it came to flying. If it came down to who of the two was the best, I'd still give the edge to Shepard, but only by a centimeter or so. John and his wife, Annie, and Anne and I and our children had a full social life at Patuxent, highlighted by waterskiing on weekends during the summer months. The Glenns lived just down the street.

I remember Glenn once expressing his love for flying and the opportunity the Marine Corps provided him to do just that. "It's a priceless feeling to look out at the airplanes parked on the flight line, knowing you were going to fly one of them that day."

I started the six-month TPS course in February 1956. The day was split half and half between ground school and flying. The curriculum began with refreshers in math and physics and then progressed to aerodynamics, aircraft performance, and a multitude of other subjects, including stability and control, which, it turned out, became my specific area of expertise. The routine was as rigorous as it was fulfilling. We worked our tails off studying and writing reports. Saturdays were the only days off, because we had to hit the books Sundays in preparation for the week that followed. When we weren't minding a classroom desk or filling a cockpit, we were sopping up every morsel of knowledge we could.

One of the hurdles we had to negotiate was writing an arduous, comprehensive Navy Preliminary Evaluation of an aircraft. I chose to do mine on the Grumman F9F-6 Cougar, a swept-wing fighter and one of the first supersonic aircraft—supersonic in a dive, that is. The aircraft was already flying in the fleet, so we knew a lot about it. I put it through all the required maneuvers, acquiring volumes of technical notes along the way. Because it had already joined the fleet, its capabilities were known. But the report was exclusively mine, based on my own observations. It consisted of an all-encompassing description in minute detail of the aircraft's performance from takeoff to landing and all points in between. It was like writing a technical manual, and it was a springboard to those meticulous and demanding reports we would have to compose as engineering test pilots on new aircraft undergoing evaluation before their introduction to the fleet.

As to the Cougar's supersonic capability, that airspeed could be achieved only by climbing to altitude, tipping over, and then diving straight down with full power on.

In retrospect, TPS was a grand prelude to what were my happiest years in the Navy. Thanks to Naval Academy training, the gift of an excellent memory, and the solid foundation in learning garnered at West End High School, I finished number one of twenty-five students in the TPS Class 16, which was frosting on the cake. My next assignment: the Carrier Branch of the Flight Test Division of the Naval Test Center.

I performed crosswind landing tests in the FJ Fury on board the USS *Intrepid* (CV-11), trying to determine the feasibility of landing on an aircraft carrier when the ship is not flying directly into the wind. The reasoning was that there may be occasions when the carrier is operating in a body of water, perhaps like the Arabian Sea, where maneuvering room is limited and the ship cannot maintain a steady course into the wind.

On one of the tests, I was on final approach to the USS *Intrepid*, nearing "low state," or low fuel condition. I also suspected the accuracy of the fuel gage. Anyway, nearing touchdown, the engineers in the bowels of the ship elected to "blow the tubes," expelling black, pent-up exhaust from the diesel engines through the ship's stack, an absolute no-no during flight operations. The black cloud of smoke obliterated the sky. Day had suddenly turned into night. I had no choice but to ram on full power and wave off, which I did. The air boss directed me to "bingo," to divert, to Naval Air Station Oceana near Virginia Beach, Virginia.

I climbed to fifteen thousand feet, aimed directly at Oceana, which was forty miles away.

Nearing the airfield, I radioed Oceana tower, informed the controller I was "low state," and requested a straight-in approach.

"Roger," the controller in the tower replied immediately, "you are cleared to land on runway 24. Proceed direct."

At one point I thought I would make it, but the needle on the fuel gage was just about pegged on empty. I descended, keeping my landing wheels retracted to eke out every foot of distance I could manage. I would extend them at the last possible moment, should I reach the runway threshold. But I didn't. The engine quit when I was several hundred feet from the paved end. I plowed into the turf and skidded forward onto the paved runway. Thankfully, the Fury did not catch fire. I was unhurt, and the aircraft was salvageable. I was incensed about banging up the jet, and it wouldn't be easy informing Anne that I had once again terminated a flight with a crash landing. But I would live to fly another day.

I gave my report to officials at Oceana and Pax, and afterward all I could think about was Anne, pregnant with Wendy, our third child. This crash landing wasn't going to set any better with her than the SNJ incident at the Kennedy Ranch in Texas and the cold catapult shot south of Hawaii in the Pacific had. It didn't, but, outwardly, Anne soldiered on. Inwardly, her comfort level with my flying had to be at a low point.

We weren't happy with the J65 engine that powered the Fury. It was manufactured by the Curtiss Wright Company but was a duplicate of a British engine. Interestingly, the British hand-tooled their engines. When Curtiss Wright built their duplicate, they employed mass-production techniques. As a result, the Curtiss Wright version vibrated because the company couldn't achieve the tolerances established by the British.

I'm not sure how many times I had to shut down the J65 because of excessive vibrations, but it was more than several and culminated in precautionary flame-out type approach, relighting the engine on final.

I conducted minimum distance takeoffs in the Fury, working out the parameters that would be entered in a particular aircraft's flight manual. This required detailed measuring of the distance needed to take off at gross weights ranging from the absolute minimum to the maximum. We varied the weight by placing such external items on the aircraft as bombs and fuel tanks.

The tests were difficult, because if you tried to lift the aircraft prematurely, it might stall with a sudden dropping of the wing, which was prelude to a colorful crash and explosion, with virtually no opportunity for escape. In addition, landing the aircraft at heavy weights called for heavy breaking, which, in turn, led to overheating the brakes and raising the temperature and pressure of the air inside the wheels and tires to the point they might explode. Inevitably, the aircraft would swerve and most likely depart the runway. On some occasions, the wheel apparatus and tires might disintegrate, hurling rubber and metal fragments in all directions, with the attendant danger to those who might be in their path.

The FJ's wheel brake system was rather fragile and thus troublesome. Twice, the wheels exploded on me after landing. It's normal for tires and brakes to heat up during landings because of the unavoidable friction produced when rolling rubber meets solid pavement. This was especially true with the Fury, because it was considered a low-drag airplane needing plenty of roll-out distance before coming to a halt.

I was returning from a flight in a FJ-4 Fury at Pax one day, having made a number of minimum-distance takeoffs at maximum weight. I landed, maneuvered onto the taxiway, and approached an intersection where a perimeter road used by trucks, cars, and other vehicles crossed the taxiway. A traffic fixture with green and red lights was situated at the intersection, and a line of vehicles was halted, awaiting my passage. As I came abreast of them, I was startled by a loud explosion. I brought the Fury to an immediate stop. I shut down the engine, climbed out to assess the situation, and found that the wheel and tire on the side facing the cars had burst, sending a shower of debris primarily at one car, beside which stood a highly agitated lady.

"Why are you trying to kill me?" she shouted.

I didn't have an immediate answer for that. She was unhurt, fortunately, but the radiator in her car had been pierced by metal fragments, causing it to leak. It took me forever to convince the lady, the wife of a fellow officer stationed on base, that I had not intentionally caused the wheel and tire to explode. The Navy paid for the necessary repairs to her car, but the woman's rage continued for a long time.

Anyway, this wasn't a fault in just the Fury. The state of the art in those days was such that landing wheels and brakes on the jets were neither strong enough nor resistant enough to heat. A wheel on a plane I was flying blew a second time during a catapult test, but no one was showered with hot rubber and metal.

I also flew the FJ configured with a small rocket mounted above the tail-pipe. At altitude I ignited the rocket to boost the Fury's speed and executed high-g pulls on the jet to measure performance at the increased velocity. We had some rudimentary telemetry in those days, which enabled the technicians on the ground to monitor, in real time, what we were doing in the sky.

During high-speed flight, we experienced aerodynamic heating caused by the friction of airflow across the skin of the plane. We learned that the heating effect is proportional to the square of the Mach number. If you're at Mach II, you're experiencing four times the aerodynamic heating you get at Mach I. It could get hot in the cockpit, especially flying from the desert at the Edwards Air Force Base complex out West.

I was no stranger to the "pucker factor," the phenomenon known commonly as downright fear. Not panic, but genuine and controlled fear. That usually happened to me booming through the ozone when the jet starts to vibrate. Any way you look at it, vibrations declare that your airplane is out of balanced flight, if only marginally. But at tremendous speed, vibrations could be a prelude to disaster, like the bird coming unglued in midair. Still, nothing was more fearful to me than the shotgun shell sounds produced by compressor stalls.

In the F8U-3, with its twenty-eight thousand pounds of thrust, igniting the afterburner at low altitude sent a burst of fuel into the tailpipe section that was immediately ignited, producing a rather jarring explosion. At supersonic speed, there is supersonic airflow at the intake of the compressor. That airflow inevitably slows slightly, and as it does, shock waves result from this sudden disturbance. Thus, ram air doors were developed to facilitate the transition from supersonic to subsonic flight, diminishing the opportunity for shock waves to form. If the ram air doors were perfectly aligned when lighting the burner, the Crusader would experience a tremendous and threatening yaw. Obviously, precision design was a must.

Al Shepard and I became pioneers in pressure suits, a dubious honor, because nobody wanted to wear the damn things. We were on the Navy Preliminary Evaluation Team for the F5D Skylancer at Edwards Air Force Base in California. The tests consisted of some high-altitude zoom climbs and engine tests, so we had to wear cumbersome partial-pressure flight suits. They consisted of a completely enclosed helmet and cloth suit, with capstans that ran down the sides of both arms and legs.

During high-altitude decompression in an aircraft, the pilot would have to "pressure breathe." When pressure breathing, the air is forced into the mouth on inhalation, and the pilot had to force it out on exhalation, just the opposite of normal breathing—a very exhausting evolution. Moreover, the capstans would fill with high-pressure air, pulling ribbonlike straps tightly across the chest, stomach, back, and legs to provide the pressure necessary to prevent formation of air bubbles in the blood.

Before each pressure-suit flight, the survival technicians would pressurize us so that we could practice pressure breathing and become familiar with functioning in a pressurized suit. During one of these sessions, Al and I were donning our partial-pressure suits, when he told the technician, "Give me full pressure today."

The technician looked warily at Al and said, "Commander, I don't think you want to do that. It'll make you real uncomfortable."

Shepard didn't hesitate. "Just give me the full pressure," he said.

The technician reluctantly obeyed, turned the pressure to full, and within seconds Al became as rigid as a robot, with arms and legs forcing him into a kind of spread-eagle stance. We had to hold back our laughter, as Al grimaced in extreme discomfort, forcing air into his lungs with painful effort and standing there like laundry hung on a line to dry.

For a month after that, Al looked like a zebra in the shower, because the straps had created red marks on his body as a result of the tight constraint at the highest pressure setting.

This was a typical Alan Shepard adventure, characterized by his pursuit of the ultimate challenge.

The irrepressible Al drove an MG sports car. Capt. Tom South, CO of Naval Air Station Patuxent, was a stickler for wearing uniforms properly. One day, as South was gazing out his office window, Al drove by at high speed in his little convertible, wearing a tam-o'-shanter and a white scarf with his uniform. South was furious, but he let Al off with a verbal reprimand. Alan Shepard was always on the leading edge.

It's fair to say test flying was a bit more dangerous than routine flying in the fleet. Yet, naval aviators tend to be optimists, confident in their ability to handle adversity should it raise its annoying head and threaten one's well-being. I wasn't naïve enough to believe I could manage any emergency. Sometimes events occur with such rapidity a pilot doesn't have time to consider corrective actions. So, I kept my personal affairs in order, wanting to assure Anne and the kids that they would be well taken care of. Most of the test pilots did the same.

We evaluated ejection seats. In jets, because of the high speed and high altitude regimes in which they operate, bailing out by manually climbing from the cockpit and pulling the ripcord à la World War II days was totally impractical. Ejection seats are pyrotechnic devices that kick you away from a stricken jet and automatically actuate the parachute, with a manual backup system available to the aviator, wherein he pulls a D-shaped ring to release the chute.

Marine major Tim Kean was flying an F8U-1 in afterburner at low altitude when he got into pilot-induced oscillations and the wing literally tore free from the jet. The jet went immediately out of control and crashed, killing Tim. We learned he probably tried to eject, but the subsequent investigation revealed that an incompatible firing pin had been installed in the seat by the technicians. Tim didn't have a chance. It was a hard way to learn a lesson.

There were many accidents in those days, and it seemed as if we attended funerals with a depressing regularity, a point vividly made by Tom Wolfe in his book, *The Right Stuff*.

There were also lighter moments. We had been coordinating tests with the Forrestal Laboratories at Princeton, where naval officers were taking postgraduate courses in aeronautical engineering. I would fly the test they desired in an instrumented airplane, then mail them the data to analyze and use as needed. On one occasion I was invited to fly to Princeton with a package of data and to visit the students and professors at the facility. I invited Pete Conrad, a Princeton graduate and "astronaut to be," to go along in a T-28 Trojan, a two-seat, piston-powered trainer. It was springtime, and we would be landing on a grass airfield at the New Jersey-based school. The officers at Princeton informed me the field had pretty much dried out from the winter rain and snow and that the turf was compact enough to accommodate the T-28.

With Pete in the rear seat, we launched early in the morning, made it to Princeton in good time, and landed quite smoothly. I delivered the data, and Pete and I spent a pleasant and informative day with our friends and their colleagues at the lab. We traded seats for the flight back, Pete flying the bird from the front. Preparing to depart in late afternoon, we were cautioned to taxi along the compacted taxiways. I noticed that Pete wasn't paying attention to the briefing. He wore an expression that said, "Oh, I've been here before, I know what to do, and this briefing really isn't necessary."

Pete fired up the R-1820 engine, completed the checks, and lurched forward. Instead of adhering to the compacted taxiway, however, Pete aimed the Trojan directly across the grass toward the takeoff end of the runway. The T-28 shortly became mired in the soft, noncompacted ground. He added power to free us, but that only made matters worse, as the nose of the airplane dipped and the propeller blades churned into the soggy sod, causing sudden stoppage of the engine. We secured the switches and got out.

"Oh brother," I thought, as pilot in command, "Two experienced naval aviators trapped in the mud. I'm in deep trouble now." Small fragments from the extreme tips of two of the three blades were missing. We'd probably need a new engine, new propeller blades, and a crew to do the repairs. This would take time, and I figured I'd be stuck in Princeton until the job was done.

The aircraft was towed back to the hangar, where an old-hand mechanic who had been at the Forrestal laboratory a long time surveyed the aircraft. He checked the oil strainer and found no metal particles, as would normally occur when there is sudden stoppage of the engine. He eyed the propeller blades for a long time in silence as I anxiously awaited his evaluation.

Finally, he said, "I have an idea. I'll use a hacksaw and cut away the jagged area on one of the blades, then make a template and cut an equal amount from the other two blades." Hopefully, this would preclude asymmetrical loads on the prop.

He did this in efficient short order, and I test ran the engine at high power, discovering happily that there was no untoward vibrations.

"You had your chance, Pete," I said to Conrad. "I'm going to fly it back."

He didn't protest.

I taxied out as twilight descended on New Jersey, lined up, added power, and commenced the takeoff roll. In the back of my mind I was uncertain about the "fix" the old hand had contrived. But the instrument readings were satisfactory, and as we lifted off and passed over power lines and trees at the perimeter of the airfield, anxiety was replaced by growing confidence. At points along the way I nearly convinced myself the engine was vibrating, but we safely—and smoothly—made it to Pax. Throughout the journey, the engine purred steadily. The fix worked and the mechs were impressed with the work of the old hand at Princeton. However, they did replace the propellers as a precaution, and that T-28 continued in service for many years.

There was a big plus to our journey, because Pete and I had an enlightening exchange with the chairman of Aeronautical Engineering Department, Court Perkins, one of the most respected men in the field.

Another lighter moment occurred when I was "chasing"—that is, flying wing—during a test in which the lead pilot was to fly the F8U Crusader at Mach 1.1 at one thousand feet altitude over Chesapeake Bay. Visibility was bad that day because of clouds and haze, forcing us a little bit closer to land than intended. The commander of the test center received a call from a high place in Washington the next day and was asked, "Did you have any planes flathatting over the eastern shore yesterday?"

"Absolutely not," said the CO. "My boys would never do that."

Apparently, we had flown over a duck blind where some prominent Maryland citizens were hunting and scared all the ducks away. Our boss's authoritative response worked, and the matter was not pursued further, so we got away with that one.

I spent a good portion of my test pilot tour with the F8U Crusader, especially the -3 version of the fighter, which was a wonderful flying machine even though it never went into full-scale production. The most salient feature of the Crusader was the two-position wing: raised for slower flight, down flush against the top fuselage for fast flight. In terms of competition, the -3 version was up against a formidable "opponent," the F4H Phantom II built by McDonnell, which eventually won the production contract. The thinking at the top level of decision makers favored a fighter with two engines and two crewmen, which was the case with the F4H. It was in a Phantom II that I met my Waterloo in Vietnam. The F8U–3 was the one in which I traveled twice the speed of sound as described in the prologue of this book.

As a project pilot for this version of the Crusader, I spent considerable time at Edwards Air Force Base in the Mojave Desert of California, where weather conditions in this remote area were ideal for flying and where the hardpacked surface of portions of the desert were perfect for landing if you couldn't make it back to the paved runways at Edwards.

The -3 version had the same platform as its predecessors, except for a thicker fuselage needed because of its more powerful J75 engine, which could produce twenty-eight thousand pounds of thrust compared to the earlier versions with J57 engines. These had approximately eleven thousand pounds of thrust. By comparison, the F4H's J79 power plant gave the Phantom II thirty thousand pounds of thrust.

The legendary Capt. Bob Elder was on our test team, flying the Phantom along with Cdr. Dick Gordon, who later became an astronaut, while Cdr. Larry Flint, Lt. Cdr. Don Engen, and I flew the Crusader. Engen was one of the Navy's most illustrious aviators. He rose to the rank of vice admiral and, after retirement from the military, held a variety of key positions, including administrator of the Federal Aviation Administration and director of the National Air and Space Museum, a tour of duty cut short when Don lost his life in a glider accident.

Sandy McDonnell, the dynamic and often crusty head of his own company, told the Phantom pilots they were not to exceed Mach 1.5 in flight. This irritated Bob Elder, because he knew the Phantom could easily reach Mach II. We had no such restriction on the -3 version Crusader. As it turned out, I substituted for Larry Flint, who wasn't feeling well on that fateful day in September 1958, and became the first Navy pilot to reach Mach II in a Navy airplane. Contractor pilots had already taken the -3 version to Mach II.

It gets a bit complicated, but a sample of the technology that was part of our daily regimen had to do with ram effect at high Mach number, ram air being air shoved into an air intake by the motion of the intake through the air. Ram effect produced a significant increase in thrust at high Mach numbers. In the -3 version, rifling along at Mach 1.8, we achieved more excess thrust than we did at Mach .9, even though drag (the retarding force acting on an airplane traveling through the air) was higher at Mach 1.8.

The powerful jet engines of the day could do wonders, but they had bugs in them that could also create sudden disasters. For example, there was a tendency to get compressor stalls when shutting down the afterburner at high Mach number and reducing power to "normal" engine operation. A compressor stall is a condition that occurs when some of the blades of the whirling turbine meet the airflow at such an angle that there is a reversal of air flow, often leading to flameout of the engine, accompanied by nerve-rattling explosive bangs as the compressor seeks to stabilize itself.

If you came out of afterburner at Mach II in the F8U-3, a severe compressor stall would occur, possibly damaging the engine. The engineers designed a bleed valve that allowed air to escape to alleviate the "transient," which occurred when going from full afterburner to no afterburner. For the pilot, this meant coming back on the throttle to a point the bleed valve kicked in, then reducing the throttle further to come out of burner.

Even as lieutenants, some of us traveled to Washington, D.C., to brief Navy leaders on the various aircraft we were testing. Having to stand at the podium and address a gathering of seniors, including flag officers, and explaining in lucid terms its pluses and minuses was an imposing but valuable experience. Even though he was from Texas, home state of the Chance Vought Company, developers of the Crusader, Sen. Lyndon Johnson, then chairman of the Senate Armed Services Committee, did not arm twist his colleagues to pick the F8U-3. It was a tough decision, but the F4H won out.

The test pilot experience enabled me to boost practical skills as an aviator while embellishing my theoretical knowledge of how an airplane works. It's like a baseball player improving his hitting and fielding acumen while grasping a greater understanding of how the whole game is played. In essence, we learned why an aircraft behaves the way it does when you manipulate it with the flight controls and the power plant.

I liked what Rear Adm. A. M. Pride said about test pilots and hoped his words applied to me, at least to some degree. He was commander of the Naval Air Test Center in 1953 when he said that test pilots had "The priceless gift of intuitive discernment between cause and effect. All the truly great test pilots have had it." Another in the pantheon of naval aviation heroes, Pride was instrumental in the development of early carrier landing systems, and he also test flew the innovative auto gyro, a combination fixed/rotary-wing aircraft.

Chapter Six

OUT OF THE COCKPIT

---

*Admiral Anderson directed, "I want the Washington Post newspaper
outside of the stateroom door of each of the visiting officers every morning.
Please see to that."*

EVER HEARD OF A BICUSPID AORTIC VALVE? I'm one of an extremely small
percentage of people who has one. It's part of the cardiovascular system, and
although I was unaware of its existence and had passed a dozen thorough
flight physicals in my career to date, it doomed me from consideration for
assignment to the Mercury program as an astronaut. The aortic valve has
three leaves that close during the breathing process. One of my leaves was
missing, which precluded complete closure of the valve, and that allowed
an almost-immeasurable amount air to leak out, creating a very slight heart
murmur, or aortic insufficiency.

The Mercury program was America's fledgling effort to put men into space.
Manned, experimental flights had probed the tropopause, up to twelve miles
above the earth, and even the stratosphere, from twelve to thirty-one miles
above the globe. In 1958 the National Aeronautics and Space Administration
(NASA) launched a search for seven aviators who would become the nation's
first astronauts. It made sense to seek these potential pioneers among the
community of experimental test pilots in the Navy, Air Force, and civilian
categories. Consequently, I became a candidate for this coveted duty.

John Glenn, Alan Shepard, and Wally Schirra, also a Test Pilot School
graduate, sailed through the qualification process, impressing everyone
with their sharp minds, physical fitness, and proven superior flying skills.
I passed all the preliminary physical and mental tests in good shape. At
Wright Patterson Air Force Base in Dayton, Ohio, along with other candidates, I was whirled about on the business end of a centrifuge arm at high-g
forces and was also placed in a chamber heated to 120 degrees for forty-
five minutes. Sensors were attached to our bodies to record how we reacted
to this rather severe stress test. NASA was concerned about the astronauts'

ability to withstand heat because of the aerodynamic heating they would experience on reentry into the atmosphere following a mission in space.

I felt fine afterward, but after studying the data sheets, the medicos and specialists who had monitored the test detected the slight heart murmur caused by the bicuspid aortic valve. The chief Air Force fight surgeon asked the flight surgeon at Patuxent River about the murmur and was told, "Not to worry. It wasn't a problem."

I was on pins and needles because astronaut duty was a dream assignment, not for the publicity it engendered but for the opportunity to be on a new leading edge, the threshold of space. I was sent to the Malcolm Grove Clinic at Andrews Air Force Base in Maryland for a personal interview with the chief cardiologist of the Air Force, where I spent an entire day being interviewed.

"You have an aortic insufficiency," he told me. "You may have had rheumatic fever in your infancy." This was news to me. I had an illness-free youth, apart from injuries related to athletics. "You're in extremely good shape otherwise. But the tolerances for the astronaut program, by the very nature of what we'll be asking the astronauts to do, are extremely strict."

In other words, it wasn't my destiny to ride a rocket into orbit. I wouldn't be part of the history-making pursuit of going to the moon. My friendships with Al Shepard and John Glenn, though everlasting, would never be the same. Less important, I would miss being there when Al, ever the clown, undergoing a proctology exam at the Lovelace Clinic in Albuquerque, New Mexico, proclaimed, "It hurts but it hurts so good." Or later on during a psychiatric test, when Pete Conrad, shown a blank piece of paper and asked what he saw, answered, "It's upside down." I would miss those shipmates.

Disappointed, I perked myself up with the realization that things usually worked out in my favor. I certainly had no complaints about my career pattern to date. In time, I adjusted and looked forward instead of back.

Cdr. Joe Moorer (USNA 1945), who was operations officer at the TPS at Patuxent, recommended me to his brother, Rear Adm. Tom Moorer, who was seeking a flag lieutenant. Tom Moorer was a phenomenon, a World War II hero who had become a flag officer in only twenty-six years of service and who now commanded Carrier Division Six, home ported in Mayport, Florida, and based on the USS *Saratoga* (CV-60) when deployed. Anne and I packed up the kids, had our household effects shipped, and motored to Mayport.

A flag lieutenant is an "aide," and the aide's duties range from valet to confidant. He's the admiral's right-hand man, oversees his appointments and meetings, makes sure the car is there to pick up and deliver him on time, and masters the protocol so necessary when dealing with dignitaries and other distinguished guests. He communicates with counterparts likewise employed and often deals directly with other flag officers. Do it right and performance as a flag lieutenant can't help but enhance a career. I rationalized to myself that this was a sound pathway for me. I had been in the cockpit for a solid eight years. This duty would broaden my experience in the Navy.

Although I was in for incredibly long work days, often eighteen hours nonstop, the job was a blessing, because I worked for Tom Moorer, a man destined to become not only the chief of naval operations (CNO) but chairman of the Joint Chiefs of Staff, from 1970 to 1974, as well. He was a respected power broker and leader of men, and the personification of a southern gentleman with a will of steel. The down side was my family situation. I didn't know it when the tour started, but I would be away from Anne and the kids for great chunks of time over the next two years.

Actually, I made it to Mayport in May 1959 before Moorer and served as temporary aide to the incumbent, Rear Adm. George W. Anderson (USNA 1927). Anderson was another front-runner, who eventually became CNO from 1991 to 1993. I was heaved into the caldron from the get-go.

The admiral was hosting a North Atlantic Treaty Organization (NATO) committee of four-star officers called the "NATO Standing Group," which was visiting the *Saratoga* while at sea off the Atlantic coast, and I was charged with handling the details of meeting. An absolute stickler for military protocol, Anderson was a picture-poster admiral, a handsome, well-built man with silver hair, a winning smile, and perfectly tailored uniforms. When he commanded the Sixth Fleet, it was no wonder his voice call was "White Charger." He could have played himself in the movie. He favored white uniforms in season, and for special occasions he especially liked the "choke collar" formal attire that most of us dreaded. Khakis were more comfortable and far easier to maintain, but the staff had to follow suit and don whites as well, a huge pain for them.

Before the NATO officials arrived for the visit, Admiral Anderson directed me, "I want the *Washington Post* newspaper outside the stateroom door of each of the visiting officers every morning. Please see to that."

That was not easy to do, but I arranged for the newspapers to be flown from the nation's capital at "oh dark thirty" to Marine Corps Air Station

Cherry Point, North Carolina. From there, one of our twin-engine Traders, referred to as the "COD"—for Carrier On-board Delivery—would collect them and haul them to the carrier. We managed to make deliveries on time.

It's best to stay on the good side of any flag officer, particularly one like Admiral Anderson, who went on to earn a third star.

I'm glad I wasn't his aide when he was commanding the Sixth Fleet in the Mediterranean. The story goes that his flagship, the cruiser USS *Des Moines*, had executed a "Med Moor" in Barcelona. A Med Moor entails backing the ship to the designated pier so that it is aligned perpendicular to it. As a result, there was a sole accommodation ladder on the fantail for enlisted personnel as well as officers and any guests. When moored parallel to a pier, there are separate accommodation ladders for sailors and officers.

Admiral Anderson had gone ashore one evening to visit a group of civilians. Unexpectedly, by the crew, anyway, the admiral invited his group to visit the *Des Moines* that night. Rather late in the evening the admiral and his entourage trooped along the pier and were approaching the *Des Moines*, when, to the horror of the admiral, not to mention his guests, they found the fantail area littered with drunken sailors in various positions of repose and disarray.

Predictably, Anderson blew a fuse. While it might have been overreaction, he ordered that senior shore patrol officers from that point on would be captains. That meant destroyer division commanders were among the four-stripers relegated to standing watches normally assigned to commanders and below. That fuse, by the way, stayed lit for over a month before tension in the ranks eased. Impulsive as he might have been, he impressed people and achieved goals on a continuing basis.

Admiral Anderson had a good sense of the spectacular. We had aboard a photo-Crusader, the camera-equipped F8U-1P. It carried flares for illuminating night photography. Ejected from the jet in the daytime, the flares produced brilliant flashes against the sky. One day he sent a dispatch to the foreign flag officer on a NATO ship and said, "I plan to salute your flag at 1420 hours." This befuddled the foreign ship, because we were nowhere in sight. But the F8U-1P was catapulted on its mission, flew to the foreign ship many miles away, and, once over it, fired fifteen flares at precisely 1420. This was Anderson's way of rendering honors at sea.

Anderson loved ice cream. While on the *Saratoga* one day, he rode a helicopter to visit personnel on an accompanying carrier, the USS *Essex* (CV-9). While there, he consumed some particularly delicious ice cream, which prompted him to send a flashing light message to the *Saratoga*, saying, "The *Essex* has good ice cream."

Capt. John Hyland called me, described what happened, and asked, "What does he mean by this?"

I said, "Captain, I think Admiral Anderson is trying to tell you that the *Saratoga* doesn't have good ice cream."

Hyland summoned his supply officer, and an ice cream improvement program commenced immediately, with, fortunately, good results

Admiral Anderson was CNO during the Cuban Missile Crisis, and after he retired from the Navy, Pres. John F. Kennedy appointed him as ambassador to Portugal.

I gained new insights into Navy operations from the vantage point of surface officers, those who run the ships. It took some time, but I qualified as a tactical watch officer, having acquired a whole new portfolio of knowledge and a profound appreciation of surface warfare operations, particularly how challenging it is to maneuver large groups of ships on the rough and busy seas.

I've read countless biographies of great leaders, especially those in the armed services, and am fascinated by the fact that each possessed a style and demeanor unique unto himself. Their common denominator was the ability to get the job done regardless of individual style.

Tom Moorer was a different animal altogether from Admiral Anderson. My days were exhausting and eventful at his side, but I wouldn't trade them for a ton of gold. Because I traveled extensively with him, we held countless personal discussions, from which I derived a kind of mental handbook of sound leadership traits. One of my perennial questions to him was, "How are you able to make decisions so rapidly?"

"The important thing is to identify a course of action and get everyone supporting it and involved in it," he explained. "The average mistake that many people make is delaying making a decision. By the time action is taken, it's been overcome by events. Don't waste time researching every possible course of action to come up with the best one. Decide on one that you believe might work and get your people started on it."

He believed that the average officer is, basically, reluctant to make a decision, that he or she will vacillate and delay. Consequently, they "delay" themselves into a much more difficult situation or risk losing an opportunity to resolve a situation. He wasn't impetuous, but he did have a way of coming up with commonsense courses of action expeditiously. Part of that is a given talent; part of it is based on experience. It didn't hurt that his breadth of knowledge on tactics was remarkable.

We participated in a major NATO exercise in 1960, primarily with the British and the French and simulated nuclear weapons strikes against the Norwegians, who played the part of our opponents. During that exercise, he and I had a two-day sojourn on the submarine, the USS *Triton,* commanded by Cdr. (later Capt.) Ned Beach (USNA 1939). Moorer soaked up every morsel of knowledge he could about the radar picket capability of the sub. He had a mind like a sponge, accumulating information and retaining it.

Moorer was always on an even keel; I never saw him lose his temper He despised stuffy behavior. He believed it important that an officer be approachable, not standoffish. He wanted his subordinates to be able to think for themselves, to take action as necessary without fear of reprimand. This attitude imbued them with confidence in themselves and their superiors and made them work all that much harder to succeed.

My family arrived in Jacksonville in May, and I deployed three months later aboard the USS *Saratoga,* our flagship. We got off to a bad start, however, because of a flooding casualty that caused the *Saratoga* to turn around for repairs. This forced us to transfer the staff to the already-crowded USS *Essex,* the other aircraft carrier in the division, where we lived in rather cramped quarters for a couple of weeks until the *Saratoga* caught up with us in the Mediterranean. The *Essex* had a great skipper, by the way, Capt. Tom South (USNA 1934), who, following his tour on the *Essex,* became Moorer's chief of staff. I developed a very close relationship with this good-humored officer. In fact, the whole staff got along well, a tribute, I think, to Admiral Moorer's demeanor and the respect he commanded.

In those days most naval aviators did not learn the intricacies of communications. Moorer, for example, had mastered single-side-band operations and knew the advantages of low frequency versus medium frequency and ultra high-frequency radios.

Captain Hyland, skipper of the *Sara* (the USS *Saratoga*) was another highly respected officer. He had privileges to play at tennis clubs on the French Riviera but had trouble finding someone to play with him. He learned that I liked the sport and invited me along when we were in port in Cannes to play at these clubs. We got to know each other well that way.

Like Moorer, Hyland was a cool customer. Entering port for a visit to

Istanbul is rather tricky because of the five-knot flow of the narrow Bosporus straits. I was on the bridge as we approached the city, and Captain Hyland was carefully executing commands, when an officer on the bridge announced, "Captain, there's a freighter in our assigned anchorage."

Ordinarily, this would infuriate the skipper of a huge ship like an aircraft carrier. Taking someone else's anchorage just isn't done. But John Hyland was not given to outbursts and calmly guided the *Saratoga* into a spot as close to the freighter as safety would permit.

Hyland, who rose to four-star rank, was a three-star and commanded the Seventh Fleet when I was shot down as commanding officer of a fighter squadron.

Naval aviation was feeling its oats in those days. The Cold War was upon us, and our carriers were roaming the seas with nuclear weapons in their arsenal ready to take on the Reds. Although a somber undertone of distrust of the Communists and lament over the possibility of unutterable destruction flavored our thoughts, naval air was a formidable power with which the enemy would have to contend.

After returning from the Mediterranean in the spring of 1961, the *Saratoga* was ordered to the Navy yard in Brooklyn, New York, for maintenance upkeep. Customarily, in such situations, the admiral's staff would remain at its Mayport headquarters while the carrier underwent overhaul or repair work. But despite protestations from Admiral Moorer, Vice Adm. Joe Rees (USNA 1926), commander Naval Air Force Atlantic, directed him and our staff to remain on the ship, an order that created a morale problem, because it meant more time away from the families of staff members, not to mention the admiral himself. The air wing flyers had dispersed to their home bases, and ship's company personnel knew well in advance they would have to stay with the ship no matter wherever it went.

When the *Saratoga* finally departed New York, it was slated to collect a load of ammunition at the weapons station near Portsmouth, Virginia. That done, we left at night for the journey to Mayport. In the middle of the night, we were awakened by the loud and frightening sound of metal tearing metal. We had collided with a German merchant ship. The overhang of the carrier scraped through the entire superstructure of the freighter. Although there were no fatalities, there were numerous injuries to crews on both ships.

Collisions at sea are never less than critical events. Admiral Moorer decided he would brief Rees directly, an action I know he dreaded. He and I flew in a helicopter to Norfolk, where Rees's headquarters was. We arrived OK, got in the official car awaiting us, and motored directly toward the headquarters building. Unbeknownst to us, Rees was heading in the opposite direction to board a helicopter for a flight to the *Saratoga* to see the damage himself. We spotted his car at an intersection, and I hurriedly got out and drew the attention of the occupants. I asked if Rear Admiral Moorer could ride with him so they could talk. But I was waved away. So Moorer and I returned to base operations for a return trip to the *Saratoga*.

It was an obvious embarrassment for Admiral Moorer to not be on board to greet Rees. But there wasn't a thing he could do about it. Nevertheless, Moorer didn't get excited about the miscue. He just didn't allow such unfortunate incidents like the collision to phase him, knowing that time suppresses, if not heals, up-tight emotions. The collision made the headlines, and the blame was placed on the *Saratoga* for a mix-up in signaling while trying to avoid the German vessel. Interestingly, Capt. Al Fleming (USNA 1936), the *Saratoga's* CO, was found at fault even though he wasn't on the bridge at the time. The event didn't preclude his subsequent selection to flag rank, a promotion that doesn't often happen to carrier skippers who have collisions or run aground during their watch.

The accident was not without humorous overtones. We learned later that at the instant of impact the German freighter was signaling "Bon Voyage!" to our ship.

We spent a long week at the Portsmouth Navy Yard while the *Saratoga* was repaired.

At the end of our Mediterranean deployment in 1960, we were coming into Mayport, and I was scheduled as the staff tactical watch officer for the 0400 to 0800 watch, during which we were to arrive in Mayport. I talked over the plan for the next day with fellow officers, absorbed their thoughts and came up with a plan. We had to launch the air group at a point corresponding to the *Saratoga's* passing a designated sea buoy marker in order to reach Mayport at high tide. Mayport has only a minimum depth of water, so if we couldn't make it at high tide, we would have to wait hours for another try. Knowing the pier would be packed with anxiously waiting dependents and loved ones, it wouldn't set well if we missed our time at the sea buoy.

We examined the predicted winds, plotted the various possible points for the launch, depending on the existing winds, considered other contingencies, and, satisfied with the plan, I went to bed.

I arrived on the bridge at 0300 just to make sure everything was under control. I noted that the officer who I would shortly relieve had not reset the dead-reckoning tracer bug on the plotting chart. This bug reacted to signals from a pitot tube in the water that detects the ship's velocity and from a gyro-compass. But the bug seemed to be indicating accurately.

A while after I relieved the flag bridge watch officer, I asked the navigator on the captain's bridge to verify the ship's position. He gave it to me, and a quick check of the chart revealed, to my alarm, that the carrier was thirty-five miles out of position. My predecessor on the flag bridge had failed to detect this error. It was nearly 0500, and the launch was to commence at 0630. We were way behind our Point of Intended Movement, or PIM. So I ordered the ship to speed up from twenty to thirty knots to close that ten-mile gap.

In his bunk, Capt. Jerry King, the staff operations officer, felt the vibrations from the increased ship's speed. He called me on the phone.

"What the hell's going on up there?" he demanded.

As I tried to explain the situation, I sensed that Jerry was half asleep, but that didn't prevent him from chewing me out. "God dammit," he said. "I thought you had all this worked out last night, and now you're out of position."

I said nothing for a moment, and then he added, "Boy, if you screw this thing up, it's really going to be bad. You know, we have all those families waiting to see the carrier."

"Yes sir!" I said, "I understand that. I'm trying to fix it."

Then Admiral Moorer called and calmly asked, "Why are we going so fast?"

I explained the situation to him. We were behind schedule, but I was doing what I considered necessary to catch up.

"Very well," he said. "I'm sure you'll handle it." Clearly, Tom Moorer's cool reaction was distinctly different than Jerry King's angry one.

We made up for the extra distance and started the launch at 0630. A few minutes later, the entire air group was in the sky, and the *Saratoga*, believe it or not, was within sixty seconds of reaching the sea buoy.

Jerry King was on the bridge by now, and we looked at each other, very slight smiles on our faces. I had the utmost respect for Jerry and had learned a great deal from him. He was a real pro. I certainly didn't blame him for being upset. But I'm sure glad we got the birds off on time and got the *Saratoga* to the pier with all those families and friends waiting.

In summary, there are going to be times in a Navy career when you find yourself in extremis. You need sound thinking under pressure to get through such occasions, but good luck and the grace of the man upstairs really help.

Being away from Anne and the kids for great chunks of time was extremely difficult during this eighteen-month tour of duty. I acquired an immense body of knowledge on shipboard operations and the multitude of formations required when two carriers and their accompanying ships function as a unit. Underway replenishment, setting screens for the carriers, and tactical dispersal of various elements in the group are challenging maneuvers. More important, I was exposed to leadership techniques displayed by the likes of Admirals Moorer and Anderson and their very talented senior subordinates. Aviators normally don't get such valuable exposure.

This experience bolstered my career but at notable sacrifice on the part of my family.

Chapter Seven

PHANTOMS AND FAMILY

There's a saying in the world of fighter pilots: "Speed is life."

I HAD LOGGED A FEW HOURS in the new F-4 Phantom fighter during test flights at Patuxent River, so I wasn't totally surprised when I got word that my services were required in Fighter Squadron 101, the replacement air group, colloquially referred to as "the Rag," at Naval Air Station Oceana. This unit was responsible for the initial introduction of the Phantom to the fleet. Oceana was a master jet base a few stone throws from what would become one of America's most popular resort areas—Virginia Beach. At the time, the skyline of the beach was barren, unlike today, with its motels, hotels, and condos towering shoulder to shoulder, one right after the other, all the way up and down the scenic stretch of sand on the Atlantic. Great potential orders, right? Back to the cockpit in the powerful and supersonic Phantom and right next to a beautiful beach. Anne and the kids would love it. But not so fast.

We had owned our home in Jacksonville for over a year and would now have to unload it and hike north to the Tidewater region for my next tour. The area itself had considerable appeal, not to mention that it was wonderfully steeped in naval aviation history. Plus, the air station was state of the art. Eugene Ely made the first takeoff from a ship just off the Norfolk coastline west of Virginia Beach, landing successfully on Willoughby Spit. Aircraft carriers were home based at Naval Air Station Norfolk and were the bulwarks of a vast naval complex. Surely, the complex was on the Russian's nuclear strike list, so important was it to fleet operations, particularly in the Atlantic and the Mediterranean. But I faced serious personal complications beyond that.

The trouble was that it took several months to sell the house. There was the frustrating fact I'd been at sea virtually the whole period of my current assignment as Admiral Moorer's aide, a long seventeen months. Then here comes another move in less than two years. There's only so much a family can take, despite the appeal of the next duty station. I was caught up in the painful turmoil of continuing my career at the expense of my young and growing family. Anne was a trooper, but she was frayed around the edges, just like any other spouse committed to the peripatetic life of a military man. More important, in the recesses of her mind, I knew she was apprehensive about my flying. Duty as an admiral's aide had a minimal risk factor.

The Phantom was a new bird, and I avidly wanted to fly it. But being new, even though we had thoroughly tested it, it was bound to involve complications and, inevitably, accidents, during the course of its introduction to the fleet. The three crashes I'd experienced, not to mention the fair number of close calls, did nothing to alleviate Anne's fears, although we didn't talk about it. She was very stoic and did not talk much about her fears, although it was obvious to me she was still troubled by my flying. And having to leave her and the family in Jacksonville didn't help matters.

The real estate market in Jacksonville was down at the time, we had trouble finding a buyer, and I had to respond to my orders to VF-101's Oceana Detachment in November. The main squadron was headquartered at Naval Air Station Key West, Florida, so I'd be spending time there as well. Consequently, I left the family behind and reported to the VF-101 detachment as a geographic bachelor. Not a good situation, but certainly one that's been encountered before and since by countless Navy families. Fortunately, Cdr. Jerry O'Rourke was the skipper of 101, a first-rate officer, a wonderful friend, and a liberally inclined aviator in that he allowed me to fly an F9F-8T Cougar to Jacksonville on weekends so that I could spend time with Anne and the kids.

In January 1961 the detachment was ordered to Fighter Squadron 121 at Naval Air Station Miramar, just north of the city of San Diego, for the West Coast introduction of the Phantom in Fighter Squadron 121, the replacement air squadron. Flyers derived from both 121 and 101 made up the fleet introduction team. The squadrons were flying the F3H Demon as well as the Phantom and were therefore conducting split or double operations.

Happily, we finally sold the house, and I was able to move the family to San Diego with me.

At Miramar, I worked closely with Lt. Ted Gordon, a shipmate from Patuxent who had more time in the Phantom than I did. We developed a familiarization syllabus for the aircraft. My focus was on stability and control and flying qualities. Other pilots more knowledgeable than I in air-to-air tactics with respect to missile operations handled that part of the training.

I had the advantage of detailed knowledge of the F-4's capabilities, how it handled, and importantly, how much fuel it would use. For example, I knew that at Mach 1.5, so many pounds of fuel would be burned up. I figured the Phantom would be flown more in the subsonic regime than the supersonic for the simple reason that, when you went supersonic in the F-4, you increased fuel consumption by 50 percent. For prolonged operations, the crew would probably fly at an average speed of .85 Mach number, a figure driven by fuel considerations.

During this period the Phantom was considered primarily as a fighter plane. A few years hence, in the skies over Vietnam, it would carry and deliver external stores, becoming, in effect, a fighter bomber.

The Phantom was a two-place fighter, with the pilot up front and radar intercept officer (RIO) in the rear seat. Transitioning to new aircraft is difficult enough, but the aircrew arrangement in the F-4—it was originally designated the F4H—was rather novel for the Navy. That is, having two flyers in a tactical aircraft represented a departure from the heretofore commonality of single-piloted fighter planes.

There had been the F3D Skyknight, with its side-by-side seating of pilot on the left and radar operator on the right. The plane performed well in the Korean War, although it was no speed merchant. Operational use of the F3D-2 version of the Skyknight in the Korean War was by Marine squadrons. Skyknights were responsible for the destruction of more enemy planes than any other type flown by the Navy or Marines in that conflict. The initial Skyknight aerial success occurred on November 2, 1952, when for the first time in history, one jet aircraft, the F3D, destroyed another jet, a MiG-15, during a night air-to-air fight. For training purposes, the side-by-side arrangement was excellent. The pilot could scan to his right and see the radar presentation the RIO was using and advise him accordingly. Also, being a subsonic and very stable aircraft, it provided a steady platform for teaching basic air-to-air intercepts and tactics.

Despite its great combat record, the Skyknight was aging, and although it had a maximum speed of six hundred knots, it was slow compared to the F-4. The F-4, incidentally, had been selected for production instead of my favorite aircraft, the F8U-3 Crusader.

There's a saying in the world of fighter pilots: "Speed is life." The twin-engine Phantom had speed, over fourteen hundred miles per hour of it—twice the speed of sound—to execute its interceptor/air superiority mission.

The F3D was, however, an excellent training platform as we tried to teach pilots and RIOs the intricacies of aircrew coordination in order to maximize the Phantom's performance. Electronic systems—black boxes—that operated the complex missile systems were continuously improving and multiplying the capabilities of warplanes. The RIO alleviated the pilot's burden, and this made the Phantom one of the most lethal weapons in anyone's inventory. I should mention that the Air Force had had considerable experience in two-place tactical planes, like the F-101 Voodoo, so we adopted some of its procedures for our pilot/RIO training syllabus.

Transitioning to the Phantom called for adjustment by pilots whose heretofore macho, lone-wolf disposition as a single-seat warrior entered the culture of two-man operations. Even so, I was not surprised to note that, with rare exceptions, pilots welcomed the arrangement, knowing that a two-man team was really needed to get the most from the Phantom. Being single-piloted may have been a key factor in the F8U-3 losing out to the F-4. Flight scheduling was often convoluted, because not only were we flying the Phantom and the Skyknight, but also the squadron still had F3H Demons on board, because some squadrons were still flying this aircraft and needed replacement pilots. It would take five years before the conversion to the Phantom was complete, at which point twenty-nine Navy and Marine Corps squadrons were flying it.

At one point, after two months at Miramar, even with Anne and the kids with me, I was stretched to the emotional limit with respect to my personal situation. My military career up to now had been successful by any measure. There was no doubt I was on the fast track to bigger things in the Navy, but the price on my family had become achingly high.

I talked with a number of people and asked Jerry O'Rourke to allow me to return to Oceana, where I would make a decision about my future course. I didn't want to leave the Navy, and Anne didn't want that either. So, I came up with a compromise. I would stay in the Navy but give up flying and go to the surface Navy. This didn't resolve the problem of being away from home for prolonged periods, but it did signal my intention to diminish Anne's fears about my flying.

My request for transfer to the "black shoe" Navy was approved, and my numerical designator, which was 1310, a number that indicated I was an aviator and a regular—compared to reserve—officer, was changed to the surface navy designator, 1100. It was with a very heavy heart that I made this decision, but I was determined to make the best of it.

I was assigned as navigator on the heavy cruiser, the USS *Newport News*, home-ported in Norfolk, and reported for duty in June 1961. Unquestionably, I went through ambivalent swings in the back of my mind as to whether I had done the right thing. I abhorred the thought of leaving aviation. Still, I owed it to Anne and the kids, especially in light of the unavoidable fact that aviation was a risky business in those days. The awful accident rate showed few signs of improving. An accident rate is the ratio of Class A mishaps compared to flight hours flown. Class A accidents in today's Navy imply costs of $1M or more; back then it was a lot less. Also, any accident involving a fatality is a Class A mishap. In 1961 the accident rate was 17.17, meaning there were 17.17 Class A accidents for 3,387,560 hours flown; we lost 603 aircraft in 1961, and 279 flyers were killed. By 1995 the rate was 2.17 accidents for 1,569,329 hours flown and seventeen fatalities.

I moved the family to Norfolk, removed the coveted gold wings from the breast of my uniform shirt, and took another major fork in the road.

Chapter Eight

BLACK SHOE DUTY

"What type of sound system does the president have in his quarters?"
My mind raced for a moment then I answered, "Well, sir," I said
uncertainly, "there's no phonograph available, if that's what you mean."
"Well, get one then!" ordered the admiral.

I ENTERED THE "BLACK SHOE" (surface ship) Navy determined to make the best of it, all the while sustaining an unspoken longing to be in the air with my "brown shoe" counterparts in naval aviation. This is not to say my new brethren of the fleet were any less accomplished or dedicated. The problem was very simple, as I knew it would be from the outset: I had gone from the swift to the slow. Cruising along in a jet at three hundred and fifty or more knots compared to maneuvering a ship at less than one tenth that speed constituted a major yet anticipated transition for me. Still, I was determined to make the adjustment.

The USS *Newport News* (CA-148) was the last of the "all-gun" cruisers and homeported in Norfolk. It was seven hundred feet long and seventy-six feet wide, displaced seventeen hundred tons, had a thirteen hundred man crew, and was powered by a 120,000 shaft horsepower steam power plant that enabled the ship to drive through the water at a speed in excess of thirty-two knots. It was a formidable warship with, eight eight-inch guns plus a dozen five-inch guns and other armaments. It was a *Salem* class vessel, the largest and most potent class of cruisers ever built. If I was going to serve on a ship, the *Newport News,* which was commissioned too late for World War II but was exceptionally capable, was as good an assignment as I could expect. It was a notable vessel beyond the norm of most ships like it, because it was employed as a flagship for the Sixth Fleet. Still, it was a far cry from the supercarriers then being built, which were crewed by five thousand personnel, displaced nearly one hundred thousand tons, were powered by 280,000 shaft horsepower engines and featured four and a half-acre flight decks measuring over one thousand by two hundred and fifty feet to accommodate eighty aircraft.

I was warmly received on board and assigned as navigator, which meant most of my days and nights would be spent on the starboard side of the bridge at opposite ends from and adjacent to the captain. I would be working over charts and maintaining a constant track of our position while guiding the ship toward assigned tactical positions or other destinations. We were not assigned as the Sixth Fleet flagship at the outset of my tour, but, rather, operated independently of the carrier group.

I plunged into my duties with enthusiasm, anxious to learn all I could. As it turned out, I loved the job. I cherished the time on the bridge and was absorbed by the actions involved in maneuvering the ship. I began to understand the attraction of driving a ship on the ocean, particularly from the vantage point of the bridge, with its open vista of sea and sky.

When I checked in, we were preparing to depart Norfolk for the Mediterranean. This meant another separation from the family now living in Virginia Beach. But, thankfully, Anne had come to terms with that, and my being on a ship instead of in a cockpit immeasurably relieved the strain she had been under when I was flying. There were far fewer funerals in the surface Navy than in aviation. Ironically, great strides were being made to improve aviation safety, and much of these were manifested in the introduction of the angled deck and the Fresnel landing system, which eliminated the need for a paddle-waving LSO on the port side of the carriers' stern. The LSO was still there, but now he did his thing via radio telephone. Moreover, the Naval Air Training and Operating Procedures (NATOPs) program was being introduced and would serve to standardize procedures throughout the aviation world, rather than having them defined by individual squadron policy. The accident rate was to take a significant downward tumble.

Like all aviators, I had a lot of experience with relative motion, and this paid dividends on the *Newport News,* especially during underway replenishment exercises, when I was conning the ship as officer of the day (OD). The bridge watch, normally four hours long, was a major responsibility in addition to navigation duties. We would approach an oiler (replenishment ship) on the designated bearing from aft on its port side, usually running at twenty-five knots. Directly upon passing a flag-bearing sailor standing on the forecastle of the oilier, I ordered "All back full," and the coxswain would signal the engine room to respond accordingly. As we settled into position abeam the oilier, I directed "All ahead standard." Smaller adjustments in speed and bearing followed until the vessels were mated and the fueling lines could be strung from oilier to cruiser. Rendezvousing in an aircraft was much the same, just faster. Sounds simple but a lot could go wrong during these exercises—and in the air, as well—so it took concentration and knowing your keys.

For much of my time aboard the *Newport News,* my CO was Capt. Thomas Kimmel, son of Adm. Husband Kimmel, who commanded U.S. Pacific Fleet at Pearl Harbor on December 7, 1941, and took the brunt of the blame and criticism for the disaster. Training for our deployment involved working with other ships of the division. We conducted a variety of operations, ranging from gunnery exercises, firing at ship-towed sleds and target sleeves towed by aircraft, to amphibious landing support.

One day during a competitive gunnery exercise using a sled towed by the ship as a target, I was unusually busy, when Vice Adm. John McNay Taylor, the Second Fleet commander, came onto the bridge and asked, "How are things going?" I didn't respond right away, somewhat surprised by the question, and before I could answer him, he got angry and said rather loudly to Captain Kimmel, and within ear shot of the others on the bridge, "It appears your navigator is not aware of what's going on up here."

Taylor's reputation as a stern taskmaster was well known, and I got a first-hand taste of it. I was embarrassed, to be sure, but I also knew this incident wouldn't alter Captain Kimmel's confidence in me. Junior officers and our young sailors, especially, avoided Admiral Taylor whenever they could. It occurred to me that if I ever did reach the higher echelons of Navy leadership, I wouldn't want that said of me.

We departed for the Med in August, made the crossing in six days, and "chopped" to the Sixth Fleet once we passed Gibraltar eastbound. We operated with British and French units, made some enjoyable port calls in Italy and the South of France, and for the most part, conducted training exercises. The Cold War was on, and the Soviet threat was ever present, yet we saw little of the Soviet navy and only occasionally were overflown by a Russian Bear.

I learned my trade as navigator with the wonderful support of the quartermasters headed by Chf. Johnny Johnson, an old-school type, who supervised his three enlisted quartermasters with an iron hand. They maintained the log, the "Quartermaster's Notebook," a key document that recorded all of the actions of the ship, including the ship's position, taken on the hour and half hour; course; and speed, changes that provided a permanent history of the ships actions.

After four months in the Med, the *Newport News* was unexpectedly ordered to return to Norfolk. The cruiser was to be converted to become the flagship of the Second Fleet, based in Norfolk, because the cruiser USS *Northampton,* which had been the flagship, was being reassigned. We were instructed to make our best time in recrossing the Atlantic, so we proceeded via "rum-line," which is the shortest traveling distance. This forced us to travel in the North Atlantic at very high north latitude, where the seas tended to be turbulent. It was imperative we achieve a seventeen knot speed of advance (SOA), which made matters worse, because the *Newport News* was unable to "sit down" in the high seas and plow steadily through them at a slower SOA. Instead, Captain Kimmel, on the bridge virtually all day and night, labored to avoid taking a wave that might damage the superstructure, not to mention other portions of the ship. We took a good pounding but made it home and tied up at the Portsmouth Naval Shipyard, where the modification process to become the Second Fleet flagship commenced. I had a welcome reunion with Anne and the kids.

The upgrade to the ship entailed designing and restructuring areas in the superstructure for the cognizant admiral's staff. The modifications took six months at the Portsmouth Navy Yard.

We got under way in June 1962 for a shakedown cruise off the Atlantic coast, which was successful and was a prelude to Second Fleet operations. As a navigator on the flagship, I was also responsible to the embarked admiral's staff for any navigation concerns. I was reporting to two seniors, so to speak, keeping both informed of the ship's position. I liked this because I got to know the members of the staff and this sort of camaraderie allowed me to serve them better. Another advantage of having the flag staff on board was the fact we were at the heart of the action. All the key orders to the fleet emanated from the *Newport News*.

In the spring of 1962, we were involved in a huge demonstration of fleet power for Pres. John F. Kennedy. The Norfolk-based carriers, the *Forrestal* and the *Enterprise*, and their accompanying ships practiced extensively for what the upper echelons of the Navy hoped would be the perfect extravaganza. It took place off the North Carolina coast and included an amphibious landing by the Marines at Camp Lejeune's Onslow Beach and a major air show. The air wings of the respective carriers were charged with conducting the airpower demo, which featured flybys and "attacks" on smoke lights in the water, using live guns, bombs, and rockets—the whole works. As a dramatic exclamation point to the show, an F-8 Crusader would whip by the carriers in pursuit of a remotely controlled drone and shoot it down with rockets in front of the president of the United States, viewing from the *Enterprise*.

I must admit I was doing well on the *Newport News,* having grasped the dos-and-don'ts of running a ship from the bridge. Consequently, Captain

Kimmel had confidence in me, relied on my judgment, and slept soundly at night. Still, I was surprised when he asked me to accompany him via helicopter to the *Enterprise* for a critique of the "dress rehearsal" that preceded the all-important Kennedy visit. For a lieutenant commander, I was in high cotton, sitting in among the two-, three-, and four-star flag officers in charge, including the DEPUTY CINCLANTFLEET.

At the postrehearsal briefing, there was some discussion of the problems regarding the air show, but I was caught completely off guard by a question directed at me. The bewildering question was, "What type of sound system does the president have in his quarters?"

My mind raced for a moment; then I answered, "Well, sir," I said uncertainly, "there's no phonograph available, if that's what you mean."

"Well, get one then!" ordered the admiral.

Is this what flag officers worry about? I could not believe all this fuss over a sound system while larger problems loomed. Especially when President Kennedy was reputed to have no interest in music. But we dutifully went out and purchased one.

The air show portion of the rehearsal had not gone well. Timing was off and there were other hiccups. It was important that each event, such as a flyby or a bomb drop, occur on the assigned time. There were a multitude of events, so the margin of error was minimal. Planners wanted one event to follow smartly on the heels of the one before it. The glitches were discussed at the meeting and tempers rose, coloring the gathering with a noticeable degree of apprehension as to how the final show would go. The powers that be wanted everything to function like a precision watch. Unfortunately, that didn't happen.

The air demonstration was fraught with embarrassing errors. It wasn't a disaster, but it was far from what everyone wanted: a polished exhibit of naval aviation at its best. The winds were strong that day and played havoc with timing. For example, in one case a shower of rockets from a diving Skyraider narrowly missed a fighter making a flyby. Fortunately, no one was hurt.

The most flagrant miscue involved the F-8 Crusader assigned to bag the drone. The drone whipped by the line of reference adjacent to the carriers, the Crusader in pursuit. The voice of the narrator on the ship declared the shoot down was about to take place. The Crusader pilot fired his high-velocity rockets. The rockets released from the fighter with an impressive whoosh! But they missed the drone! The drone continued undisturbed as the volley of rockets fell into the sea. On the internal radio circuit, the drone operator wisely asked the controllers of the show, "Do you want me to crash the drone?" This query brought an immediate, "Affirmative." And the drone was destroyed.

I never did learn the president's reaction to this, but I don't think anybody got fired. Yelled at, maybe, but not fired.

At night, during the visit, we formed a column of twelve ships for a pass in review for the president. The column of ships formation dates from before World War II. It is a difficult procedure, particularly in turbulent seas, because maintaining "nose-to-tail" clearance is a challenge when you're directly behind of one ship and in front of another. Captain Kimmel admitted it was a "tricky" maneuver. We got through it OK, and I believe the president was impressed, though he made no comment.

Routine operations followed through early summer of 1962, when we were assigned to conduct a NATO exercise in Northern European waters. Although I didn't participate in the actual operations, I prepared the necessary charts and navigational procedures. The *Newport News* journeyed to Halifax, Nova Scotia, en route to Europe, and I left the ship there in July. I simply had to get back into aviation and, luckily, my request was approved.

In retrospect, this black shoe tour was invaluable to me. I certainly learned a lot more about the Navy at large than the average naval aviator would. It's a shame that career progression requirements for the flyers don't allow time for a black shoe duty tour when they are junior officers. At the same time, with respect to career patterns, carefully selected aviators command aircraft carriers after attending a sequence of pertinent schools.

I believed my *Newport News* experience would enhance my prospects of gaining a carrier command were I to return to aviation duty, assuming I didn't screw up in the next ten years or so. Of course, I didn't anticipate my career would be disrupted by a period of detention in North Vietnam. This imprisonment precluded my shot at command of a deep-draft ship, a necessary prelude to carrier command, and carrier command itself.

I have particularly warm memories of the quartermasters, those sharp enlisted personnel who assisted me on the bridge, and the boatswain's mates, that seemingly roughshod cadre of sailors who compose the very heart of the Navy. In my day, the boatswain mates tended to have less education than those of other ratings did, but they were no less dedicated. The quartermasters, however, had to master celestial navigation and some other rather complicated procedures such as Loran (long-range navigation). They tended to be more academically astute than the boatswain mates, but the two worked together very competently. I loved being around both, because they made the shipboard tour of duty both worthwhile, for the new knowledge I acquired, and reassuring, having witnessed close up the wonderful mix of sailors who keep the ships afloat and ready.

In aviation I had gotten used to be out there "on the edge." That is, we were reaching out to new frontiers in the blooming jet age, and the excitement of going higher and faster was fulfilling. At the same time, I loved being on the bridge of a ship and working as a black shoe, even though simmering inside me was a degree of frustration at the slow pace of surface operations compared to air. Most of my fellow black shoes, however, had no similar feelings. They didn't miss flying, because they hadn't experienced it in the first place. They were no less committed and dedicated to fulfilling an important part of the Navy's mission.

As I look back on my career in college and after, I was no great star. A wise man once stated that 75 percent of life is showing up. During my college career, I never missed a practice. Aboard ship I never missed a muster. In the final analysis, the pleasure and satisfaction of the Navy career has been the camaraderie and bonding with my fellows, male and female, that occurs. I'm blessed with having made lifelong friends who will be with me through thick and thin. I could not have had a better career.

Chapter Nine

BACK INTO THE COCKPIT

I had to slow down and extend the flaps to stay with it.
As I described the aircraft's markings to the controller on the ground,
I was startled to look up and see the skyline of Havana
about fifteen miles on the nose.

IT WAS AS IF I HAD MENTALLY HEAVED a huge sigh of relief. I gazed at the F3H Demons in perfect alignment alongside Fighter Squadron 14's hangar at Naval Air Station Cecil Field, Florida, and knew I was home again, and where I belonged. The jets had been in the fleet nearly ten years and were rather antiquated, but that didn't matter, because ours would be the third squadron to receive the new F-4 Phantom IIs. My orders to VF-14, via the Replacement Air Group (RAG) squadron VF-101, meant Anne and the kids could stay where they were, I'd be donning a flight suit and oxygen mask again, and all was right with the world. Part of me regretted the departure from the surface Navy, but I was overwhelmingly certain the air Navy was for me.

It was the fall of 1962. VF-74 and VF-102 were ahead of us in gaining the F-4s, and VF-14 would have to make one more Mediterranean deployment with the Demons before acquiring the Phantoms. I did have a measure of experience in the bird from my test pilot experience, which should prove valuable to the squadron when the Phantoms arrived the following spring.

I was ordered to Naval Air Station Key West for refresher training in the Demon before linking up with the squadron and was there when the Cuban Missile Crisis occurred in October. The base was gridlocked with aircraft from the Navy as well as the Air Force and the Army as tensions mounted between the United States and the Soviet Union. Our syllabus training was put on hold for a time, so, as a volunteer, I assisted in air operations, keeping track of the elements involved in the buildup. I was not alone in believing that the likelihood of a nuclear confrontation was real. Fortunately, the crisis was resolved with the removal of the missiles. Our group finished training at Cecil Field, capped by carrier qualifications aboard the USS *Antietam*.

I had accumulated a few hours in the Demon at Patuxent test work and was aware of some of the jet's deficiencies, but when I joined VF-14 aboard the USS *Franklin D. Roosevelt,* the shortcomings in that airplane manifested themselves more noticeably than earlier. It was too heavy for the thrust available with the J71 engine. Regardless of the weapons and fuel load we carried, every catapult shot had to be made in afterburner. We were so concerned with the airplane's lack of range—or, in the vernacular, "legs,"—that we flew virtually every mission at maximum endurance power settings. Not a good way to do business in any aircraft, much less a warplane. If we ever did have to jump or dog fight Russian MiGs, we'd be at a disadvantage from the get-go.

VF-14's aircraft availability rate was poor. Too many aircraft were "down" at any one time. Assigned as maintenance officer with a cadre of about two hundred personnel under my purview, I learned right off the bat that two major discrepancies were the principal cause of this: a leaking hydraulic system and communications, the latter dominated by TACAN and ultrahigh frequency (UHF)radio failures, twin bugaboos that plagued the unit. I noticed that hydraulic problems most often occurred after an in-port period, during which the idle jets were never turned up. I ascertained that the hydraulic seals were drying out during the lull in activity. Inevitably, when we resumed flying at sea, the seals leaked.

As a department head, I had direct access to the executive officer (XO) and CO. When I suggested to the skipper, Cdr. Cal Buck, that we start the Demons' engines and turn up each aircraft daily during in-port stays to keep the seals moist, he hesitated, knowing this wouldn't set well with the air boss, Cdr. (later Vice Adm.) Beetle Forbes, much less the pilots who would have to do the turning. Nevertheless, after a moment, he gave me the simple go ahead, "Do it."

But first I had to explain to Commander Forbes why we wanted the turn ups. He resisted, because he knew the sounds of all those engines turning would carry across the harbor to the shore and disturb the local citizens. That wouldn't set well anywhere, especially in places like Cannes on the French Riviera.

With a bit of boldness, I said, "Commander, if you want these Demons to fly, we've got to turn 'em up." He shook his head in dismay but ultimately agreed to our request.

Commander Forbes wasn't the only one troubled by the turn ups. My fellow pilots hated them, because it meant rising early after a night of shore leave to man aircraft and run the engines for a few minutes. This action alleviated the hydraulic leak problem, however, because the seals stopped leaking.

In retrospect I believe there was a sense of complacency under the previous leadership in the squadron. I had learned that other Demon commands were also turning up their birds in port but not VF-14. To me that meant the previous CO was less than dynamic in maintaining a high state of readiness. He was willing to accept missing sorties on the flight schedule. Commander Buck felt otherwise, and that, combined with a dedicated cadre of maintenance troops, resolved the problem.

As to the TACAN and UHF radios, they were the very lifeblood of our capability to navigate, especially at night or in bad weather. TACAN provides bearing information from the ship or points on land as well as distance through its distance-measuring equipment (DME) imbedded within. With these two elements, unless you're beyond the range of the signal emanating from the TACAN station, usually the ship when at sea, a pilot always knows where he or she was. Keep in mind that these were the days before global-positioning satellites. If a pilot lost his TACAN at night, he was in a legitimate emergency situation. To recover on board the carrier, he would have to be led down by a wingman until radar control took over. A double whammy occurred if you also lost your UHF radio. It could get very lonely up there with twin failures.

The squadron's avionics officer, Lt. Frank Taylor, was an LDO lieutenant and a fine officer. LDO—limited duty officer—is an unfair title, because LDOs were usually experts in a specific technical field and were indispensable in any unit. LDOs are highly qualified, former enlisted personnel selected for commissioning as officers. Usually, they are experts in a particular field such as aviation electronics, or ordnance/weapons handling. Anyway, to reduce the communications failures, he and I decided to "turn to" the aviation electronic technicians, the "ATs." We directed them to remove the UHF radios and TACANs and, basically, to overhaul them insofar as their training and experience allowed. Now aircraft maintenance is carried out under a three-level system—organizational (squadron level); intermediate (aircraft intermediate departments ashore and afloat); and depot (major overhaul and repair facilities). Each element has increasing capabilities. Back then, squadrons did what they could to repair equipment in-house. What we couldn't fix we transferred to more capable facilities ashore, hoping to get the repaired part returned in reasonably good time.

After a couple of weeks of focused effort on the communications systems, our aircraft availability rate improved substantially. Combined with the turn ups and a more concentrated tweaking of Demon systems, we began to lead the air wing in flight hours and sorties completed, which was a nice turnaround compared to the commencement of the deployment. There was a price to pay. As much as I would have liked to visit Pompeii, or lounge on a Riviera Beach, most of my time was spent working on the Demons. My reward came in witnessing the squadron meet, if not exceed, its flight requirements during the remainder of the deployment.

Tragically, we lost two pilots on the deployment, both as a result of misfires on the catapult. This was a mystery, because the F3Hs had been flying from the carriers for six or so years without major catapult problems. Along with ship's company personnel and a technical representative from the Navy's engineering facility in Philadelphia, I became immersed in the investigation to figure out what was going wrong. The culprit turned out to be holdback rings.

Basically, an aircraft is catapulted like a sling shot by a steam-powered piston below the flight deck. A shuttle in the groove of the catapult track was connected to the jet by a heavy cable. The cable was pulled taut—tensioned up—around the forward lip of the shuttle, with the cable's ends connected to fittings on the aircraft. The cylindrical-shaped holdback ring, with flanges at each end, was attached to the deck aft of the aircraft's tail via a cable affixed to a holdback fitting. On signal from the flight deck officer, the aircraft was "tensioned" on the catapult, the cables pulled taut. Next, the pilot was signaled to add full power. With checks complete, the flight deck officer, wearing a yellow jersey, cranial helmet, and goggles, exchanged salutes with the pilot, indicating the catapult was cleared to fire. At a certain designated pressure for the Demon, the holdback ring would break, releasing the jet down the track.

The investigation revealed that, under tension, a twisting phenomenon took place that rolled the holdback fittings out of the holdback apparatus. We never did figure out what precisely caused the twisting, but we altered procedures during the tensioning up process to resolve the problem. That is, we imposed the tension load at a slower rate so the wire would stretch slowly without a twisting-type action.

One pilot dribbled off the bow and was killed because of the holdback problem. During a night shot, a second pilot slid with his aircraft into the catwalk that ran parallel to the catapult track and was uninjured. The second fatality occurred following a successful catapult shot in which the pilot flew, inexplicably, into the water. We collected debris from this accident and found an airplane part for a generator still in its packing box, which was another mystery, because we couldn't figure out how this part, if not installed, could have caused the crash.

Although the basic principal is the same, launching systems on today's carriers are much improved and far more reliable.

The *Roosevelt* was roomier than the *Essex,* and its angled deck and steam catapults made it operationally safer, despite the losses mentioned above. There were some exciting moments with the F8U Crusader squadron, VF-11, on board. The Crusader was tough to handle at night, so when VF-11 flew after dark, getting back on deck was always an adventure. Plus, we had VAH-11 aboard, the heavy attack squadron that operated the huge A3D Skywarrior. I really admired the guys who flew that bird because of its size. It weighed in excess of thirty tons and had a seventy-two and a half-foot wing span. When the Skywarrior grabbed a wire on landing, you could feel it throughout much of the ship.

We were extremely lucky to have Cdr. Bud Nance as air operations officer. A 1945 graduate of the Academy, Bud's coolness under pressure and ability to control aircraft at night very likely averted an untold number of accidents. Bud reached flag rank, and when he retired from active duty, he became the nonpaid chief of staff for South Carolina senator Richard Helms.

A realization came to me from this deployment that I believe is crucial to the understanding of leadership in the Navy. It is of huge benefit for the naval officer corps to be crewed not only by Naval Academy graduates, but also by men and women from other sources, ranging from Ivy League schools to diminutive or large colleges and universities across the country. The Aviation Officer Candidate (AOC) program, which converted college graduates into commissioned officers in four months, is an excellent source of talent, as are the multitude of NROTC programs in many of today's learning institutions. The diversity of commissioning sources is a healthy process. This sort of cross-fertilization strengthens the officer corps and makes it better. It was true in my day and remains true today.

The Cold War was certainly ongoing in the early 1960s. For us, it was manifested in the occasional overflights of U.S. ships by Soviet Bear bombers in the Atlantic. These incidents worried Navy officials, because they feared the Air Force could proclaim our carriers vulnerable to enemy attack. For a time, carriers intentionally traveled a longer southern route from the United States to the Mediterranean, remaining just beyond the range of the bombers, which launched from Russian bases.

We returned to Cecil Field in April 1963 anxious to take on the hot new Phantom, now identified as the F-4, rather than the F4H, because of a revised designation system for naval aircraft. Our transition took place primarily at Key West in the RAG, VF-101. The Demons were phased out. Because I was familiar with the Phantom from my Patuxent River days, I was helpful to the pilots and a new brand of officers in the squadron, the RIOs. The RIOs are naval flight officers (NFOs) who controlled the fighter's weapons from the rear cockpit. The Phantom represented a quantum leap in technology from the Demon in terms of complexity and performance.

From a maintenance officer's viewpoint, this presented a huge challenge. But I was blessed with the arrival of a mustang officer (one who begins his career as an enlisted person and qualifies to become an officer), Ens. (later Lt. Cdr.) Harry Errington. Harry was worth his weight in gold. He made all the difference in getting our expanded maintenance department up to speed and beginning the arduous process of learning all about this high-tech, high-performance flying machine.

We applied the Navy's new maintenance inspection system—"phased maintenance" on the Phantoms. Heretofore, when an aircraft was scheduled for a periodic inspection, it was placed in a "down" status for days, if not weeks or more. In effect, with the Phantom, we conducted the same maintenance but on a piecemeal basis, accomplishing repair or upkeep tasks in briefer periods. This reduced the down time and increased availability.

The influx of RIOs, doubling the officer complement in the squadron, was not only a plus for the tactical employment of the Phantom but it also increased manpower, thus relieving some of the administrative/paper work load that goes with being an aviator in a squadron. In the process I learned that, generally speaking, NFOs, who wear their own exclusive set of gold wings, take a more rational approach to paperwork and ground duties than pilots do. Pilots, conversely, especially young ones, naturally just want to fly and not be encumbered with satellite duties outside the cockpit. Happily, this did not produce discord. Rather, at least in our squadron, there was excellent rapport among the pilots and RIOs.

One salient reason for this, of course, was the valued presence of the RIO "in the back." His handling of the weapons systems relieved the pilot so that he could concentrate wholly on flying this powerful and capable fighter jet. When facetious remarks flew around the ready room to the effect that pilots were truck drivers while RIOs did all the work, I, for one, took that in stride. It was fine with me.

While at Key West, we were assigned "hot pad" duty. There were lingering tensions from the previous year's Cuban Missile Crisis, so we stood watches in a trailer near the flight line and could crew up and scramble into the air in minutes. We were "exercised" with some frequency to test our alertness, thus acquiring welcome flight time. One day, in my haste to get airborne, I discovered that my parachute harness was not hooked up. This could have been disastrous, to be sure, but after considerable sweat and squirming in the confinement of the cockpit, I got it hitched up properly.

On another occasion I launched to check out a bogey—an unidentified aircraft—in the area, a C-46 twin engine transport from El Salvador Airlines, traveling, we conjectured, from Miami to some point in Central America. I had to slow down and extend the flaps to stay with it. As I described the aircraft's markings to the controller on the ground, I was startled to look up and see the skyline of Havana about fifteen miles on the nose.

"Break it off!" ordered the controller simultaneously with my sighting of the city. "You're heading straight for Havana." Naturally I complied.

Chapter Ten

FROM FIGHTERS TO FARAWAY PLACES

*He was hospitalized temporarily, and it was during this interlude
that I was shoved into the breach.*

FIGHTER SQUADRON FOURTEEN became the first F-4 Phantom squadron
located at Naval Air Station Cecil Field in Jacksonville, Florida, an excellent location for jet operations. There were outlying fields, like nearby
Whitehouse, available for "bouncing"—field carrier landing practice—and a
spacious working area off the Atlantic coast. Conversely, being the first unit
of its kind at the base meant problems with maintenance supply support and
acclimating to the way routine daily flight operations were conducted with
respect to ground handling of the Phantoms.

At Oceana we conducted "hot refueling." Pilots landed and, before entering the parking ramp, halted at the "refueling pits," a designated area adjacent to the taxiway, where the aircraft stopped and kept their engines running
while a crew of maintenance personnel plugged huge hoses into the aircraft
and filled the bird with jet fuel. This was a carefully practiced evolution, but
it worked beautifully, because when the jet was finally shut down after the
pilot taxied it back to the squadron's parking area, it was gassed up and ready
to go on the next hop, assuming there were no other discrepancies.

Cecil Field did not advocate hot refueling. After shutdown, the crew had
to hitch the plane to a tow tractor, tow it to the fuel farm, attach an external
power unit to the aircraft to ensure that all the F-4s internal pumps were
working, pump in the fuel, disconnect from external power, and tow the
Phantom back to the line—obviously, a time-consuming and manpower-
intensive exercise.

As maintenance officer, I was convinced this had to change, so I set about
trying to convince base personnel that hot refueling was a sound practice. I
was rebuffed initially. It was as if I was trying to deviate radically from time-
honored naval regulations. A succession of meetings with the fire marshal

and safety staff followed, but we finally got hot refueling approved, a change that measurably increased the efficiency of our operations.

My Cecil Field experience was very positive except for one unforgettable day of national significance that, like many Americans, became fixed in my mind forever. It was a Friday in November, a week before Thanksgiving in 1963. I had returned from a flight and entered the ready room. Instead of the lively repartee characteristic of this normally vigorous space, a glum and dejected collection of officers sat sullenly or moved slowly and without energy.

One of the officers said to me in a soft monotone, "The president's been assassinated."

I was stunned, of course, and remember going home and watching television all that weekend and often thereafter, seeing Jack Ruby shoot Lee Harvey Oswald, trying to grasp the significance of the tragedy, and seeing Pres. John F. Kennedy laid to rest in Arlington National Cemetery.

I participated in the flyover at Arlington National Cemetery when President Kennedy was buried, and it was a challenge. It was to be a combined U.S. Air Force and Navy event. Coordination was a nightmare, because we were to fly in a formation of "Vs," three aircraft per division, with an Air Force lieutenant colonel leading. We rendezvoused over Langley Air Force Base, north of Oceana, somehow got aligned with the other twenty-four airplanes, and circled east of the nation's capital until called in. We streamed over the gravesite at the designated minute, but it was a struggle.

I loved the Phantom. It was a mighty machine with plenty of power—a pair of J79s, each producing twenty-eight thousand pounds of thrust, and maneuverability. It served dual roles as a fighter for air-to-air engagements as well as a bomber for attack missions. Those were good days at Cecil. The family liked it there, the folks of Jacksonville appreciated the military, and the weather, though blisteringly hot in the summer, was fine most of the year. The kids went to the air station swimming pool every day in the warm seasons, and the flying was wonderful.

The squadron successfully completed carrier landing qualifications aboard the USS *Forrestal*, commanded by Capt. Mike Hanley, and in January 1964, we were slated to go to the Caribbean for more training aboard the USS *Franklin D. Roosevelt*, commanded by Captain (later Vice Adm.) Jerry Miller. We were slated for a Mediterranean deployment.

I had been maintenance officer for more than a year and was to become the operations officer, replacing Lt. Cdr. Dick Thompson, who was leaving the squadron. But a phone call from the personnel detailer in Washington changed all that.

"How would you like to be the executive assistant to a four-star general?" I was asked.

I had a sinking feeling in my stomach. I was in a flying squadron, doing what I loved, was supposed to stay in the outfit for at least another six months, and now an outside force was getting in the way of that.

Without hesitation I replied, "I would *not* like to be the executive assistant to a four-star general. Moreover, you know from looking at my record I've already had a tour as admiral's aide with Admiral Moorer." I added that I was about to become the squadron's operations officer, we were going to sea, and I was really needed here. I had been told earlier that after the squadron's deployment, I would be ordered to attend the Naval War College in July, a sound step in terms of career progression. Moreover, the executive assistant's job would cut short my squadron tour and deprive me of six months of flying duty.

I was given some time to think this over and consulted Capt. (later Adm. Mickey Weisner, the CO on my first squadron, who was the senior aviation detailer in "BuPers."

"Skipper, I think this is unfair," I said. "I've already had an aide's tour."

Weisner replied, "I'll look into it and get back to you."

Next day he called me and explained, "You've been personally picked by Vice Adm. [William] Smedberg." Smedberg was the chief of naval personnel. He knew me slightly from my Annapolis days, but his son, Bill, was my classmate, and we were friends.

Weisner amplified, "It's a very sensitive situation, Bill. General [Paul DeWitt] Adams, a four star, is commander in chief of the U.S. Strike Command and has just been given full unified command status with purview over the Middle East, Africa [South of the Sahara], and South Asia [Pakistan, Iran, and Iraq]. The Navy is concerned about carriers and other assets deploying in this area under his operational control."

The Navy was also upset that an Army general gained control of the Middle East, a responsibility heretofore handled by a Navy flag officer based in London.

The Navy, including Adm. George Anderson, CNO at the time, had misgivings about this authority, and as a result, tensions existed between the upper echelons of the two services. Some in the Navy were adamantly opposed to the unified command status, an initiative pushed by then Secretary of Defense Robert McNamara and authorized by President Kennedy.

Gen. Paul Dewitt Adams, a West Point graduate (1928) and the four-star to whom I would be assigned, was known as a gruff, demanding officer, very tough on people and a man who viewed time as a precious commodity that should never be wasted. More important, he was not on friendly terms with his Navy counterparts, Adm. Don Felt, commander in chief, Pacific, and Adm. Page Smith, commander in chief, Atlantic. Both were old-school naval officers, just as General Adams was an old-school Army officer, with an esteemed combat record in World War II. Indeed, he even resembled German general Erwin Rommel, the "Desert Fox," was impeccable in his appearance, freshly creased from top to bottom, and always carried a swagger stick, the army mark of authority.

Understandably, Felt and Smith abhorred the notion of an Army general ordering our warships around, particularly the aircraft carriers. The situation was so strained that Felt and Smith wouldn't even speak to Adams, which meant there was virtually no interface among Navy unified commanders and the Strike Command. This was an acutely unhealthy situation for our national defense. General Adams knew this, of course, and sent letters to both Smith and Felt suggesting an exchange of liaison officers, a standard practice at that level of command. Neither of these letters was answered, to the detriment of our country. Yet the liaison did take place, and I was part of it.

I remained baffled by my selection for the job. A lieutenant commander simply does not pull much weight in dealing with flag-rank personnel. I was a mouse among the elephants. In retrospect, I believe it was because of my previous affiliations with the likes of Admirals Moorer and Anderson. Adm. David McDonald succeeded Admiral Moorer as commander Carrier Division Six, and I got to know him during the turnover—and, to some extent, Smedberg. My plan was simple. I would do the best I could, and if I failed, I figured the worst thing they could do was to send me back to a fighter squadron.

It turned out that a lowly lieutenant commander can influence a situation, if only in a subtle manner. Whenever I perceived an area where communications with the Navy could be improved, I jumped on it. I sought opportunities for General Adams to visit naval shore commands (he had already been on a number of Navy ships) and to meet senior naval officers at social events as well as official occasions. If I could inject into his speeches favorable comments toward the Navy, I did so.

The purpose of Strike Command was to develop a Rapid Reaction Force that blended elements of the three services into a flexible and lethal, joint, quick-strike unit. It had to be capable of moving to a trouble spot in a hurry and taking whatever actions were necessary to resolve a crisis.

Very aware of the ongoing tensions, and to demonstrate good faith, General Adams was pleased that a flag officer was assigned as his chief of staff. That duty fell to Rear Adm. Forsythe Massey, a naval aviator. Admiral Smedberg also felt I could contribute to smoothing the troubled waters between Adams and his counterparts. I wondered how in heck a lieutenant commander, yours truly, could be counted on to assuage hard feelings at a level of authority far beyond mine. But I would give it my best shot.

Admiral Massey and I were dispatched to Strike Command Headquarters at MacDill Air Force Base in Tampa, Florida, reporting in January 1964. We were warmly received, although I felt I was entering a cauldron of controversy that could easily have a detrimental effect on my career if I wasn't careful. I hated leaving my fighter squadron, and I'd have to move the family again, but there are far worse places than Tampa. I had no choice but to make the best of it.

I took over the job cold. A timely turnover with my predecessor, Richard Harris, was impossible, because he, an Army major and, ironically, a 1951 West Point graduate who finished second in his class, didn't get along with Adams and had been transferred to the (J-3) division on General Adams's staff. The major was considered an up and coming superstar who had been handpicked for the job. The pressure got to him, however, and he was unable to bear up under it (although it didn't prevent him from recovering and become a two-star general later in his career). He was hospitalized temporarily, and it was during this interlude that I was shoved into the breach. You simply could not relax around the general, and that went for seniors as well as juniors.

General Adams was just getting the Strike Command under control when I arrived. The Air Force and the Army had made progress in developing rapid reaction tactics and were responding well to General Adams's direction, although the Air Force folks felt they really worked for the commander in chief of the Tactical Air Command, while the Army people believed their true boss was the commander of the Continental Army Command. Both were four-stars and West Point graduates. At least they were talking to Adams and operationally came under Adams's purview. Sound complicated? It was. There were plenty of ingredients for turmoil.

I was determined to avoid the politics of the situation, if that were possible. What followed was an abundance of long, hard working days and nights. Indeed, for the first year of my tour, we worked seven days a week, and seldom less than ten or twelve hours a day, including Saturdays and sometimes

Sundays. There was much to do, moving the Rapid Reaction Force beyond the initial setup phase. We were plowing new ground with respect to this "unified command" philosophy. Not only did we have to prepare contingency plans, but we also had to manage the military assistance programs that would inevitably follow a conflict. The administrative detail was mind-boggling. There was an incessant flow of paperwork, trying to get each of the multitudes of participants on the same page. The number of plans we prepared was sizeable.

We were also responsible for the Joint Test and Evaluation Task Force, which focused on developing helicopter mobility tactics, an effort that led to the creation of the first air cavalry division being formed by the Army. Secretary of Defense McNamara actually conceived the idea of Strike Command. In short, we had a tremendous amount on our plate.

In the summer of 1964, traveling via a noisy but reliable four-engine U.S. Air Force C-118, Henry "Hank" Ramsey, a State Department official assigned to Strike Command; Army lieutenant colonel Joe Miller; yours truly; General Adams; and other staff members departed MacDill for a lengthy trip to Europe, the Middle East, and Africa. We made an en route stop in Paris, where the general met with top officials from U.S. and European commands. Admiral McDonald, now chief of naval operations, having relieved Admiral Anderson because of a scuffle Anderson had with Secretary McNamara during the Cuban Missile Crisis, was there. We were able to arrange a brief window of time for an unplanned visit with him. McDonald was a fellow southerner, from Georgia, and they hit it off well, which was a plus in the quest to ease the strain between the Navy and Strike Command.

We also made a side trip to Monte LaMar in southern France. When the general commanded the 136th regiment of the 36th division during the war, his command post was in a chateau owned by a family friendly to the Allies. The family was still there, and the general presented a plaque to them in commemoration of his stay. A very nice touch.

There was another window of time that would allow for a side trip to Naples. "It might be a good idea," I suggested to the general, to meet with the commander in chief southern area, Adm. James Russell (USNA 1926). Russell, I knew, was a gracious and popular officer, and although there was no direct link in the chain of command between the two, it wouldn't hurt for the pair to get to know each other. In fact, there was an indirect link between the commands in that Russell would provide contingency support to Strike Command as necessary.

Admiral Russell took the general on his boat for a ride to Capri, which was relaxing and conducive to forming a comfortable relationship between the two senior officers. It was another approach to mending fences.

Subsequently, we traveled to the Paris of the Middle East, Beirut, then a lovely coastal city, brimming with fine hotels, tourists, and attractions of historical interest. The general had been deeply involved in the Lebanon crisis of 1958, so he was quite familiar with its surroundings.

After Lebanon came Saudi Arabia, Ethiopia (where the general met Haile Selassie, then monarch of that country), Nigeria, Senegal, Liberia, and Nigeria. And from there we went to the Republic of the Congo, which had recently won its independence from Belgium. In Leopoldville, the capital city, the general met with U.S. Amb. George McMurtrie "Mac" Godley and, later, Pres. Sese Seko Mobutu, the opportunistic Congolese army sergeant who made his brutal way to the top post in the country. While the general dined with the former sergeant, I was hosted at a dinner in the city and consumed some beef that didn't taste quite right. I was ill, off and on, the rest of the journey. I wasn't alone in this discomfort. We drank distilled water, which helped, but most of us in the party experienced various degrees of dysentery throughout the portions of the trip. On arrival at McDill, my temperature soared. I was injected with a significant volume of penicillin, and after a couple of days, I returned to the job.

In retrospect, this journey was as educational to me as a course at the Naval War College in Newport, Rhode Island. Every day we received a voluminous number of messages from the intelligence network describing critical events all over the world. We were tracking not only the conflict in the Congo but also the growing controversy involving India and Pakistan, Rhodesia's declaration of independence, and so on. Hank Ramsey, incidentally, was in his element during the trip and produced a number of beneficial briefings from his State Department perspective that were most helpful.

In the second year, we scaled back to six days a week, taking Sundays off. We made progress, slowly but surely. And in the spring of 1965, we exercised the Rapid Reaction Force when a crisis occurred in the Dominican Republic. There was a rebellion against the government, and it was our task to support the incumbent leaders. Interestingly, in the midst of the encounter, Adm. Tom Moorer relieved Admiral Smith. One of the first calls Moorer received was from General Adams, something Adams would never have done with Smith or Felt.

"I want to assure you," Moorer told Adams, "that I will work with you and that we've got everything under control." Moorer asked for more helicopter support and Adams OK'd same on the spot. The two officers struck up an excellent working relationship, one that went a long way toward resolving the crisis in our favor. It didn't hurt that both Adams and Moorer hailed from Alabama.

When the crisis subsided, General Adams traveled to Norfolk to make a call on Moorer, who returned the visit to our headquarters shortly thereafter. The difference in the atmosphere that prevailed once Moorer was in the saddle was as amazing as it was welcome.

In retrospect I was very disappointed in Admirals Smith and Felt. The Rapid Reaction Joint Task Force concept was sanctioned by the highest authority, the president of the United States. It was to be implemented, not tried out as an experiment. It is still used today.

Adams was a stickler for proper correspondence and paperwork. He had a tendency to mumble when dictating a letter, but his secretary, Betty, had a magical ability to interpret those muffled sounds. I would help her finalize her notes, and because I did have some facility with words, I inserted my own phraseology here and there to make the document read as smoothly as possible. Incredibly, once we got into a groove, we seldom, if ever, had a letter or document returned to us for rewrite. The general was so busy he often signed the letters without reading them. That was a good sign. Yet Adams hated to relax, much less take leave.

Despite this, I couldn't help but respect the man. In early 1942 he was a lieutenant colonel assigned as executive officer in a commando unit—the first special forces unit—a joint venture with Canadian troops. They formed up and trained in Helena, Montana, conducted cold weather and mountain training, and were initially dispatched to the Aleutian campaign in Alaska. After that they were ordered to Italy and fought their way up the boot from Salerno, much of the time behind enemy lines. The general used to jokingly boast, "I've spent more time forward of our own artillery than any other officer in the Army."

His rise to prominence was somewhat meteoric. He became regimental commander of the 36th Division, was promoted to brigadier general by the end of the war, and in the process, earned a reputation as a hard-nosed, if impersonal, warrior with a minimum of close friends but a special knack at getting the job done.

He had a temper and would dress down anyone who erred. I once saw him brace a three-star general against the bulkhead, forcing the poor man to stand at attention like a plebe at West Point. He was not a "hail fellow well met" and did not belong to any "old boys club" of Army officers. In this sense he was a loner and not well liked. But he had been handpicked by Secretary of Defense McNamara for the Strike Command job. General Adams's leadership philosophy boiled down to one theme: subordinates had to prove themselves before earning respect rather than the more common practice of assuming personnel were competent until proven otherwise.

I worked the general's schedule, and he'd become irate if anything went wrong with it. He made it very clear that I must learn his requirements and standards very quickly. And Lord help the man or woman who, in one way or another, cost him time he didn't want to spend. He usually saved a few minutes after lunch for his personal "quiet time" and considered it inviolate. No one dared to disrupt that silent interlude.

Henry Ramsey, the political adviser from the State Department, a "Foreign Service Officer One," which is one grade below ambassador, was a bit of a thorn in Adams's side. He was a bachelor and a gentlemanly and verbose man, inclined to writing lengthy messages. He did not use the terse military style Adams preferred. I knew Adams didn't want to waste any minutes with Ramsey, so we put Ramsey off by referring him to subordinates in the command. But Ramsey was persistent, and one day he came into my office and said, "This is an absolute, dire emergency. I must see General Adams!"

So, with reluctance, I entered the general's office. "Sir, Mr. Ramsey insists on seeing you."

Whereupon the general took the container full of number two pencils, which were religiously sharpened for him every morning, raised it to shoulder height, and slammed it down with a loud clack on his Plexiglas-topped desk. "Goddamit!" he said. "Can't you keep that son of a bitch out of here?"

Then he heaved the pencil he was writing with onto his desktop. It ricocheted from the desk and whizzed by my head. I defensively fell to the floor, successfully avoiding the missile, and scampered from the office. I told Ramsey the General couldn't see him today. I advised Ramsey that the general preferred that he make his remarks at the morning staff conferences.

Ramsey angrily said, "Commander Lawrence, you are not letting me do my job!"

So I was a bit of a scapegoat in this fracas.

Incidentally, the general never apologized for pitching that number two pencil at me. He was not an apologizer.

As to the Navy's role in Strike Command, General Adams finally acceded to the fact that naval forces and the carriers would stay under the operational control of a naval commander. Operational Control is a term that describes how those elements in the chain of command respond to a reporting authority. In this instance, Admiral Moorer had conceived of a way to have naval forces "in support" of army operations rather than under their control. This new concept was agreed to by Gen. Earle Wheeler and approved by Secretary McNamara.

There was an exception. In the Middle East, a seaplane tender and two destroyers were permanently based at Bahrain, under the commander Middle East Force. Through a quirk in the overall arrangement, these ships came directly under the control of General Adams. We called it his "Little three-ship Navy."

Although I wouldn't want to emulate General Adams's style of leadership, I admired and respected him for his achievements. Though he always called me "Lawrence," never by my first name, I sensed he had warm feelings toward me. I noticed he never used first names. I asked a fellow officer about this, and he told me, "Welcome to the club. As far as we know, the only people he calls by their first name are his wife and children."

The war in Vietnam was heating up as my tour at Strike Command ended in January 1966. Adams, who was a student of warfare, had carefully studied the French experience in the Indochina War, which lasted from 1946 to 1954 and ended in defeat for the French. Consequently, he was very wary about America's entry into a conflict in Vietnam. He felt we could win there but that it would take a long time and be very costly. He wrote many letters to the Army chief of staff, General Wheeler warning that American involvement in Vietnam would be lengthy, frustrating, and costly in both lives and money.

When I was ordered to a fighter squadron, which, in all likelihood, would be sent into combat because of Vietnam, he was happy for me. He knew how much I wanted to fly again. There was a touch of sadness in his eyes when we made our good-byes. He was a time-tested warrior, who knew close up the horrors and tragedies of armed conflict. He feared America was in for a dreadful experience, and I read in his expression a genuine concern for my future well-being.

Memorably, some time after I was released from captivity in North Vietnam, I visited Adams in Tampa. He called me "Bill."

Chapter Eleven

COMBAT

Abeam the beach, with a sizeable crowd watching, he started a roll.
Something went wrong, and the F-4 slammed into the sea,
killing both men and destroying the aircraft.

"HEY, I THINK I HEARD A HEART MURMUR," said the young Air Force flight surgeon. I was undergoing my annual physical before my departure from Strike Command at MacDill Air Force Base, and the last thing I wanted to hear were those words, heart murmur. I'd paid my staff duty dues and craved climbing into a Phantom and bursting back into the sky. Moreover, I had been promoted to commander and had screened for command, which meant I would join a fleet squadron as executive officer and, after a year in that billet, would "fleet up" to command of the unit and more than likely be involved in the fighting in Vietnam.

The words followed me to Naval Air Station Miramar, where the doctor there declared, "You need a complete cardiology workup at Balboa," the major naval hospital in San Diego.

At Balboa, a physician, who was not a flight surgeon, said, "Your heart murmur is a disqualifying condition. Were you to try and enter the service today with this problem, you couldn't get in." Dark clouds loomed on my horizon, but I wasn't going down without a fight.

I called Cdr. Frank Austin, a friend from Patuxent River days now serving in the Navy's Bureau of Medicine. Frank was a flight surgeon who had also gone through flight training to become a fully qualified naval aviator. I explained my dilemma to him. He listened carefully and then decided my case should be resolved by a board composed of flight surgeons at the Naval Aviation Medical Institute (NAMI) in Pensacola. Consequently, in February 1966 I was ordered temporarily to Pensacola for the evaluation. I was not optimistic, a feeling made all the worse because I felt perfectly fit and was really anxious to get into combat in Vietnam. Like every naval aviator—and just about anyone who enters military service, I was committed to the warrior mode. As much as it might sound like something out of a John Wayne movie, we were trained to kill and destroy. Volumes of pilots and backseaters go through their careers without tasting combat, although it seems as if there's war for every generation. It's all a matter of timing, and my time had come.

After another thorough examination that focused on the state of my ticker, the board met and carefully reviewed my situation. "Commander Lawrence," the head of the board began rather somberly when we went one on one in his office at NAMI, "you've been in naval aviation for fifteen years." He paused, and my heart sank, murmur and all. My one year of black shoe duty apparently was included in the fifteen. "But you're healthy," he went on, "and your heart murmur is what we call 'human dynamically insignificant.'"

My heart sank no further, but it wasn't rising yet.

The doctor then smiled and said, "We're going to give you a waiver to stay in naval aviation, service group one!"

The old ticker leapt, and I sat straighter in my chair, elation building.

"Furthermore," the doctor went on, "you're the first guy on record to have a heart murmur who has been allowed to stay in a military field, aviation in particular!"

Thank you, Frank Austin. I also thanked the Lord for providing me an otherwise excellent cardiovascular system. The board had compared my NASA physical records in 1959 with the current readings and there had been no change in heart size. I was allowed to continue as a Navy pilot.

I was rushed through the training syllabus at the Fleet Replacement Squadron (FRS) at Miramar, a kind of graduate school tailored for the Phantom. But the family was with me, and we made the most of our time together, knowing I would deploy immediately after completing the curriculum. In July 1966, being slated to be the XO to Cdr. Tomas Townsend, I stuffed a couple of duffel bags with flight gear and uniforms, said goodbye to Anne and the kids at our rented Solana Beach home overlooking the beautiful Pacific, and traveled via military transport from Travis Air Force Base to Danang, South Vietnam, then via a carrier on board delivery aircraft to the USS *Ranger* in the Gulf of Tonkin. Because the ship and squadron had already been deployed for over two months, I was anxious to get into the fray. "Dixie Station" operations (which encompassed bombing targets in South Vietnam) for the Navy had been terminated, and all carrier assets were now dedicated to bombing North Vietnam, operating from "Yankee Station," a geographical point off the central North Vietnamese coast.

The Phantom's punch was being felt. In my first F-4 tour, the aircraft was purely a fighter. We didn't carry ordnance, even though we knew the capability existed. No fighter pilot would consider himself a bomber pilot in those days. But the Phantom had been transformed in reality to a fighter bomber, arguably one of the best combat machines ever built.

For tactical planning purposes, North Vietnam was divided into six zones beginning at the demilitarized zone (DMZ —the 17th parallel) with "Package One" to "Package Six," the utmost northern portion of the country, which encompassed the port city of Haiphong and the capital, Hanoi, sometimes referred to as Indian Country because it was so heavily defended and patently dangerous to enter.

I didn't know it at the time, but target selection was actually determined in the White House and, as was later confirmed, Pres. Lyndon Johnson himself made a lot of the target assignments. Hard to imagine, but true. Most of our objectives were in packages two or three during the 1966 deployment. They ranged from suspected truck parks to bridges and barges suspected of transporting the supplies of war by the enemy. The surface-to-air missile (SAM) threat was not significant at the time. SAM sites existed but were sparsely positioned throughout the country. At the same time, you could expect to be shot at anytime you went over the beach, usually by 85-millimeter antiaircraft artillery or smaller guns.

If there were two carriers on station, one would operate from 1200 to midnight, the other during the next twelve hours. If there were three flattops, one would fly midnight to noon, the second would operate noon to midnight, and the third would fly from 0800 to 1800. The worst schedule from most everyone's standpoint was the midnight to noon. It was notably more difficult to adjust to it than the other periods. You just couldn't seem to adjust your sleep pattern.

We didn't realize it at the time, but the pace and intensity of this deployment could be described as benign compared to our next turn on Yankee Station in 1967. For one thing, there was a lack of electronic countermeasures—the technology to break the enemy's radar lock on our aircraft— although the A-4 Skyhawks and A-6 Intruders did have ECM equipment that told pilots when they were "receiving radiation" and the direction of site from which it was coming. They could also break the lock.

For us, in 1966, this wasn't a critical deficiency, but that all changed a year later with the proliferation of surface-to-air missiles in the North. Fortunately, our CO was Cdr. Doc Townsend; a technically oriented officer who made sure our aircraft were upgraded with the APR-25 Electronic Countermeasures (ECM) system, which was designed to detect a basic search radar signal. Once that signal locked on an aircraft, the defensive system would try to break that lock. A pulsating tone would alert aviators of an active radar signal. When that happened, a pilot might transmit, "I've got a chirper." When the signal intensified and lock-on was imminent, the chirper became a warbler, meaning a high pulse rate frequency (PRF). A very scary sound. Our ECM system would provide the direction of the threat as well as the audio signal.

When we returned to Miramar following the 1966 deployment, we had to transfer our Phantoms sequentially to the Naval Aviation Depot at North Island, California, for electronic upgrades that would better serve us in the increasingly hostile SAM environment in North Vietnam. Our F-4 "availability" rate plunged, and that translated to less flying time and a reduced state of readiness. This was the down side of the "fix," but we had no alternative. We did try to give the nuggets—newly arrived aviators—some priority to tune them up for their baptism in combat.

It was hectic. Even though there was a war on, we had to undergo an administrative inspection, a real pain in the posterior, because it entailed a review of all our instructions, personnel data, operating procedures, log books, the whole nine yards. On our deployment, paperwork took a back seat to combat operations. Ashore now, we were paying for that with frantic updating of the records, a lot of scurrying about, and elevated tensions, because these "admats" were serious business. A team of inspectors from Commander Fleet Air Miramar would swoop down on the squadron and go through all our data inch by inch. We spent long hours at the squadron getting our paperwork into shape. On top of all these, we had to conduct weapons training at the Marine Corps Air Station Yuma complex in Arizona in preparation for the forthcoming deployment.

By 1972 Navy aircraft were equipped with an affective array of ECM equipment, but in 1966 we were on the backside of the learning curve. Because we were dealing in technology that could spell the difference between survival and the dreaded alternative, there was a deepening intensity toward getting our jets ready for the next tour on Yankee Station.

In peacetime, a Friday night—and a few midweek days—wouldn't go by without an exuberant gathering at the officers club for happy hour. During our turnaround, there were no happy hours. Men were predisposed to spend what precious free time they had with their families. We weren't in a somber state of mind, but knowing we would soon be going back into harm's way took some of the humor, normally free-flowing in a cadre of aviators, out of the workplace.

One of our new pilots, an Ensign Brown, was a quiet sort but a pretty good stick. He had flown well around the ship, day and night, and we were quite impressed with him. One week before we were to set sail for the Pacific, he was sent to the overhaul and repair facility at North Island to collect one of our Phantoms freshly upgraded with the new gear to fend off the SAMs. His RIO was a "mustang" lieutenant, an officer who had begun his career as an enlisted man and had a wife and several children. They manned up, launched, and headed north toward the coastline at La Jolla. Brown accelerated and kept the Phantom down low. Abeam the beach, with a sizeable crowd watching, he started a roll. Something went wrong, and the F-4 slammed into the sea, killing both men and destroying the aircraft.

It's hard to imagine an event more devastating just prior to deployment—losing a crew and a refurbished warplane. Flathatting is a cardinal sin, and when it terminates in disaster, it is costly beyond measure. The families suffer, all that training and experience is lost, and you must add in the lofty cost of the multimillion dollar jet itself. But it happens, and the effect of this tragedy set us all back at a time when we were already pent up in anticipation of going back into harm's way.

In addition to my other responsibilities, I had to spend the succeeding weeks preparing the Judge Advocate General (JAG) investigation on the incident, which is conducted in parallel with the official accident investigation, the latter being a more technically detailed and lengthy process.

Chapter Twelve

MIDNIGHT TO NOON – NOON TO MIDNIGHT

---

*"Better proceed to the alternate target, Bill," he radioed.
This is when I sighed guiltily, knowing we would not have to duel with
the dreaded SAMs that had proliferated in the Hanoi-Haiphong area—
"Indian country"—since our last deployment.*

I BREATHED A GUILTY SIGH OF RELIEF. It was early morning and Haiphong was socked in—cloaked by heavy cloud cover. The CAG Cdr. (later Rear Adm.) Gene Tissot, a superlative officer, was in an F-4 Phantom farther back in the flight, but I was the designated flight leader and was at the apex of the thirty-plus aircraft formation. My job was to navigate us to the target, which was a complex of transshipment points in the Haiphong area on the Red River. My F-4 and seven other Phantoms were to pounce on enemy gun sites as flak suppressors, clearing the way for the Skyhawk and Intruder bombers to make their attack. My RIO was twenty-four-year-old Lt. (jg) James Bailey from Kocuusko, Mississippi.

The flak suppressors carried six to eight five hundred-pound cluster bomb units (CBU) with proximity fuses. These were pressure-sensing devices that caused the bombs to detonate slightly above the ground, sending hundreds of lethal steel fragments over a wide area at tremendous velocity. The CBUs were ferociously effective as antipersonnel weapons. On this day they were intended to debilitate crews manning enemy antiaircraft artillery (triple A—AAA) and SAM sites. We also carried four Sparrow and two Sidewinder missiles each. After the flak suppression runs, we would become the MiG Cap element, swiftly climbing to altitude to do battle with any MiGs that might be in the sky.

In addition to the A-4 Skyhawks and the A-6 Intruders, RA-5C Vigilante photo-reconnaissance jets would transit the target area right after the strike to obtain bomb damage assessment (BDA) imagery. The transshipment points were temporary holding facilities for supplies that came in via ships we were not allowed to target. Ridiculous, but true. The supplies were subsequently loaded onto trucks from the transshipment points and delivered to Communist units positioned throughout North Vietnam, more often than not in the darkness of night.

We prided ourselves on the ability to launch and rendezvous a large group of warplanes in a relatively swift and orderly manner under "zip lip," or radio silence. I'm not the only Alpha Strike leader to be awestruck by the sheer drama of this undertaking. As I circled high overhead, the jets, weighted heavily with bombs, drew toward me like obedient geese joining on the leader of the flock.

Circling over the ship, I could see them, one after the other, catapulted from USS *Constellation* (CV-64), our new ship, and climbing toward me in the cylindrical chamber of airspace above the carrier. I was imbued with a sense of power, purpose, and responsibility that was as uplifting as it was worrisome. I had to be smooth at the controls, maintaining proper airspeed and altitude as we collected ourselves for the inbound leg to the target. Any roughness on my part would cause a domino effect throughout the formation. And I knew darn well that should my basic air work be rough, the word would get around and diminish my reputation as "a good stick."

The rendezvous went like clockwork; I took up a northwest heading and reported, "Taproot [our call sign] departing." A voice from the combat information center replied with the time-honored term, "Roger." We shifted to our tactical radio frequency for the business portion of our mission.

About fifty miles from Haiphong, however, the towering mass of clouds along our course was like one huge stop sign. I verified with *Constellation* that there was no ingress route to Haiphong clear of clouds. The CAG read my mind.

"Better proceed to the alternate target, Bill," he radioed. This is when I sighed guiltily, knowing we would not have to duel with the dreaded SAMs that had proliferated in the Hanoi-Haiphong area—"Indian Country"— since our last deployment. For this day, anyway.

I clicked my mike twice in agreement and began a turn toward Nam Dinh, forty-five miles south of Hanoi, and a thermal power plant within the small city, our secondary target. Forays into Indian Country always invited doom, but Nam Dinh, which is also on the huge Red River Delta, did not pose a SAM threat. Triple A, certainly, but not the rocket-driven telephone poles with devastating warheads at their tips.

Let me digress and detail events prior to my moment of truth over Nam Dinh. The last time we were on Yankee Station, the SAM threat was minimal. Our flights usually consisted of two-plane sections or four-plane divisions seeking out a designated bridge, roadway, suspected truck park, or ammo cache for targets. In the interim between then and now, the air war had intensified dramatically. Now we flew thirty-plus aircraft Alpha Strikes against key targets heavily defended by AAA, ranging from 37- to 85-millimeter guns and a growing danger of SAMs, especially around Hanoi and Haiphong.

Our squadron had left San Diego in good shape but for the terrible loss of Ensign Brown. The time-consuming burden of writing the JAG report on the accident was left to me, not to mention preparation for the all important ORI—operational-readiness inspection, a kind of final exam before we went into combat. We had experienced a manageable turnover of pilots, our Phantoms were equipped with the ARE-25 ECM gear, and we had a nice mix of combat-experienced and "new guy" personnel.

When we reached Hawaii, we worked our way through an ORI, a kind of final exam before proceeding to the combat zone. CAG Tissot, a razor-sharp officer, pilot, and veteran of the Korean War, wanted an advance look at operations on Yankee Station. Cdr. Gene Profilet, skipper of VA-196, the A-6 squadron on board the USS *Constellation,* often referred to as the *Connie,* and I were selected to accompany him. We flew from Hickam Air Force Base in Hawaii via a commercial charter transport, landed at Clark Air Force Base in the Philippines, and motored the relatively short distance to Naval Air Station Cubi Point, located within sight of Corregidor, where many American servicemen in World War II were swept up by the Japanese and became a part of the ignominious Bataan Death March. From Cubi, which was the air side of a huge complex adjacent to Naval Station Subic Bay, a major shipyard and gathering place for Navy surface ships, we then hopped into a twin-prop C-1 Trader for the rumbling four-hour flight to Yankee Station. Yankee Station was the strategic point in the Gulf of Tonkin from which the carriers and their supporting ships operated.

We visited the carriers *Kitty Hawk* and *Enterprise,* the latter commanded by the remarkable Jim Holloway III (later admiral and chief of naval operations), affectionately referred to as "Triple Sticks," because he was the third "James" in the family line, his father, James Holloway II, being a four-star surface officer before him. Adm. Tom Moorer was always a cool, enthusiastic, and self-confident man, and Jim Holloway is right up there with him in my estimation. He was something to observe. The crew's morale was high on the "Big E," and Holloway came across as a dynamic and respected leader, quick to smile and a man who clearly loved the challenge of handling a huge nuclear-powered warship, especially in wartime.

The three of us from the *Connie* flew "indoctrination" flights to acquire the flavor of the operations it would be our duty to execute. This was an invaluable, if further sobering, experience as we garnered information that was bound to help us get quickly acclimated to the escalating tempo of the conflict. I believed our squadron would do well despite the challenges reflected in our looking glass.

With respect to scheduling, we would alternate the midnight-to-noon, noon-to-midnight schedules with a sister carrier. Daytime was devoted mostly to the Alpha Strikes, while at night, using flares, we flew reconnaissance flights, looking for targets of opportunity along the roadways, or "sky spots," which entailed straight and level bombing from altitude under the guidance of a forward air controllers such as A-3 Skywarriors from Electronic Countermeasures Squadron One (VQ-1). At night we primarily sought out truck movement along Highway One, the Ho Chi Minh Trail. Rolling stock made its way from north to south or south to north almost with impunity, so difficult were they to find, much less bomb. It was tough making a bomb run on a moving target at night, even if it was illuminated by the one-million candle power flares we deployed; this was a far from cost-effective method of stopping the flow of enemy supplies.

The daytime Alpha Strikes could be fraught with confusion, particularly when the ground fire sprang up from below. It was virtually impossible to maintain formation integrity with SAMs flung at us from the ground. It seemed no matter how well the "Iron Hand" jets struck the SAM sites with their Shrike and High Speed Anti-Radiation Missile (HARM) ordnance, a number of SAMs inevitably got through and wreaked havoc. To protect themselves, and still try to put bombs on target, pilots literally functioned on their own, weaving to avoid streaking SAMs and working their way back to the bomb line for a run on the target. Collectively, we were all going in the same direction, but individual tracks through the sky were often erratic. The radio chatter really stepped up as we tried to help each other out. On occasion, it was like trying to listen to a dozen radio programs simultaneously.

The first line period went well, and when the ship retired to Cubi Point for a rest and recreation, "R and R," break, I relieved Doc Townsend as commanding officer. It was June 1967. We returned to Yankee Station and were soon in the thick of it. Despite some success with targets, I began to sense we really weren't hurting the enemy, no matter the abundance of iron bombs we heaved at the North Vietnamese. More troubling was the way the targets were determined.

In the first place, an Alpha Strike target would seldom be assigned before 1 AM our time. Reason: it took that long for the chain of command to decide on what target to hit. What bothered the heck out of me was that we believed the decisions were being made at the White House level and that President Johnson was at times the final arbiter on what we could and couldn't hit. Once the White House decided, the word was passed to the Pacific fleet commander, then down the line to the *Constellation.*

For the most part, junior officers got sufficient sleep while on Yankee Station, although we were all a bit run down from the pace of operations. For commanding officers, it was a different story, because we were the flight leaders, responsible for planning these elaborate intrusions into the breach. Sleep was at a premium for us. Twenty minute catnaps in my stateroom helped me recharge batteries. We seldom got six or more consecutive hours of slumber. But the late arrival of the target assignment, especially if we had a morning launch and a time on target (TOT) of, say 0730, meant we'd be lucky to get an hour or two in the sack before donning flight gear, getting breakfast, and briefing.

It was critical that flight leaders knew the terrain they would overfly nearly by heart. Then, they had to visually sight the target and establish a proper roll-in point that was workable not only for them, but also for the rest of the entourage. The thirty-plus guys trailing the leader had a tough enough time staying in formation, particularly when jinking—changing altitude and heading to prevent enemy gunners from drawing a bead on their aircraft—not to mention avoiding collisions with shipmates. Wingmen simply could not shift their scans from outside the cockpit to within to check a navigational chart. They relied on the flight leader to get them to the roll-in point. The leadership and tactical guidance imparted to the wingmen was critical to life and limb. I had led several flights up to this time.

In my case, I never spent less than thirty minutes focusing just on the target and its immediate environs. I wanted to know every nook and cranny of the landscape surrounding the target. Where were the SAM sites? Where would the sun be at our TOT? What egress route was best? On top of this, were all the other elements of concern: quickly rendezvousing thirty or more airplanes, ensuring the combat air patrol was positioned properly, rolling in as precisely as possible at our TOT, knowing emergency procedures, and so on.

Even more infuriating—and this has been hashed and rehashed since the debacle of Vietnam—was the list of targets that were verboten, that is, off limits, for us. For example, we could strike a storage area like the transshipment points, but not the piers where Chinese or Russian ships delivered the war cargo that was transferred to these points. The powers that be didn't want to antagonize the Russians or the Chinese. A singular exacerbating issue was the fact that we could not mine Haiphong Harbor. What a difference that would have made in shortening the war. Simply put, we could have interdicted the Communists' primary source of war materiel.

One day, one of our young RIOs, Jim Falvey, asked for a private chat with me. He was feeling the pressure of combat early in the deployment and was progressively having second thoughts about continuing to fly. I had had several long talks with him, hearing him out and encouraging him as best I could. On this day, Jim seemed especially down.

We were in my stateroom when Jim nervously proclaimed, "I'm seriously considering turning in my wings." The tone of the statement indicated to me he had not fully made up his mind but was teetering on the edge. He was driven to the precipice by fear coupled with the sense we were in an unwinnable conflict. Once you've slipped through a sky full of SAMs and popcorn clouds of AAA and got away with it, you wouldn't be human if you weren't scared. It was natural to believe that one of those missiles or rounds might have your name on it.

"You're experiencing what we all do at one time or another," I told him. "It's natural and nothing to be ashamed of." These mundane words certainly didn't persuade him to change his mind. But the fact I spent time talking to him made a difference, and he changed his mind about unpinning his wings.

In fact, Jim stuck with it, and years later, when I got out of prison, he was one of the first to look me up. "God," he said, "I thank you for giving me the strength to keep going and hang in there during combat. If I'd pulled myself out and quit I'd never, ever have felt the same about myself as I do now."

Our Phantoms were in good shape. The maintenance personnel outdid themselves in getting our electronics equipment up to speed and operating consistently well. They were the manifestation of what the American sailor can do when you put him (and nowadays, her) on a carrier, with no place else to go, working twelve hours or more a day. Fortunately, our troops were motivated regardless of the grinding schedule. They were acutely aware of the direct relationship between their maintenance of the airplanes and our safety when flying them. The F-4, to be sure, was proving itself a durable, workhorse warplane, capable of flying cover against enemy fighters or unleashing sizeable bomb loads on ground targets.

As great an airplane as it was, with fully loaded external tanks the Phantom had a dangerous tendency to pitch up nose high on catapult shots. The position of the tanks on the swept wings moved the aircraft's center of gravity slightly aft. The effect of the center of gravity exacerbated the nose up attitude. A few of our pilots tended to overrotate when fired into the air, and this portended disaster if forward, or nose-down stick wasn't immediately applied. They would hold onto the stick and pull too far back once airborne, particularly at night.

Most of us made hands-off catapult shots. That is, we did not have our right hand on the control column during launches but would grasp the stick once airborne. In effect, the airplane was better at taking off on its own, at least in the immediate early stages of the takeoff, if you set the trim properly. I prepositioned my hand behind the stick and, once catapulted, used the attitude gyro to track movement of the F-4's nose as it rose. When it reached the proper position on the gyrohorizon, I grasped the stick and took control from there. This procedure was particularly helpful at night, when carrier flying calls for extra concentration.

Just like any other aircraft, the Phantom was vulnerable, to AAA or SAMs, as I found out the hard way on the day we diverted from our primary target in Haiphong to the alternate in Nam Dinh, twenty miles inland from the Gulf. We paralleled the coast, staying out of the SAM envelope until reaching a point abeam of Nam Dinh, where I turned west and began a descent. I felt pretty good, although I'd had only two hours sleep. The weather was clear, and I sighted several of the landmarks I'd studied the night before. Because this was a delta region, the landscape was checkered with flat, green, rectangular or square rice paddies, bordered by brown, nearly orange-colored berms that allowed access to the paddies.

The target was a cinderblock structure with a tall smoke stack, indicative of the coal-fired power plant within. Our plan was to roll in from ten thousand feet at five hundred knots, execute the attack, and egress rapidly eastward, getting back over the relative sanctuary of the sea.

"This is Taproot lead, approaching target," I radioed to the formation. "Check your [armament] switches." There was no AAA yet. We gathered speed rapidly, and I felt my Phantom gripped by the compressibility effect of fast-moving air over the airframe. I was at five hundred knots, nearing ten thousand feet and five seconds from my planned roll-in point, when I was enveloped by flak—lethal steel and smoke blossoming all around me.

I felt a jolt to my airframe. My immediate wingman, Tom Rodger, transmitted, "Hey, skipper, I think you've been hit!"

I felt like saying, "Tell me something I don't know." Still, the Phantom seemed to be flying. At the roll-in point, the hydraulic pressure warning lights illuminated. But the controls felt normal. I made a snap decision not to pull myself out of the flight and head back to the ocean. I believed I could complete the bomb run.

I rolled the F-4 onto its back, pulled the nose through, leveled the wings, and settled into the run. Out of the corner of my eye, I couldn't help but note the red warning lights on the instrument panel. It appeared both my primary and secondary flight control systems were damaged. On the way down, the Phantom started to feel mushy—unresponsive to my control inputs. I was able to get my gunsight pipper on the plant and released the CBUs.

Then real trouble began. I was headed directly toward the ground, and using all available strength, I could barely get the nose to come back up. Somehow I managed a slight climb and got to ten thousand feet, headed for the water, the Phantom streaming smoke. Hydraulic pressure was now zero.

I went into a very flat spin. The F-4 wallowed clumsily as it swung around and around. I had no more influence on the controls and became a passenger rather than a driver. The engines were still working, and I tried using alternate afterburner to stop the spin, but this didn't work. Plummeting through three thousand feet, I knew the Phantom was doomed.

"Eject, Jim!" I ordered. He responded immediately. There was a startling pyrotechnic charge behind me, as Jim was fired up the rails of his ejection seat into the bright blue sky. At eighteen hundred feet I pulled the lower ejection seat handle and punched myself out. Our equipment worked as advertised, and our parachutes blossomed nicely.

I grasped my handheld, walkie-talkie-type radio, secured to my survival vest via Velcro, yanked it up to my lips, and reported, "Taproot lead has a good chute. I'm OK." It was critical that I let the flight know I survived the ejection. I saw Jim's chute, and he appeared OK as well. Even though I was still floating in the sky, I could almost feel the earth quake as our Phantom smashed into the ground in a ball of yellow-red fire fringed in black.

I was thankful to be alive, but knew I would not be able to exercise any escape and evasion skills this day, because unfriendly people were waiting for me, and there was no place to hide on the pool table-flat terrain of the delta. I was about to become a prisoner of war.

Chapter Thirteen

INCARCERATION

"You are an air pirate!" he declared vehemently.
"You are not a prisoner of war. The Geneva Convention does not apply to you."

I LANDED THIGH-DEEP SMACK in the middle of a rice paddy. As I struggled to untangle myself from the parachute's shroud lines, I saw a man in khaki militia garb standing on the adjacent berm, brandishing a rifle at me. The rifle looked like one Sergeant York might have used in World War I. The man was thirtyish and had a look of uncertainly in his eyes, but his finger was on the trigger, and I had no doubt he would pull it if I made any threatening gestures. I had no chance of escape, a reality that sunk in even as I descended in the chute. I stood there in the mud hardly able to move.

The transition from the relatively comfortable confines of the Phantom's cockpit to the wide open, if alien, countryside with a gun pointed at me was so extreme it seemed surreal. My heart was beating like a trip-hammer. At the moment, the only thing I had going for me was that I had not been hurt during the ejection.

As an aviator expected to fly over enemy country, I had trained at two of the Navy's survival, escape, resistance, and evasion (SERE) schools. The first was during the Korean War at a complex set up at a city park in Alameda, California; the second, a far more sophisticated operation, in the mountains near Warner Springs, California, not far from San Diego. (Today, a second school is located near Naval Air Station Brunswick in Maine. The Air Force and Army have similar facilities.) Escape and evasion were, for the moment, out of the question. Survival and resistance, however, were achievable, and those challenges lay ahead. Whether I could succeed with those two elements, I did not honestly know. My immediate concern was to abide by the Department of Defense-sanctioned Code of Conduct.

As I extricated myself from the rice paddy, a rifle was continuously aimed at my chest. In the periphery, people were gathering on the surrounding berms. I was the center of attraction and probably the first American most of them had ever encountered.

I was marched toward a nearby hamlet, which was hardly more than a collection of hooches—small, wood-framed huts that looked as if a swift wind would blow them away. I was motioned into a side section of one of the huts, which turned out to be a pigpen occupied by a sow, who must have tipped the scales at no less than four hundred pounds. The sow eyed me curiously and, I judged, with a bit of indignation for crowding up her quarters. She seemed to be thinking, "What are you doing in my bedroom?"

An hour or so passed, during which countless thoughts raced through my mind. Anne would be getting the news soon, then the kids, my parents, and the many friends with whom my life had been blessed. But mostly I thought about Anne. She'll be all right, I thought. My transmission that I was OK in the chute would at least let her know I survived the ejection. She was a solid Navy wife, even with the worry and strain that accompanied marriage to a flyer.

After a time, a man who seemed to have more authority than the others arrived and took me in custody. I was stripped of my harness, (my pistol had already been taken), my handheld radio, watch, boots, and flight suit, leaving me in my skivvies, barefoot. I had left my Naval Academy ring back in my stateroom, or that would have been raked off my finger. The man looked into my mouth, presumably to see if there was gold or silver in there. Fortunately, there wasn't, otherwise I'd have had an immediate dental extraction.

I was prodded into a run across the countryside, which took several minutes, until we arrived at a point on a dirt road, where I was loaded into the back of a truck. I was soon joined by Jim, and the truck headed north. When he and I tried to talk, we were struck with the butt of a rifle from one of the guards who accompanied the truck.

Young kids seemed to be everywhere, laughing and cutting up as if our capture was a huge social event. The older people, however, gazed at us, most with genuine hatred in their eyes. They tried to hit us with sticks and stones.

En route to what I was certain to be Hanoi, the truck stopped at an intermediate point, and I was roughly ushered into what seemed like a small guard station. Another member of the militia sat behind a table and placed a typewritten questionnaire before me. It was written in English, and he motioned me to fill it out. I refused. Under the Code of Conduct, I was not required to comply. I gave him my rank, serial number, and date of birth.

The man put on a forlorn and disapproving expression, as if he'd gone through this before, but didn't press the matter. "Maybe this is the way I'm going to be treated," I said to myself. "They're going to abide by the Geneva Convention after all."

Wrong.

By the time we reached Hanoi, it was growing dark. The truck proceeded through a guarded entranceway in a walled structure into a courtyard area with various other separate buildings situated throughout the complex. This was unmistakably the Hoa Lo prison, which the American inmates had come to identify as the Hanoi Hilton. The basic sections of Hoa Lo were Little Vegas, also called Camp Vegas; Unity; Heartbreak Hotel; and New Guy Village. Many of the early prisoners were Air Force flyers who had trained at Nellis Air Force Base in Nevada, not far from Las Vegas. The familiarity of the casinos, coupled with the arrangement of separate compounds within the basic sections of the prison complex Hoa Lo complex, inspired the titles of those various compounds. For example, the compounds within Little Vegas included Stardust, Desert Inn, Mint, Thunderbird, Riviera, and Golden Nugget.

We were ordered from the truck, and I was led into an orientation room, where a North Vietnamese officer, dressed in a uniform that was a slight improvement over that of the militiamen, sat behind a crude wooden desk flanked by two other officers. He fired a sequence of questions in English at me, and I responded to each with name, rank, serial number, and date of birth.

"You are an air pirate!" he declared vehemently. "You are not a prisoner of war. The Geneva Convention does not apply to you."

"William P. Lawrence, commander, 410 443 3904, January 13, 1930," I responded.

"What was your target?" he demanded.

I continued with my litany.

"What type of aircraft were you flying? What targets did you plan to strike in the future?"

I stood my ground and he, his. This fruitless exchange created a tense impasse, which I don't think surprised my interrogator. He stood up abruptly and left the room. I stood there at attention in my skivvies, wondering what came next.

Enter "Straps and Bar," also known as "Pig Eye," one of the more memorable, if intriguing, characters of my incarceration. Straps and Bar was a professional torturer. I was unaware of his sobriquet at the time, but I was about to learn in unassailable fashion how he earned it. I was also going to be deeply grateful to those "two-a-days" at Annapolis during preseason football practice.

Straps and Bar was a medium-size Asian with noticeable muscle tone and a phlegmatic demeanor. In this same room over the next three days, I became very well acquainted with him, but purely in the physical sense. He never changed his stoic expression, never exhibited any emotion, including anger, and simply went about his business with the aplomb of an assembly-line worker in Detroit. He was an expert at inducing pain without maiming or killing. The North Vietnamese did not want us dead. In their eyes, we were valuable hostages. He put my legs in shackles affixed to a long, horizontal bar and pushed my head down to go underneath the bar. He then pulled my arms behind me, secured them with a strap, laced another strap tightly around my neck, and left me there, twisted like a pretzel, and in inexorable pain.

This was a first in a series of contortions Straps and Bar engineered on my person. Over the next three days, I passed out several times. I distinctly remember blacking out when the strap around my neck cut off the blood flow to my brain. Expertly, the pressure of the strap was released before fatal damage was incurred. Periodically, an interrogator came into the room and fired questions at me. I believe I resisted as well as I could and don't recall answering the questions to the interrogator's liking. Indeed, recollections of this period remain dim in my memory, because I was in and out of consciousness throughout the three days. I don't even remember having anything to eat or drink during this period.

Primarily, the interrogators wanted to know what targets we were planning to hit. Having become a POW, I certainly had no knowledge of what was being planned back on the carrier. But the torture was taking its toll, and I was reaching a breaking point. I finally accepted the fact that I had to tell my captors something. So, I just started picking out the targets that would do the most damage to the Communists, such as the piers in Haiphong; the fighter base at Phuc Yen, north of Hanoi; and government headquarters in Hanoi.

My captors seemed satisfied, even though my response had no validity. They backed off on the torture. I was quietly pleased, because I was very worried they might learn that I possessed highly classified knowledge about some of the systems used in electronic countermeasures. Most of this knowledge was acquired through my experience with the F-4 Phantom at Patuxent and in the fleet. In the end, the questions were very basic.

In dark retrospect, I appreciated the professionalism of Straps and Bar. He could have made a mistake, gone too far, and did me in. I learned what it feels like for one human being to be totally subjugated to the will of another, and it was a terrifying experience.

After my fellow POW, Capt. Jack Fellowes, was released in 1973, he told an interviewer that when he was shot down in 1966, he felt he would be a prisoner for only six months that the war would be concluded by then. Jack, one tough customer, persevered throughout captivity, despite his earlier prediction. My perspective was different and largely influenced by Gen. Paul Dewitt Adams. He had clearly feared that United States involvement in Vietnam would become a costly and lengthy quagmire. I had no doubt that he was right, and that I was in for a long, tough haul.

Chapter Fourteen

1,900 DAYS

One of our most familiar and reassuring phrases, passed on liberally throughout imprisonment, was G - B - U. God Bless You. It helped.

I WAS TRANSFERRED FROM HEARTBREAK HOTEL to Camp Vegas in the Thunderbird cell block, and in the days of misery that followed, I fought back the notion that I made a huge mistake when I continued the attack on the thermal power plant after my aircraft had been hit by what I presumed was a single 87-millimeter shell, fired by a marksman who was either incredibly skilled or unbelievably lucky. Had I allowed this really unanswerable question to linger in my mind, it might have had a devastating effect on my disposition, which was already being tested to the maximum. On top of this, I had to fight the realization that I would not be allowed contact with my family via letters.

Had I turned back immediately upon being hit, I might have made it to the sea and friendly hands. But the Phantom was still flying, I had bombs on board, and I was the leader of the attack. I believed then as I do now that I would make the same decision again, not because it was the heroic thing to do, but because it was the right thing to do. Thus, I rid myself of the element of self-doubt that could have been mentally debilitating over the long haul. I didn't want any "What ifs" pestering me in the long days ahead.

So began my more than nineteen hundred days of captivity. We were fed two meals a day, one at 10 AM, the last at 4 PM, usually consisting of weak, unseasoned pumpkin soup and a small loaf of bread made from coarse brown flour, probably derived from some Russian, Chinese, or Eastern Bloc country. Occasionally, we'd get a handful of rice. These meals provided us seven hundred calories per day and was our steady diet up to six months before our release in 1973, when the cuisine improved, with more substantial food.

I was extremely fortunate in that I experienced dysentery only two or three times while in prison. Others fared far worse. Each of us had to struggle to survive, employing every iota of the will to live. The absence of a proper diet was a continuing challenge. The other was communication. Hermits are rare in any society. Most of us are social animals and like to talk to one another, whether it's in passing at the grocery store, at work, or on social occasions. When you are secluded, enclosed by four walls, and unable to talk to anyone but yourself, day in and day out, for hours on end, your mind grows weary and confused. The tendency to daydream and fantasize and to lapse into the "why me?" syndrome has to be fought.

We devised a tap code, somewhat similar to Morse code, involving a sequence of taps spelling out the alphabet and, ultimately, words and sentences. This tap code has been well chronicled in numerous books. Suffice it to say our ability to communicate via this code literally saved us from a different kind of starvation—that of no contact with fellow detainees. We rapped knuckles on cell walls, coughed the code, even swept floors using the sound of the broom brushing concrete floors to send a message. Our ability to converse in this rudimentary yet clever fashion was essential to survival.

I was installed in a one-person cell in the Thunderbird cell block. This began six months of solitary confinement. I was banged up after my three days with Straps and Bar and had very limited use of my limbs. It would actually be several months before they were back to a reasonably functional status. Turns out I had a fractured bone in my left shoulder, plus I had lost the feeling in the outside of my right leg.

Crippled as I was, I was able to work myself over to the door of the cell, where I detected other POWs talking. From this, I learned that the senior officer in Thunderbird was Navy Commander (later Vice Admiral) Jim Stockdale, an old friend from test pilot days, who was shot down in September of 1965. I hadn't learned the code yet, but I was able to get word to him piecemeal through various other POWs that I had seen his wife, Sybil, four months before at a change of command ceremony at Naval Air Station North Island, that she looked great, and that all four boys were doing fine. I also notified him that his name had appeared on the latest captain's list and that he had been promoted to captain a year ahead of his Naval Academy class. I learned later this was a huge boost to him, because he hadn't heard anything from his family but for a "carbon" letter from Sybil the previous December.

The days and nights were long and lonely. Thank heaven for the tap code, which I was able to pick up rather quickly. It was a relatively simple system. Picture a matrix with twenty-five of the twenty-six letters of the alphabet (we left off the K and allowed C to stand for both letters). There were five lines of five letters each. Line one across was for *A-E*; line two, *F-J*; line three, *L-P* and so on. To send a word, we tapped once for line one, twice for line two (next line down), and so forth, then worked horizontally. The phrase "OK" would be tapped as follows: three taps for the third line down (which contains the *O*) then four taps to select *O*. Next, one tap for the first line and three taps for the third letter going from left to right. It was amazing how proficient we became with this simple system.

At one point I was moved to a cell that had a common wall with another cell wherein resided U.S. Air Force lieutenant Ron Maston. Ron and I had an active exchange of information via the tap code, which we exercised with increasing proficiency.

I slept on a bare wooden bunk in debilitating heat. I developed bad sores on my scalp, although my broken shoulder was healing. The overriding ambiance of our prison life was characterized by the unending filth and rats. It took a while to realize that the standard of hygiene in the prison camp was hardly different from what the general population in Hanoi experienced. Once, I was spread out with my head close to the slight gap between the bottom of my wooden cell door and the cement floor. I was trying to see what I could see and endeavoring to transmit a message. I had left a chunk of brown bread on my bunk, and when I turned back from the door I was startled to see a foot-long rat nibbling at the bread. I shooed him away, but I knew he or his pals would be back. I'd never seen a rat as big as that one.

We had rudimentary medical care; a North Vietnamese "corpsman" had some medicines. I was extremely lucky to never have gotten really sick during captivity. But I did contract a viral infection in my left eye. I was taken to the corpsman, who used a big needle to give me an injection of penicillin. I was allergic to this medication in large doses, but that's what I got. My eye got better, but I traded that for a really bad rash. I cannot stress enough how valuable it was that I was in top physical condition when I was shot down. Those POWs who were less fit physically had a huge strike against them at the outset. In some cases, because of the dreary and continuing poor conditions, dysentery became commonplace, and malaise set in, seriously eroding the all-important will to survive.

I was in solitary confinement through the summer and was periodically moved from one seven-foot-square cell to another. The furnishings were inevitably the same—a slab for a bed and a bucket for human waste.

We communicated well in Thunderbird for that first month, but almost suddenly, "conversation" was ceased. Apparently, the camp commander perceived that the courageous Jim Stockdale had established some sort of network through which he could put out orders to fellow POWs who were subordinate in rank.

The guards removed a dozen prisoners who they believed were at the heart of the network and segregated them in another section of the prison complex called Alcatraz. From July to October there were virtually no communications.

One day I looked out through the bars of the small glassless window of my cell, a forbidden practice, and caught a glimpse of Byron Fuller, a Naval Academy classmate. He had been injured and was being helped along by a fellow POW, Wayne Waddel, of the Air Force, assigned to him by the North Vietnamese as Fuller's nurse.

Another time when I surreptitiously peeked out the window, I was caught by a guard. For punishment, I was placed in leg stocks, iron shackles rigged at one end of the wooden bunk. I could raise up and my arms were free. But being secured to that slab and unable to move about was terribly demoralizing. The immobility, the heat—which led to the eruption of sores all over my body, not to mention a relentless armada of flies and mosquitoes—the inability to communicate with anyone, not to mention the absence of letters from home, or the opportunity to send one myself, and the inexorable discomfort took their toll. I was two months into captivity and I felt myself growing despondent. I recognized this as a danger point, as if I were lowering deeper and deeper into a darkening well. It was very easy to feel sorry for myself. In retrospect, this was the lowest point of my tour in the Hanoi Hilton. Fortunately, I never completely slipped off into the abyss.

In October, an escalation of the bombing resulted in an influx of prisoners. Several times a day air raid sirens wailed across Hanoi, announcing the arrival of American bombers. As more and more aircraft flew into the dangerous skies, more and more aviators were shot down, increasing the POW population. This became an ironic blessing for me, because I was let out of the stocks. To my unfathomable relief, I was placed in a cell with three newly arrived flyers, one of them another classmate, Cdr. Chuck Gillespie, commanding officer of Fighter Squadron 151, flying F-4 Phantoms. POWs Bryon Fuller, Al Brady, Jim Mehl, and now Gillespie were fellow classmates at the Academy. Also, there were Lt. Col. Tom Kirk, U.S. Air Force, and Lt. Cdr. Verlyne "Red" Daniels, U.S. Navy. Being with other human beings was an emotional lift, a feeling unlike any other I'd experienced in my relatively brief lifetime.

Off and on the four of us would be together for most of the remainder of our incarceration. Tom Kirk and I, especially, were cellmates for the duration. I briefed the newcomers on the tap code and tried to get an update on what was going on in the outside world during those rare moments when we figured the guards were out of earshot.

Perhaps because of the influence of the French Colonists, the North Vietnamese took a siesta from one to two in the afternoon each day. The camp was eerily quiet then except for our innovative tapping, either by knuckles against stone or wood, the flick of bamboo brooms against the pavement, or the discrete sequence of coughing that could be heard from twenty feet away. One or two coughs signaled the first and second lines of the matrix; a clearing of the throat meant the third line; a deep hack was for the fourth line, and a distasteful but significant spitting sound stood for the fifth line. To keep the guards confused, we orchestrated almost constant sneezing and coughing. We actually badgered the guards into letting us use the brooms to keep our cells neat and orderly. The guards came to believe we Americans were absolute cleanliness nuts.

One of our most familiar and reassuring phrases, passed on liberally throughout imprisonment, was *G - B - U*. God Bless You. It helped.

Still, the state of confrontation did not abate. The North Vietnamese constantly tried to pressure POWs into making propaganda statements. Two among the prison population eventually acceded to the pressure. I noticed one of the two. He had stopped communicating, a behavioral trait that sent up a red flag. I implored him as best I could through the tap code to stay the course, but he did not. He was removed from our presence and collaborated with the enemy, gaining better treatment for himself. This was obviously disappointing, but in retrospect, none of us knows if and when we would give up under the unrelenting pressure. Fortunately, very few of our number went over to the other side.

While the first sign that a man's resolve was disintegrating was the failure to communicate, the second was the failure to eat. After meals, our bowls were stacked on a table. If we saw that a man's bowl still contained food, we knew he was endangering himself. We used whatever persuasive lingo we could contrive to urge him to eat, to hang in there. In most cases, this group "therapy" worked, and the prisoner got back on track. Yet, some POWs caused their demise through failure to eat.

Chapter Fifteen

VISIT TO CALCUTTA

For example, we could tap on one wall for fifteen minutes, acquiring a poem and then go to the opposite wall and repeat the message for the next guy, having rapidly committed the newly received item to memory.

IN THE FALL OF 1967, I relieved Jim Stockdale as the senior officer in Camp Vegas. Jim and some others had been transferred to another section called Alcatraz. In that capacity, my biggest challenge was keeping everybody on line, communicating, getting the word out. The North Vietnamese knew we valued this capability and were determined to stop it. They also continuously tried to identify individual POWs who might be lured into making a propaganda statement. Fortunately, no one under my command agreed to be seen by any of the various "peace" delegations who came to Hanoi. One of my directives was, "No one is to go out and see a delegation," such as Jane Fonda.

We prided ourselves on our tough resistance posture, and, in my view, the North Vietnamese figured Camp Vegas wasn't a promising source for their propaganda purposes. I did not totally originate the policy on POW behavior at Camp Vegas. Instead, it was in part an extension of Jim Stockdale's initiatives, with some amplification by yours truly.

One dictum I authored had to do with withstanding pain. If it came to torture, I conveyed to the POWs, "Don't hang in there until you lose your rationality. Have a cover story, but before you start using that cover story, endure as much pain as you can stand." If a man's rationality deteriorated, he would not be able to maintain his planned cover story, and the North Vietnamese would know he was lying and make life even more miserable for him, and for the rest of us.

Sadly, we did lose one of our POWs in my group, Air Force First Lieutenant (later Captain) Lance Sijan. He had evaded capture for a long time after being shot down but suffered from extreme exposure, a broken leg, gangrene, and other maladies. He was with us in Camp Vegas for about two weeks of great suffering. After hearing his painful moaning for several days, I exhorted the camp authorities to give him urgent medical attention, but to no avail. I never did get face to face with him, but we realized that, because of his condition, his days were numbered. He was removed from his cell still alive, but he was not returned when we were released. It was determined he died in captivity. He was given the Medal of Honor for his bravery and perseverance in avoiding capture. A hall at the Air Force Academy is named in his honor.

Each person had his own threshold for pain. One of my cell mates had an absolute fear of any pain whatsoever, for example. As the senior officer, I was, in practical terms, a cheerleader, trying to boost spirits whenever necessary. My cell mate, Tom Kirk, ultimately persevered.

I was a fan of the poet Sir Walter Scott. His lines, "The Stag at Eve had drunk his fill, / Where danced the moon on Mona's rill, / And deep his midnight lair had made / In lone Glenartney's hazel shade," were favorites of mine, especially because they were written in the rhythmic phrasing of iambic pentameter. One of the mind games I played in an attempt to distance myself from the pain and physical misery I was experiencing was to compose poems in my head. I was no Sir Walter Scott. He was a genius. But I had time. One of my earliest efforts was, "Oh Tennessee, My Tennessee," an ode to my home state, which I composed over a three-week period while in solitary confinement. After my release, I was asked to address the Tennessee state legislature and took the opportunity to recite the poem to the lawmakers. I didn't garner great applause, but two weeks later I learned the poem had become the state poem of Tennessee. Tennessee doesn't produce many poets, and the state did not have an official state poem, so it's not as if "Oh Tennessee, My Tennessee" was going to earn me a Pulitzer. Besides, country music reigns in that part of the country. I felt honored by the gesture nonetheless and was happy I could enhance the image of my state, if only in a small way.

It was amazing how sharp our memories became in captivity. Three of us in Camp Vegas were designated to memorize the names of every POW we were certain was in the camp. I developed my list gradually and every third day would repeat the names to myself over and over. I maintained the list in groups of five, alphabetically. We got so skillful at this that, when a new name came to our attention, we could insert it in place and regroup the list, in "fives" again, in a flash.

Memorization was a big help in keeping us mentally sharp. When a POW passed on a new poem or some other writing, we would grab onto it eagerly and commit it to memory. I memorized Rudyard Kipling's "Gunga

Din" in its entirety along with other works by that great writer. Keep the mind working, that was the key.

I designed houses, replayed football games, reflew flights I had made, anything to keep the brain cells mobilized. For example, we could tap on one wall for fifteen minutes acquiring a poem and then go the opposite wall and repeat the message for the next guy, having rapidly committed the newly received item to memory.

Obviously, the average person in an everyday, normal environment simply doesn't exercise his or her mind as we did in the prison camp. There is no need to. In the prisons cells of North Vietnam, it was a dire necessity.

One day I was caught placing a note in a special spot in a common area where POWs occasionally moved about—the outside bath stalls. The guards had suspected I might be a leader in promoting communication among prisoners, and placing the note was proof. Furious, they transferred me to a six-foot-square cell that was unventilated, unlighted, and had a tin roof. Temperatures were soaring to a hundred or more degrees during this time. Jim Stockdale had been sequestered there and later described it as a "torture pit." We called it Calcutta, and I was there for two eternal months.

The pain, solitude, oppressive heat, and loneliness took their toll on me. I forced myself to continue playing my mind games, creating poetry, building houses, remembering names and faces from my earlier years, and so forth. This helped get me through the ordeal. It was with a significant measure of relief that I was sent back to Camp Vegas. I found out later that I had been moved from Calcutta because they had another candidate they wanted to install in the black hole, Cdr. John McCain. McCain had gotten in some sort of trouble and had to be punished. It sounds like black humor, but I felt indebted to John who, at this writing, is an esteemed United States senator from Arizona, for relieving me in the torture pit. At Camp Vegas I was placed in a cell with my old roommate, Tom Kirk. It turned out that Tom's earlier cell mate had been John McCain.

You had to fight the tendency to lapse into self-pity. The worst question you could ask yourself was, "Why me?" Moreover, you had to take it one day at a time. Each morning when I woke up I told myself, "Today is umpty-ump, in the month of umpty-ump, in the year of umpty-ump." I was in my middle thirties and had enough experience to be a senior in the camp. Yet I was young enough to be healthy and vigorous, commodities that helped me withstand the poor diet, bad sanitation, and terrible treatment.

There's no doubt my Naval Academy training helped me live up to my responsibilities as a senior officer.

Chapter Sixteen

PERSEVERING

We hope you are well. We are fine and have escaped the flu so far.
We are beginning to have some spring like weather. Everyone is praying for you.
Much Love, Mother & Dad

A NAGGING DEFICIENCY during our captivity was the absence of knowledge of what was happening in the world beyond ours. We didn't learn about the first landing on the moon in 1969 until well after this historic milestone. We were, however, witness to the antiwar demonstrations that were plaguing America, which I considered a case of bad news being better than no news at all. One night in 1970, we were taken from our cells and seated apart from one another to view a movie of a demonstration in San Francisco. We read the placards people held up. One of them read, "Hey Dick, you can put a man on the moon, but you can't stop the Vietnam War." In subsequent communication we wondered what this meant. Dick, we figured, was Pres. Richard Nixon.

I said, "God, you think we really put a man on the moon?" I remembered that in 1967, before I was shot down, this was a goal; we wanted to have a man on the moon by the end of the 1960s. I considered this too much of a technological feat within that time frame. We queried each other about this for months.

There had been a bombing halt as a result of peace talks in 1968, but when the bombing started up again in the spring of 1972, more flyers were shot down, and from them we confirmed that, indeed, the United States had put Neil Armstrong and his crew on the moon in July 1969. That's nearly three years from the event to our learning about it.

Using amplifiers of very poor quality, the North Vietnamese blared propaganda speeches from the Voice of Vietnam for a half hour each morning and a half hour each afternoon. Hanoi Hannah was a featured performer for the network. She spoke in good English with a slight Asian accent, always emphasizing the discord that was raging in the United States. I learned about all the calamities and adverse events in America from Hanoi Hannah and the Voice of Vietnam. To me, though, I savored every word of it. Taking into account the source, I could derive a sense of how the war was progressing. The casualty counts were so outrageous, however, that we decided to divide the number provided by four.

We were issued a propaganda newspaper that described ongoing battles throughout the country. This, coupled with the broadcasts, and with our concerned doubts considered, helped us learn the course of the conflict. In effect, after two to three years, the North Vietnamese recognized that our resistance to torture and the concomitant pressures of captivity weren't doing them much good in the brainwashing war. The propaganda briefings and the newspaper, they felt, would have to take up that cause.

I did not receive a letter from home until I'd been imprisoned for three years. Mail call was a haphazard affair, but it usually came once about every three months. I was able to write letters early on but not receive them. I was uncertain where Anne and the kids might be, so I addressed their letters to my mother and father in Nashville, hoping they would relay information to Anne. When I did get a letter, it was from my mother. I was exhilarated to hear from her, but her message was so bland and uninformative, the only satisfaction I derived from it was knowing they realized I was still alive. I'd been listed as missing in action (MIA) until late 1969, when, at the urging of Sen. Ted Kennedy and others, the North Vietnamese issued a list of our names.

In all my time in the Hanoi Hilton, I never heard from Anne, but I did learn in a letter from my parents that she had moved to California. The letters were brief and written in a proscribed form, with the content of the letter limited to a four- by five-inch block of lined space. My address was:

William Porter Lawrence 543032
Camp of Detention of U.S. Pilots
Captured in the Democratic
Republic of Vietnam
c/o Hanoi Post Office
Hanoi, D.R.V.

Inscribed to the left of the address my mother had written:

Air Mail
Via Moscow
U.S.S.R.

Here's an example of one of the letters, written in script with a blue ball point pen, from my mother.

> Dear Bill: We are all well. Hope and pray you are. We have had our first frost and cold weather past weekend. Bobby [my brother] & Brad [his son] came down Friday for V.U. [Vanderbilt]—KY [Kentucky] game on Saturday. KY won 14-7 in last 36 seconds on intercepted pass. V.U. has a 2-7 record. They are adding an Athletic Dept. next year. All send love, Dad and Mother.

Another letter from mom was carefully printed in capital letters. She wrote:

> WE ENJOYED SO MUCH YOUR FINE LETTER OF JULY 23. WE IMMEDIATELY CALLED ANNE TO READ TO HER. WE ARE ALL WELL AND ACTIVE. AUNTIE WALLIS WAS BURIED LAST WEEK AFTER A LONG ILLNESS. 90 YRS. TOM MARRIED NEIGHBOR GIRL JUNE 6. TERRY STEELE WHO LIVES ACROSS HI-WAY. TOM GOT HIS DEGREE & WKS FOR 1ST AM. BANK. LOVE FROM ALL. MOM AND DAD. [September 25, 1970]

One more, in script:

> We hope you are well. We are fine and have escaped the flu so far. We are beginning to have some spring like weather. Everyone is praying for you. Much Love. Mother & Dad.

Following is a sample of one of my letters to the folks. I made sure my handwriting was neat and legible to convey to them that my physical and mental status was OK:

> Dear Mom and Dad: I'm fine and hope you are active and well. Have enjoyed very much your letters and Christmas color pictures. Tom's wife is very charming and pretty. Await your news on where Bill's [my son, Bill] in school now and what study fields he is in. Did Anne buy the house she lives in now in Solana Beach. I also would like to thank you for such tasty gift items. I surely hope that on Christmas most of your family is with you. Please send more pictures. Dad, enjoy your retirement. You earned it. Love to all. Bill

One more from me to them, this time in printed letters:

> Don't worry about me for I'm in fine shape in all respects. I hope you are in
> very good health and spirits, are enjoying life, and are able to travel much
> both in and out of USA. If Dad is retired now, an interesting project would
> be to write a family history. Dad, I would highly value your analysis and
> advice in helping Bill to make a decision on his college. I also thank you
> for the help I know you are giving Anne and the children. I wish you both
> late happy birthdays and many pleasant years ahead. Give all the family
> my love. Bill

The North Vietnamese delighted in giving us bad news collectively and individually. Navy lieutenant Edward Alvarez, who was imprisoned longer than any of us, had the terrible misfortune of being divorced by his wife and the enemy knowing it. With satisfaction, they informed Ev, a debilitating blow to any person in a position helpless to do anything about it. (Ev prevailed, however, and subsequently became very successful as a consultant in medical qualifications for military retirement, remarried, and has been a dear friend over the years.)

Despite our miserable conditions and the sheer awfulness of being confined, we held up, determined to one day return home. We continued communicating, fighting torture, and caring for each other. And as the months and years passed, I believe that our captors developed a grudging respect for our toughness and resolve. Gradually, around 1969, when Ho Chi Min died, our treatment improved. A sailor, Doug Hegdahl, was released in a propaganda event in the summer of the same year, and he gave the U.S. government a nearly comprehensive list of all POWs as well as conditions of treatment.

One guard, however, never changed his coarse mind-set toward us. We called him "Big Ugh." He had a vicious streak, which manifested itself when he struck us on the head with his keys. He never changed. But the others did. I came to believe that, under any other circumstances, the Vietnamese are an inherently gentle people.

As I mentioned earlier, we did have two American prisoners who opted to cooperate with the enemy in exchange for better treatment: Col. Ed Miller, USMC, and Capt. Gene Wilbur, U.S. Navy. In addition, three other POWs were inclined to follow Miller and Wilbur. No one knows how he or she would respond to the adverse conditions inherent in being a prisoner of war.

I hold no animosity toward these men. We tried very hard to keep them in the fold, but they refused. We did succeed in getting the other three to stay.

I've been asked about the usefulness of the Code of Conduct that outlines behavior expected of captives. We were "bound" to provide name, rank, serial number, and date of birth, with the understanding we would resist giving any other information to the utmost of our ability. However, following an evaluation of the code after the war, the word "bound" was eliminated from the text, easing somewhat the rule of disclosure. It gives a prisoner just a little more leeway in his resistance posture. The code still works, but I would have preferred keeping the word "bound" in the text.

The code also tells us to try to escape from and evade the enemy. That wasn't much of an option for us, because the compound was so heavily guarded, and as most of us were Caucasian, we would stand out in the Asian community rather than blend into it.

Nonetheless, Capt. John Dramesi and Capt. Ed Attabury, both U.S. Air Force, spent months planning an escape and actually got away from the compound called the Zoo. They made it to the Red River and worked their way south but were captured. It is believed that Atterbury died at the hands of the North Vietnamese from his subsequent punishment. Dramesi survived. Consequently, though, as a signal to all of us that escape attempts would not be tolerated, torture and brutality increased.

In November 1972 the famous raid on the Son Tay prison, located twenty miles northwest of Hanoi, took place and startled the enemy. The mission failed because all prisoners had been removed well before the raid, but it alarmed our captors, and about Christmas time, POWs from outlying prisons were pulled into a central location at the Hanoi Hilton. At first we didn't know the reason for this sudden influx. But there were some South Vietnamese POWs among us who managed to get the information from the guards that a rescue had been tried.

As might be expected, religion played a major role in our lives in Hanoi. Indeed, it was the sustaining element of our lives. For the first four years, we were not allowed to conduct any religious activity. I thought it critical that we be able to do so. For a long time, each man conducted his own private service, if only in his mind. In 1972, when larger numbers of POWs were placed in bigger cells accommodating forty to forty-five men, precipitated by the Son Tay raid, we started group services. A stalwart in this effort was one of my heroes, USAF colonel (and Medal of Honor awardee) Robbie Risner. He led a service for the group that was seen by the guards, and once they realized what was happening, they panicked.

Within minutes, the guards hurried into the cell, grabbed Risner, Capt. Howie Rutledge, U.S. Navy, and George Coker, who were assisting Robbie, and hauled them away. This infuriated us, and after a brief confab, those of us who were seniors decided to go on a two-day fast. We sent word around the camp about what happened, which got everyone pumped up in anger. That evening, after the sun had gone down and things were a bit more settled, we stood up in unison on a prearranged signal and, at the top of our lungs, sang the "Star Spangled Banner" so loud I thought it might have been heard on the streets of Hanoi.

As a consequence, the North Vietnamese selected out the seniors in the group, still fasting, and removed us to small one-person cells. In essence this was solitary confinement. This gesture allowed them to save face, but the upshot was that, in time, we were allowed to have group religious services, a major victory for our side. We ended our fast after five days.

Actually, this was the second time I was involved in a fast. A few months earlier, Capt. (later Sen.) Jerry Denton had returned to Vegas from Alcatraz, and because he was senior, I turned over command of Vegas to him. He ordered a two-day fast to protest solitary confinement for certain POWs. We called Denton "Low Cholesterol Commander." In retrospect, I have my doubts about the fasting. When you're already receiving fewer than the required calories for sustenance, it didn't help to go without any calories at all. Still, it had its advantages. We were not only POWs, but, as time went on, the North Vietnamese came to accept that we also were hostages, and, as hostages, we were of value to our captors. It was not in their best interest to let us perish behind prison walls.

Chapter Seventeen

SOMETHING IN THE WIND

*It was personally reassuring to note that many of the boldest leaders
in the camps were Navy men, and many of them were
Naval Academy graduates.*

BEFORE 1971 WE WERE OCCASIONALLY let out of our cells for brief periods
in the Hanoi Hilton courtyard for a "horse trough" bath. The guards remained
antisocial and maintained a rather cocky attitude even when strike groups
swarmed in and unleashed untold numbers of bombs on North Vietnamese
targets.

After the religious service fiasco, things tightened up when the seniors,
including yours truly, were abruptly transferred away from the larger body of
POWs and kept in two- to three-person cells. That lasted until our release.
In early 1971, however, our captors began to loosen up a bit, and we were
allowed into the courtyard en masse, a special treat, because it allowed us to
mill about and talk to each other.

Toward the end of 1972, the seniors were released from the smaller cells
and placed into larger ones that accommodated up to twenty-five POWs.

This progressive liberalization made us wonder if external political events,
particularly peace talks under way in Paris, had something to do with this
change. Paraphrasing the words of Winston Churchill, this wasn't the beginning of the end for us, but it certainly seemed like the end of the beginning
of our long captivity. Something was in the wind.

That something turned out to be raids by U.S. Air Force B-52s, the aging
but amazingly effective heavy bombers. These raids struck close to Hanoi and
its environs and dramatically changed the state of the war. Had we mined
Haiphong, cut the two main rail links to China, and employed the "Buffs,"
as the B-52s were called, earlier, the war certainly would not have lasted as
long as it did. But better late than never.

It began one night. We heard this tremendous rumbling. It continued
for half an hour. I remember somebody calling out, "God, what do you think

that is?" No one perceived or even guessed that it was a bombing attack.

"Must be an earthquake," declared another man. We just had no sense that a bombing raid had taken place.

The guards began to wear worried expressions. You could see fear in their faces, particularly after a thunderous peel of iron bombs exploded in sufficient proximity to shake the earth. The propaganda broadcasts continued, and the North Vietnamese revealed their country was being bombarded by the B-52s. Their confidence became a fragile thing. They frantically began digging holes in the ground as refuge points against the bombing. With the onset of dusk, they scurried into these makeshift bomb shelters.

"Why is your country doing this to us?" one guard cried out. For me that was a question that needed no answer.

Did we fear the prison itself would be hit? Not really. I suppose we were inherently eternal optimists. The bombing had been going on for years, albeit not in the immediate vicinity of the Hanoi Hilton, and we were never hit. U.S. intelligence certainly knew where we were, and the prison certainly would not be considered a strategic target.

Not too long after the B-52 raids began, the food began to improve. I had lost forty pounds since the shoot down but started to gain some of them back. While anxiety began to embrace our captors, we had a sense that maybe, just maybe, the end was near. Visions of a return with honor to friendly shores were on the horizon. Then, in late January 1972, the propaganda broadcast proclaimed that a peace treaty had been signed between the United States and North Vietnam.

One of the stipulations of the treaty was that POWs were to be provided details of the treaty. This information was conveyed via the normal broadcasts plus a mimeographed sheet. It did not specify a release date, but it certified that we would be released in the order that we were shot down. Obviously, we were delighted but remained subdued. It was too early to shout with joy. On the one hand, we were optimistic, but on the other hand, skepticism lingered. We were still enclosed by those thick and formidable walls of the Hilton.

I began to contemplate the heroes among us during our lengthening captivity. Men like Jim Stockdale; Jerry Denton (for whom I served as a deputy commander in our area of the camp for a time); John McCain, a very strong and active resistor; Jim Mulligan; Harry Jenkins; Howie Rutledge; Jack Fellowes; Red McDaniel; Bob Shumaker; and so many others who each in his own way was a tower of strength. Robbie Risner of the Air Force, a Medal of Honor recipient, was a standout and inspiration to all.

It was personally reassuring to note that many of the boldest leaders in the camps were Navy men, and many of them were Naval Academy graduates. I later calculated that, although Naval Academy graduates composed less than 5 percent of the POW population, they earned 50 percent of the Medals of Honor (Jim Stockdale) and Distinguished Service Medals.

It seemed the senior naval officers were more caught up in the aspect of taking command, which is inherent in our training from the get-go. In my view, Air Force officers, in contrast, considered themselves pilots first, with leadership a second duty. This is not intended as a slight, but rather an observation of the "way it was" from my perspective, and reflective of Air Force training policy rather than a matter of courage or determination. Commanding a squadron, an aircraft carrier, or any unit in the Navy is a foremost goal. At the time, the Air Force didn't have screening boards for command as does the Navy. My sense was that commanding a squadron in the Air Force was considered less critical to career progression than in the Navy.

The Air Force Academy produced its first graduating class in 1959. As a result, there were several Air Force captains in captivity who were graduates and who demonstrated superlative toughness, like Medal of Honor recipient Lance Sijan, mentioned earlier in this narrative. In a way, these younger officers seemed better prepared to withstand the challenge of captivity, a tribute to the Air Force Academy curriculum.

From the announcement of the signing of the peace treaty, we knew our prospects were more positive than at any other time. We had become masters of patience over the years and would have to exercise that attribute a little longer.

Chapter Eighteen

GOING HOME

With the utmost kindness and sensitivity, Ross said,
"I'm very sorry to have to tell you this, Captain,
but your wife divorced you while you were a prisoner of war."

STIPULATIONS OF THE PEACE TREATY signed in January 1973 were read to us over the loudspeaker system several times. Concomitant with the issuance of the treaty, a strong sense of urgency came over the North Vietnamese with respect to getting us out of their country as soon as possible. It would take some weeks, but preparations quickly began for our release.

We were to be let go in a sequence of four groups in order of our shoot-down dates. Those who had been imprisoned the longest would get the first flight out. About a month before release, we were sequestered by chronological order, regardless of rank. The first group left in February, and I was let go in March, with the third of four contingents.

We were an emotionally hardened assembly of military men, so we took the treaty and the subsequent actions with some trepidation or disbelief. Peace talks had begun way back in 1968. We got up for that, only to be let down. When the food improved at one point, we figured this a good sign, only to be let down. Up until the time we actually stepped out of the buses onto the tarmac at the Gia Lam airfield in Hanoi, we were skeptical.

I trained my mind to deflect any visions of reuniting with Anne and the children. I didn't want to get excited about seeing them again only to have the carpet hauled out from beneath me. Wait and see, I told myself, wait and see. I'd received but a handful of brief letters from my parents containing hardly more than mundane remarks. I did not receive any mail from my wife or children for the whole six years I was there. In the last three years of imprisonment, I mailed ten very brief letters to Anne but got no response.

I had absolutely no idea how Anne and the kids were doing. Nevertheless, I held the optimistic hope they were all OK, that the government and other family members would have pitched in to ensure their well-being.

When the time came for our departure, we shed our striped prison garb and were issued cotton trousers, shirts, jackets, and leather shoes—quite a treat after living with sandals. We were bused to the airfield and moved in formation. As our names were called, we proceeded to a desk, where a North Vietnamese officer checked our name from a register, with a U.S. Air Force officer monitoring. As soon as I was cleared, another Air Force officer took me by the arm and escorted me to the waiting C-141 transport, a remarkable, bigger-than-life experience. We remained silent throughout the process, uncertainty lingering in the mind of each and every one of us.

I had served over six years in captivity, which included fourteen months in solitary confinement.

Once on board we were still a bit insecure and itching to get into the sky. With all hands on board and ready to go, the C-141 taxied to the approach end and took the runway. When those engines powered up and the huge bird lumbered forward, we knew the long-awaited day had come. But it wasn't until we lifted off, started a magnificent climb away from the country of North Vietnam, and shortly went feet wet over the Gulf of Tonkin that all the pent-up exuberance released itself. Collectively, we shouted for joy. It was a long, continuous happy hollering, the memory of which has stayed with me to this day. Next stop Clark Air Force Base in the Philippines.

En route to Clark, an Air Force lieutenant colonel approached and told me, "You know, my wife is from your hometown of Nashville." He mentioned her maiden name.

"Yes," I said, "I remember that family."

"Well," he continued, "I understand that you're going back to the naval hospital in Memphis."

I was momentarily startled. I thought, why I am going to Memphis when my family is in Solana Beach? Moreover, my squadron was based at Miramar. I had figured I was destined for the Balboa Naval Hospital. Curious.

Our reception at Clark was very, very warm. Adm. Noel Gayler, commander in chief Pacific Command, and Air Force lieutenant general Bill Moore, his deputy, greeted us as we descended the ladder of the C-141. I learned I had been promoted to captain, which was a plus. Television cameras were all about, and a large crowd cheered our arrival.

We were bused to the base hospital, where a large assortment of amusing, uplifting, and heartfelt welcoming posters created by schoolchildren were all over the place, a pleasant touch. It was late afternoon by the time we were taken to our assigned ward, four men per sizeable room. There were no activities scheduled for us, so we loitered in the passageway, chatting, with hospital personnel amongst us, ready to assist in any way.

It was during this lull that I inexplicably developed a sense that I was being observed in a peculiar way. There was nothing specific about a gesture or expression here and there, but something in the looks of the staff members, if conveyed only with a fleeting glance, fueled my curiosity. However, I let it go, faulting my imagination. Perhaps the excitement of being on friendly soil was getting to me.

After a time, Capt. Ross Trower, a chaplain from the Service Force Pacific Fleet Staff (who later became the Navy's chief of chaplains), came up to me, wearing a serious expression, and said, "I'd like you to come with me." I followed numbly as we entered a nearby private room. He asked me to sit down. He remained standing.

With the utmost kindness and sensitivity, Ross said, "I'm very sorry to have to tell you this, Captain, but your wife divorced you while you were a prisoner of war." He let that set in for moment, and I eyed him in stunned silence. He then added, "She is now married to a minister of the Episcopalian church named Ralph Haines. They are living in Encinitas, California." I insisted he repeat what he had just said. I was bewildered. I felt my whole body shiver. This was such an unbelievable announcement that I couldn't immediately react.

As the shock of the moment swept through me, I remembered Tom Kirk, my POW roommate for over three years, who never stopped worrying that his wife would divorce him while he was in the Hilton. "Quit tormenting yourself," I reassured him, day after day, "she'll be there for you." And she was.

Now here was I, totally discombobulated over the very fate Tom Kirk feared but happily avoided. What had Anne done? Who was Ralph Haines? How were the children? The elation that came with the end of my ordeal was obliterated by this dark and totally unexpected news.

Ross sat with me for quite a while as the weight of this terrible truth and destroyed plans for the future swept over me. My Anne had been an honorable person and a devout Christian. I had been totally confident she would measure up to the challenge of caring for the children and maintaining the family unit without my presence. Somehow I went to bed, but I wept through a night of fitful sleep.

When morning came, my brain must have been working overtime through the night, because I remember saying to myself, "I've been through a hell of a lot for six years, but I've got to face up to this problem and some-how get it behind me. I cannot let it pull me down and out." This may be difficult to believe, but it's the way it was. For the most part, I was able to discard, temporarily at least, the dreadful emotional impact of the divorce. After all, I had the tools to make a good life for myself: my loving parents, brothers, the children, an excellent education, and the hope of continuing my naval career.

In a telephone call to my children the next day, all three seemed stoic. I expected a bit more enthusiasm from them, but my perception was they were in a state of bewilderment over my return, coupled with what happened to their mother. They were fine and exuberant kids when I left but didn't seem so now. I realized right away that, on my mental checklist of things to do, the first priority was to get straight with Bill, Laurie, and Wendy.

In a telephone call to my parents, I explained I would be in Memphis in about three days. The children would be sent there to meet me. In a subse-quent phone call, there was a measure of joy in the voices of the kids, which was uplifting.

I also made it a point to inform Tom Kirk, who had become like a brother to me, and the other POWs, with whom I was close, about the divorce. I sought not sympathy, but rather, wanted them to know I'd be OK.

We had three busy days at Clark. We underwent physical examinations, dur-ing which we were all found to have intestinal parasites that had to be treated. It would take two to three weeks to liberate our bodies from those vermin, during which we were not allowed to consume any alcohol. It would interfere with the medicine used against the parasites. My eyesight had diminished somewhat, so I got glasses, and I had some dental work done. Part of the problem with my eyesight, by the way, had to do with lack of nutrition and spending untold hours in small cells, wherein the eyes did not get the exercise they should have. We had one trip to the Navy Exchange, where, assisted by a tailor, we were outfitted with new uniforms—one set of khakis and one set of blues for us Navy types. I also bought a watch. Those who organized and planned our activities did a great job. Rear Admiral Don Shelton, who com-manded Naval Forces Philippines and was an old friend from test pilot years, stopped by for a visit.

As to the immediate adjustments to a radical new lifestyle, I remember being asked some time after we got home, "How long did it take you to get acclimated to eating American food and sleeping on a soft bed?" My answer, "About five seconds."

Some had trouble adjusting to beds, but I wasn't one of them. As to food, I really didn't want to gorge myself. I craved certain items for sure, especially fruit, vegetables, and salads, which I did devour with some intensity. We had been on a low-fat diet in North Vietnam, but I didn't have an acute craving for beef. When Capt. Jack Fellowes was asked what was the first item he wanted to eat, he promptly answered, "A good old American hamburger."

Although cholesterol certainly wasn't a concern (most of us had readings of well below two hundred upon our return), I ate little beef and have more or less continued that trend through the years.

We flew from Clark to Hickam Air Force Base in Honolulu, arriving at two in the morning. Despite the late hour, a crowd met us with enthusiastic cheers. Academy classmates took the time to greet and chat with me, which was a wonderful gesture on their part.

Next stop was Scott Air Force Base in Illinois, jump-off point for those POWs who were to convalesce in the central part of America. The C-141 was configured with individual bunks, which made for very comfortable travel. As we crossed the California coastline, it was daylight, and I marveled at the sight of San Francisco and the Bay area. Only those who have been away from home for a long time can comprehend the thrill of such a beautiful image.

At Scott we proceeded to separate C-9 transports, one of which hauled a group of us to Memphis. Realizing I was the senior officer in the group and would be expected to make a brief address on arrival, I practiced the few remarks I would make, none of which were very memorable.

In Memphis, I was led out first, the others following in trail. I was ushered toward a waiting microphone and rather nervously gazed at the crowd, only to spot my smiling parents and the children. With them were Bob, my oldest brother, and Tommy, my younger brother, who had returned from Vietnam in 1971 following duty as an officer in the Army's 82nd Division. Yet, here I was, making a speech before I had even embraced my family.

My address was brief, but the subsequent reunion with my family was happily the opposite. It was composed of a heartwarming round of powerful embraces, an abundance of tears and a multitude of joyous "welcome back" expressions. The children were animated, which made me feel better than I did after speaking to them on the long-distance line. However, I noticed my daughters were overweight, and again, I sensed things just weren't right with them.

I was assigned to the hospital at Naval Air Technical Training Center Memphis but received permission to stay with my family in the Navy Lodge on base, a motel-type facility, which we used for a few days.

I underwent a comprehensive physical exam and was interviewed at length by intelligence officers, to whom I provided all the POW names I held in my memory bank. There was a question as to whether some POWs were being left behind in North Vietnam. In my view, no one was left. I've always been taken aback by the notion held in some quarters that our government would turn its back on prisoners. The North Vietnamese seemed eager to rid themselves of POWs. Why would they want to retain any? For what purpose? Certainly not propaganda value.

Later on, when I became chief of naval personnel, I received comprehensive briefings by intelligence officers, and I came away from those presentations with no feelings of mendacity in their reports concerning POWs. Among other groups I know that Red McDaniel, who was in the Hanoi Hilton, and Ross Perot sincerely believed Americans were left in Southeast Asia. Indeed, Pres. Ronald Reagan asked Ross to head up a group appointed to investigate the possibility of men still over there. I suppose this is an issue that will endure for a long time to come.

My son, Bill, had let his hair grow long, and I was advised that female skirt lengths were on their way down compared to what they had been during the peak of the war. There were countless blanks in the six years of history I had missed, and I wanted desperately to fill them in. But there wasn't time. Although the family reunion was a priceless experience, I realized I had much to do. I had to get on the fast track to resolve family issues.

Midshipman Bill Lawrence (front row, third from right) as Brigade Commander in his senior year at Annapolis. He was also president of the Class of 1951 and finished 8th academically out of 725 midshipmen. *U.S. Navy photo*

A star high school athlete in Tennessee, Lawrence also excelled at the Naval Academy. He's number 34 (second row, second from left) in this photo of the 1949 varsity basketball team. *U.S. Navy photo*

Lawrence, shown here in the 1950 varsity football team photo, also played baseball at the Academy. He had to forego participation in sports his senior year in order to attend to brigade commander and class president duties. *U.S. Navy photo*

Right: First-tour jet pilot Bill
Lawrence when he was in
VF-193 in 1953.
U.S. Navy photo

Below: Family man Lawrence
with daughter Laurie and
son Bill Jr. at their home in
Patuxent River, Maryland,
in 1955. *Photo courtesy
Lawrence Collection*

142

Lawrence, in 1963 with the Phantom Fleet Introduction Program, following a
flight in an F-4B that belonged to the VF-14 Tophatters fighter squadron.
U.S. Navy photo

Lawrence was reunited with his family in 1973 in Nashville. (Seated, left to right)
Son, Bill Jr., and his wife, Jenny, Bill, daughter Wendy, and daughter Laurie.
Standing are brothers Bob and Tom and Bill's mother and father. *Photo courtesy
Lawrence Collection*

Captain Lawrence speaks to an audience of well-wishers in Memphis, Tennessee, on March 7, 1973 upon repatriation from captivity in North Vietnam. Shot down as a commander, he was promoted to captain while incarcerated. Note wristwatch he bought at the Navy Exchange in the Philippines on his first stop en route home. Nashville Banner *photo*

Lawrence and Admiral Thomas H. Moorer, one of Lawrence's heroes whom
he revered as a role model, exchange smiles outside the Tennessee legislature in
Nashville. Admiral Moorer was Commander Seventh Fleet and was listening on
the tactical radio frequency when Lawrence was shot down in his F-4 Phantom.
He traveled to Nashville to greet Bill upon his return from Hanoi in 1973.
Nashville Banner *photo*

Rear Admiral Bill Lawrence poses with an A-7 Corsair II attack aircraft in 1974 at Naval Air Station Lemoore, California, where he served as Commander Light Attack Wing Pacific Fleet. *U.S. Navy photo*

Diane Lawrence and Bill in 1979, just after Diane put on his new shoulder boards as a three-star admiral. *U.S. Navy photo*

On November 19, 1980 the Hamilton Watch Company presented a Hamilton Chronometer to the Naval Academy in honor of Admiral Arleigh Burke (left) in ceremonies at Bancroft Hall. Admiral Burke posed with Superintendent Lawrence on the occasion. *U.S. Navy photo*

Vice Admiral James Stockdale, former POW and recipient of the Medal of Honor for his performance as a prisoner, congratulates Wendy Lawrence upon her graduation from the Naval Academy in May 1981. *U.S. Navy photo*

On July 20, 1984 a ceremony recognizing National POW/MIA Day was held on the south lawn of the White House. Vice Admiral Bill Lawrence, then Deputy Chief of Naval Operations for Manpower, Personnel and Training, was seated at left and behind President Ronald Reagan as Secretary of Defense Casper Weinberger spoke to the gathering. Seated at right are First Lady Nancy Reagan and Vice President and former naval aviator George H.W. Bush. *White House photo*

Above: Bill and Diane enjoy a light moment in the garden of Buchanan House, the Superintendent's quarters. *U.S. Navy photo*

Right: Superintendent Lawrence, Diane, and their Irish Setters, Max and Maggie, in the library of Buchanan House. The portrait above the fireplace is of Commodore David Porter (1780-1843), a former superintendent. *U.S. Navy photo*

Among the notable guests Lawrence hosted at Annapolis was the indomitable Bob Hope during Commissioning Week, May 1981. *Photo courtesy Lawrence Collection*

As Commander Third Fleet, Vice Admiral Bill Lawrence bundled up in a dogsled with Third Fleet's meteorologist, Commander Maurice Gibbs (behind), during a visit to Scott Base, near McMurdo, Antarctica, circa 1981. *Photo courtesy Lawrence Collection*

152

In October 2000 Lawrence was among five "Distinguished Graduates" of the
Naval Academy honored at a ceremony with the brigade of midshipmen present.
(Left to right): Former Naval Academy and Dallas Cowboys football star Roger
Staubach; astronaut Major General William A. Anders, U.S. Air Force; Lawrence;
Admiral James L. Holloway III, former Chief of Naval Operations; Commander
John J. McMullen, USN (Ret.), owner of the New Jersey Devils hockey team;
Captain George Watt, USNR (Ret.), President and CEO of the U.S. Naval
Academy Alumni Association; and Vice Admiral John R. Ryan, Superintendent of
the Academy. *U.S. Navy photo*

Lawrence and Senator John McCain in the Naval Academy Superintendent's tent at the Army-Navy game in Baltimore, December 2, 2000. *U.S. Navy photo*

Wendy Lawrence (center) with crew members of Space Shuttle Mission STS-114, February 2004. *NASA photo*

Lawrence with fellow Academy graduate H. Ross Perot, who was an avid supporter of Lawrence and his family throughout Lawrence's career and retirement. *U.S. Navy photo*

Lawrence greets President George W. Bush at a Naval Academy graduation ceremony. *U.S. Navy photo*

Chapter Nineteen

AFTERMATH

*I was transfixed by the sight of her, lovely as ever after six years,
but her apprehension was almost palpable. The situation was surreal.*

WE LEARNED A BIT OF THE HISTORY that took place during our hiatus in Hanoi from newspaper clippings of key events and other documents, nicely categorized by subject (people, politics, international activities, sports, etc.), and provided by the team set up to reacclimatize us to current life in America. We also underwent extensive intelligence briefings, downloading those events of our captivity best kept classified. And we were interviewed by psychiatrists, I supposed, to make sure our heads were still on straight. On a dark note, once all our inputs were compiled, it was determined that 113 POWs died in captivity from torture, malnutrition, or other factors. In a sense, our camp was lucky, because our torturer, Strap and Bar, was a true professional. He knew when to stop before he killed us.

As to my physical condition, apart from the parasites, presumably spawned by our diet of wormy bread, watery pumpkin soup, and occasional fish heads, and needing to add weight, I was in fair condition. That aortic insufficiency detected when I applied for the astronaut program was no worse and would not be an impediment to continuing my naval career. I suffered numbness in my outer right calf as a result of nerve damage presumably sustained when I was in leg irons. My broken shoulder had not healed correctly, but it wasn't limiting to me. I also had resorption, an unexplained phenomenon that caused my teeth to slowly dissolve away. Fortunately, this problem dissipated, but it took ten years to finally stop. I was told resorption could be caused by trauma, and there was plenty of that to go around in the Hanoi Hilton.

A major public affairs program called for us to make appearances and give speeches at a variety of events. This was necessary, but for me it was rather intrusive with respect to my personal goals of squaring away the situation with Bill, Laurie, and Wendy. I had to give priority to them.

I gave talks now and then, the most prominent of which was an address to the Tennessee legislature. It was here that I recited the poem I had composed in my mind while I was secured to a bed slab by ankle chains in the blistering heat of my single cell in Calcutta. I told listeners how I had leaned and twisted onto my side and stretched my body to the maximum; how this contortion allowed me to catch a glimpse of the outside world through the makeshift window of my one-man cell. I was able to see the top of the courtyard wall and just above it, a patch of brilliant blue sky. That patch of blue lifted my spirits, and in that one beautiful moment, I felt as if a wondrous flow of cool water washed over every part of me. To this day, I vividly remember the sensation of those precious seconds, because I believe God had placed his hand on my head.

As to the poem, my imagined mentor, Sir Walter Scott, need not fear competition from yours truly. I had sought to emulate the magical cadence of his poems and was proud of what I had composed, because "Oh Tennessee, My Tennessee" came straight from the heart. It would not win the Pulitzer but by an act of the state legislature in 1973 it became the official state poem of Tennessee. It follows:

Oh Tennessee, my Tennessee,
What love and pride I feel for thee,
Your proud old state, the Volunteer,
Your fine traditions I hold dear.

I revere your many heroes,
Who bravely fought our country's foes,
Renowned statesmen, so wide and strong,
Who served our country well and long.

I thrill at thought of mountains grand,
Rolling green hills and fertile farm land,
Earth rich with stone, mineral, and ore,
Forests dense and wild flowers galore,
Powerful rivers that bring us light,
Deep lakes with fish and fowl in flight,
Thriving cities and industries,
Fine schools and universities,
Strong folks of pioneer descent,
Simple, honest, and reverent.

Beauty and hospitality
Are the hallmarks of Tennessee.

And o'er the world as I may roam,
No place exceeds my boyhood home,
And, oh how much I long to see
My native land, my Tennessee

Our oldest daughter, Laurie, was a high school senior and wanted to get into nursing. She and I visited the director of admissions at Vanderbilt in Nashville, even though when she lived on the West Coast, she had applied to UCLA. She was readily accepted at Vanderbilt. I must admit the fact her father was a returning POW helped. She went on to earn her BS in nursing, which she followed up with medical school, also at Vanderbilt, and that led to her very successful career as a physician.

Young Bill was without direction. He'd been out of high school two years, had married his high school sweetheart, Jenny, the year before when they were nineteen and eighteen, respectively. Because of their youth, this union displeased me. Plus, Bill was working a minimum-wage job as a gardener at the church where his stepfather, the Reverend Haines presided. With respect to the future, any sense of purpose had alluded Bill, although he loved music and wanted to study it. I jumped on the chance to get him started in the field and, with his concurrence, enrolled him at Peabody College in Nashville to study music. This meant moving from California to Tennessee, but Bill didn't hesitate about moving. A career in the world of harmony and composition did not materialize for him, however. Bill Jr., instead, entered the world of computers and has carved out a remarkably successful career as a master of computer science and has written five books on computer netware.

I had a bit more breathing room in developing a plan for Wendy. Because Anne and her new husband didn't object to my taking custody of our youngest child, I ensconced her with my parents, and she attended the eighth grade at Brentwood Academy in Nashville. She eventually attended the Naval Academy, where she graduated with the class of 1981. She requested and received orders to flight training, became a helicopter pilot, had squadron duty, sought assignment to the astronaut program, and was accepted as a mission specialist. At this writing, Wendy has made three flights into space, logging 789 hours beyond the stratosphere.

As I was setting in motion these plans, which I hoped would set our children on a positive course for the future, I made an extremely unsettling discovery. One of the reasons the kids reacted to my return with a kind of reluctant suspicion was because they had been told I was dead! They had no idea I had survived the ejection and was imprisoned. For several years, I admit, my fate was unknown. I had been listed as MIA—missing in action—for three years, which should have been a hint. But in 1970, my name was on a list of detainees that Sen. Ted Kennedy was able to glean from the North Vietnamese. I didn't receive any letters from Anne, but I had written her and presumed she received the letters, because my parents had received mine. Surely, Anne must have known I was alive.

"Didn't you see the letters?" I asked the children. They collectively shook their heads.

Laurie said, "We saw only one letter from you, and mother told us it appeared to be contrived. It didn't look like your handwriting, and it didn't sound like you."

Oddly, my father and mother had talked to Anne at least once a week and even visited her once. Yet, they had no inkling of her plans to wed Haines.

I learned Anne had not shown the children nine of the ten letters I had sent her from prison. Moreover, I learned she had destroyed all my letters to her and the children dating back to my time in the Korean War. Anne knew I had always anticipated these letters would be of historical value, to me and my family, anyway. This was unbelievable. The Anne I had known was a fine, honorable person, totally incapable of acting in this fashion.

"I can't believe your mother did this," I told the kids.

When asked what she thought when she found out I was alive and coming home, Laurie explained, "I was riding my bike with my friend, Susan, when Father Haines drove up and nervously told me that I had to go straight back to the house—that my mother had just received word my father was coming home. I knew this must be a true God-given miracle—my father had come back from the dead. Father Haines looked shocked, but I remember Susan saying, "Hey, that's really cool!"

I talked with Anne's father, Rear Adm. Macpherson Williams, who was awarded two stars upon retirement—making him what is called a "tombstone" admiral—in honor of especially great service to the Navy, and my mother-in-law. To my amazement, Admiral "Mac" and Mrs. Williams, too, thought I was deceased. They weren't aware of the POW office in Washington established to assist relatives and dependents of POWs. My own parents were very aware I hadn't gone to the deep six.

Talk of failed communication, this was a classic example of it. The Williamses were genuinely delighted about my survival and just as genuinely sorry about what happened with Anne. It didn't hurt them that Anne had remarried, because she had her life to live and they had accepted I was dead. But they were terribly shaken when they realized Anne divorced me when she must have known I was alive.

Three weeks after my liberation, and after profound consideration, I decided the best thing to do was to confer with Anne directly about the whole situation. My father was vehemently opposed to my going to California, but I felt I had to make the trip. I set up the visit through the children, and my son Bill arranged for us to meet in his apartment.

Anne was a casualty of the war like me. The normal and anticipated disruption in our lives, which Navy families experience every time a ship goes to sea, was exacerbated by my shoot down, extending that disruption to six eternally long years.

From various sources I put together a kind of scenario of what had happened while I was in the Hilton. While stationed at Miramar before the deployment to Yankee Station, we rented a home in Solana Beach, a lovely community along the Pacific coast north of San Diego. We attended St. Peter's Episcopal Church in nearby Del Mar, influenced by the fact that retired Navy chaplain, Cdr. Matt Currey, who married Anne and me, was the pastor there. Matt had actually helped us find our house in Solana Beach.

The Episcopal bishop of Southern California visited the church one day, and Matt made a point of introducing Anne, me, and the children as a "model" family.

Unfortunately, St. Peters experienced some terrible internal problems while I was overseas, and they became so severe Anne decided to attend an Episcopal church in Encinitas instead. Ralph Haines was the reverend at this church. Haines had recently lost his wife to illness, leaving him with two young sons.

After I was shot down, Haines, as part of his ministerial duties, visited Anne to render solace to a POW's wife. Over a period of time, they apparently fell in love. Laurie, our oldest, was mature enough to comprehend what was happening; that this minister was violating his position of trust. But Laurie was powerless to do anything about it. Anne was in a profoundly vulnerable state, and Haines, intentionally or not, took advantage of it. Haines and Anne had a full-fledged, formal church wedding while I was sequestered against my will on the other side of the world.

Anne entered Bill's apartment so terribly choked up she could hardly talk. I was in casual clothes as was she. I was transfixed by the sight of her, lovely as ever after six years, but her apprehension was almost palpable. The situation was surreal. I wanted to take her in my arms, but I feared that would make matters even worse. Here we were, two grown-ups who had shared a major part of our adult lives together, created three new lives, yet now met as strangers. We sat down and were uncomfortably silent for a moment. Anne couldn't seem to talk, so, with a level tone, I started.

"You are a victim of the war just like me," I said. What you have done is so unlike you. . . . well I've always perceived you as an honorable human being and . . ."

Mine was a stumbling dialogue, but I continued. "I don't really know what to say, except, I really would like for us to be together again, especially for the sake of the family. It's the best thing to do."

The wariness in her expression intensified.

"I'm sure an annulment can be arranged," I continued. "Or, under the circumstances, I believe you could seek a divorce without a lot of complications."

From the despairing look on her face, I knew in my heart of hearts there was little, if any, hope of reconciliation, but I pressed on. "We can put this behind us," I said, "and start over."

Finally, with a faltering voice and on the brink of tears, Anne said, "Look, Bill, I really tried hard. I really tried to be strong. I'm sorry I couldn't. I just couldn't. I just want you to know you are the finest man I have ever known." And with that she rose and left the room.

The memory of that time Matt Currey held Anne and me and the kids up to the bishop as a model family flitted through my mind. Any hopes of a reiteration of that honor were certainly erased from the realm of possibility, but I honestly believed an accommodation could be reached.

It was obvious she was truly in love with Ralph Haines, was content with her decision to share his life, and was not even remotely inclined to consider divorcing him and returning to me.

I can't say I was surprised by her adamant stance. I held out hope she would reconsider. I looked at her, resurrected the vision of her as my lovely bride, and allowed images of our happy past together to make their way through my mind. She was the mother of our children, and I still felt warmth and longing for her that equaled in intensity my disappointment over what she had done.

The California trip did yield one rather positive thing. After I was shot down, my clothing had been shipped to Anne. The clothes, I learned, were in a California neighbor's garage, still secure in a metal cruise box.

In retrospect, an element of this tragic fiasco was that the POW office in Washington knew that divorce proceedings were under way but never advised my parents. It's hard to say, but had Mom and Dad known, they might have intervened to stop the divorce. Water over the bridge.

To this day, I am convinced that this Episcopal minister, who was supposed to provide solace and support to a prisoner of war's wife, seduced Anne. In my view, he violated his position of trust and responsibility as a minister. Anne was in an awfully vulnerable situation. She had been an honorable person, but once she compromised herself, the situation went downhill from there.

During the divorce proceedings, Anne took the position that our marriage was irrevocably broken before I left, which was utter nonsense. My children and Father Currey, who knew us very well, would attest to that.

Under California law, if a woman in a situation like Anne's initiates divorce proceedings against her husband, she must prove desertion. Her attorney advised her to put an ad in the paper requesting that I appear in court, and that ad had to run for a certain number of weeks. She also had to show evidence she had sent a letter to my last-known address and that the letter was returned unanswered. So she sent a letter addressed to me aboard the USS *Constellation,* and sure enough, it was returned to her.

Before leaving California, I paid a visit to her attorney. "You knew I was a POW," I stated. "How could you, with any sense of ethics, be complicit in such an action? You know, I could have you disbarred!"

He retorted with lawyerspeak, said something about California being a community property state, and when he finished, I vented some fury about his actions and threw out the word "dishonorable" somewhere in my diatribe. He reacted with a shrug, not at all bothered by my charges.

I wrote a letter to the area's Episcopal bishop, the same one to whom Father Currey introduced us as a model family. I suggested the church conduct an investigation into the ignominious actions of Ralph Haines. I outlined the whole scenario, the letters withheld from our children, the shielding of the truth about my so-called death in combat. Haines had to know. Father Currey aggressively supported me in this action. I still held the unrealistic notion Anne might change her mind and return to me.

Meanwhile, my father took the case to some prominent Episcopal friends in Tennessee, who alerted the senior Episcopal bishop in the area.

"I'm sorry," said the bishop, "but each area bishop is totally autonomous in his own diocese. "I have no authority over the bishop in Southern California, nor does anybody else. He acts as he feels he should. I cannot bring any pressure to bear on your behalf." This bishop did write a letter to the cognizant bishop out West and in no uncertain terms said any minister in his region who did what Ralph Haines did would have been defrocked.

Ultimately, I received a response from Hayne's bishop, which, in effect, stated the marriage between Anne and Haines should be preserved. He wrote, "I welcome you as you return to observe the culture which has developed in your absence. My heart goes out to those who have experienced pain and suffering."

I considered this a mealy-mouthed response. I was still hot under the collar. The Vietnam War had soured huge numbers of Americans. I knew servicemen returning from Southeast Asia were spat upon and ridiculed, that the conflict had bred hate and confrontation. But I believed I had a case.

"Unless you take some corrective action in this case, I am going expose what you have condoned," I wrote in return.

He came right back with, "Don't do anything like this. It could have an adverse impact on your family."

As if it hadn't already had an adverse impact on my family. Incredible.

Some time went by, during which Anne and Ralph Haines talked with their bishop, and any hope I held out for reunification was dashed. Anne conveyed through our son, Bill, that she did not want to come back to me.

As furious and disheartened as I was, I delved into some deep soul-searching. I concluded I was in a fight I could never win. Anne had been a good wife. She had hung in there with me for twenty years, and she had been, up to a critical point, an endearing mother to our children. Wouldn't I just be making things worse for her if I elevated my fuss with the Episcopal Church?

"I no longer intend to take action in this case," I begrudgingly wrote the bishop, but I am resigning from the Episcopal Church.

To Ralph Haines I wrote, "I accept what has happened, and I am not taking any other steps to attempt to reunite with Anne."

Meanwhile, Anne's parents had disowned her, severing all relationships with her. To the Williamses I wrote, "Anne is your only child. Please don't do this. Accept what has happened as an unfortunate occurrence of the war. I strongly urge you to reestablish your relationship with her and help put all this turmoil behind us." In the summer of 1973, they reunited with their daughter.

One positive aspect of my real-life soap opera was gaining custody of Wendy through a court order, which Anne did not oppose. Bill and Laurie were technically adults and could do as they wished. Fortunately, they soon became engrossed in their studies, a prelude to their successful careers. Wendy, as I mentioned, stayed with my parents and attended a private school. I found it reassuring that all three children were now in Tennessee, with my parents nearby, and their lives on a more productive track. Meanwhile I was ordered to the National War College in Washington, D.C., where I hoped to restart a career interrupted by a well-aimed 87-millimeter shell six years earlier.

Chapter Twenty

ORDERS

"I've got to introduce you to Diane," John McCain started on me one day.
"But I've got so many other things to take care of . . ."
"Trust me," he said, "you will like this lady."

THE NAVY TOOK REMARKABLY GOOD CARE of its POWs and pretty much gave
us orders of our choosing, particularly with respect to locations. Left unsaid
were the questionable prospects of those of us who had been "out of the Navy
for years," missing out on assignments considered necessary for advancing
our careers. Most of us were convinced there was no way to catch up. Yet
Adm. Elmo Zumwalt Jr., CNO, and Adm. Tom Moorer, chairman of the
Joint Chiefs of Staff and former CNO, made it clear POWs were to receive
every opportunity to reestablish their careers.

The National War College, located at the Army's Fort McNair in
Washington, D.C., was a good step for me. I had "screened" (qualified in
accordance with a board of officers who review candidates for command billets and gives them a thumbs up or down) for a carrier command. This meant
at the completion of war college, I would return to sea duty. With studies,
reconciling a multitude of personal affairs, answering the demands for speaking engagements, and weekend commuting to Nashville, my plate was full.

Fellow POW, war college student, and Naval Academy graduate Jim Bell
and I shared an apartment in Alexandria, Virginia. Despite the heavy schedule, my energy level was way up, and I felt as productive as ever. The disaster
of the divorce lay heavy on my mind, but I was resolute in putting it behind
me and getting on with duty. I even pursued and achieved a master's degree
in political affairs at George Washington University and wrote a thesis titled
"The Deep Sea Bed, the Current Status and Future Prospect."

While this was going on, John McCain, who was also attending the war
college, kept bugging me about a lady he wanted me to meet. John needed
extensive therapy because of the severe injuries he sustained during his shoot
down and captivity. He could have received therapy at the National Naval

Medical Center in Bethesda, Maryland, but an outfit in Alexandria called Rehab Incorporated offered to treat him at no charge, and its location was convenient for commuting to Fort McNair. His therapist was a lovely and lively woman named Diane Rauch. She had been married to a nuclear submariner, but that union ended in divorce.

"I've got to introduce you to Diane," John started on me one day.

"But I've got so many other things to take care of. . . ."

"Trust me," he said, "you will like this lady."

Like his father and grandfather before him, both renowned Navy admirals, John is a persistent man. John's knee was essentially frozen, and Diane was determined to work aggressively with him until he could achieve a full ninety-degree flexion (enabling him to successfully complete the required physical exam to return to flying). This endeavor took four hours a week for nine months. During those strenuous sessions, he was working Diane the same way he worked me, playing the matchmaker role with his special kind of eloquence and persuasion.

On her part, Diane told John, "I really don't want to become involved again with another naval officer; I was a Navy wife for twenty-three years."

Finally, after four months of badgering, Diane and I met at a dinner party staged by John. We were seated next to each other, and from the outset we hit it off. Not only was it easy to engage in conversation, but I also was impressed with her beauty and classy demeanor. Still, my main focus was on Nashville and matters military, and not much happened between us immediately after that first encounter.

A month later I finished my thesis at GW and was near completing the war college course in international relations. Thankfully, the kids were doing well, although the dramatic swing from the "loose" California culture to the more staid environment of a Bible Belt state created difficult pressures for them. Thank heaven for my parents and the magnificent job they did as surrogate parents when I wasn't around.

The upheaval of my reentry into the free world had dissipated, like soup reduced from bubbling to a quiet simmering. I asked Diane for a date, she assented, and the courtship began.

As the song says, "Love is better the second time around." That applied to both of us. When Laurie and Wendy visited me in Washington and met Diane, they immediately took to her, and another domino felled en route to our ultimate marriage. To my welcome surprise, I was also selected for flag rank while at the college.

I did not get a carrier command, a disappointment tempered by my promotion to admiral. Commanding a warship with eighty-plus aircraft and five thousand people on board is one of the greatest leadership challenges one could face. But it was not to be for me. Instead, I was assigned as commander Light Attack Wing Pacific Fleet at Naval Air Station Lemoore in the San Joaquin Valley of California. In retrospect, I believe my elevation rather quickly to flag rank was an early promotion, which was enhanced by fitness reports written in my behalf by Col. John Flynn, the senior Air Force POW, and from Jim Stockdale, Jerry Denton, and Robbie Risner. I was humbled by the manner in which they sang my praises. John Flynn wrote in my fitness report, "Among the group of heroes Captain Lawrence was the most heroic of all."

I also felt indebted to Admiral Zumwalt, who clearly wanted to demonstrate that he was willing to bet on the POWs. His rationale was that, even though we missed valuable assignments, the value of the POW experience and the leadership we demonstrated compensated for deficiencies.

Chapter Twenty-One

VALLEY OF THE JETS

I was in the Pentagon for three years, felt confident I knew how things got done, or undone there, and learned much about dealing with Congress.

THE LEMOORE ASSIGNMENT WAS LIKE A BOLD, refreshing tonic to me. I was back among the operational aviators. Just the sound of the Skyhawks and the Corsair II's launching and recovering and streaking overhead was invigorating. I had twenty-three squadrons under my command plus cognizance over Naval Air Station Fallon, Nevada, where air wing weapons training took place, and Naval Air Station Alameda across the bay from San Francisco, a major carrier base and home to active and reserve squadrons.

Lemoore was composed of two major sections: the operational end, with the runways and hangars, and, three miles away, the administrative portion. In between and expanding across a huge area were cotton fields, where farmers were allowed to work the land.

A-7s were king at the time, while the legendary A-4 Skyhawks were going away, with only two fleet squadrons left at Lemoore, a far cry from the abundance of these units prominent during the war. (The Skyhawks remained on duty in training and "adversary" capacities for many more years.) Two of the squadrons, referred to as RAGs—and technically known as FRS today—were training units for the A-7B and A-7C versions of the Corsair II.

I thoroughly enjoyed visiting each of the commands, sitting down with the COs and the flyers, and talking aviation. Interfacing with the young pilots was uplifting. I flew in a two-seat Skyhawk to keep my hand in and for business travel. What a great way to go!

I readily adjusted to the operational aspects of naval aviation despite my six-year hiatus. I had to catch up on things like drug problems and the Z-Grams published by the CNO, Adm. Elmo Zumwalt But for the most part, the assignment was free of major troubles. The Z-Grams were designed to alleviate racial tensions, which created immense turmoil during the war (crises aboard the *Constellation* and *Kitty Hawk* were especially troubling) and to "liberalize" the way the Navy did business. They promoted a major improvement in equal opportunity, particularly for blacks.

I did notice a trend, hard to put a finger on, but a trend nonetheless, that bothered me. With respect to running their units, I detected reluctance on the part of commanding officers to take forceful action when the normal precepts of discipline were violated. The COs feared toughness on their part in dealing with enlisted personnel would backfire. Using a hotline, enlisted people could call in any complaint directly to an office in Washington, and the Inspector General Hotline, without using the chain of command.

In my periodic inspections, I found there was a distinct lack of basic cleanliness. The overall condition of the barracks was poor because of improper upkeep by the troops themselves. It was apparent to me the chain of command had weakened over the years. I met with the COs and tried to turn things around by directing them to take more initiative in correcting discrepancies. In other words, they needed to be more hard-nosed in order to get the sailors back into a mode of taking better care of their facilities and respecting military discipline. With the help of the base commander, Capt. Jack O'Hara, we instituted strict security and decorum in the enlisted men's club and reenergized the shore patrol to maintain same. Overall, we were fortunate in that the racial discord prominent in major facilities like Norfolk and San Diego did not exist in Lemoore. In fact, I believe that, overall in the military, racial problems were on the downswing, certainly because of the end of the Vietnam War and Zumwalt's determined efforts. Being a southerner, I was happy to see the increased number of African-Americans in the Navy and their apparent good morale. The Navy was finally coming into the twentieth century.

Another key adjustment had to do with the resurrection of our focus on the Cold War. We needed to put the conventional war in Vietnam behind us and concentrate more on nuclear strike planning and issues related to the global challenge of the Cold War. This occupied much of my time. We also took the lead in improving electronic countermeasures at Lemoore, a significant step forward for the Navy in the Cold War.

Diane, Wendy, and I loved this tour of duty. The people of Lemoore and the surrounding community were enthusiastic supporters of the military; collectively displayed a strong work ethic, as patriotic as any group of people I ever knew; and were as friendly as could be. The whole area was an agricultural mecca, part of the great breadbasket of the West, which was the San Joaquin valley.

Alas, it wasn't to last. Only ten months into the tour I was ordered to Washington, D.C., as director of the Aviation Programs Division (OP-51), under the deputy CNO for air warfare (OP-05B), Vice Adm. Bill Houser. Bill Houser was one of naval aviation's finest; I could not have asked for a better boss.

I no sooner got there than I was handed a proverbial hot potato. I was to draft a response to Sen. William Proxmire concerning a Government Accounting Office (GAO) report on the Tailhook Convention in Las Vegas in 1974. Seems the Navy authorized thirty-two C-9 flights to transport aviators from across the United States to Las Vegas for the annual gathering.

It was recommended I explain away the flights to the GAO as training sorties. That, to say the least, would be an enormous stretch and lack credibility. Proxmire at the time had garnered enormous national visibility with his periodic Golden Fleece Awards—presented to the individual or group that pulls off a boondoggle, or takes advantage of the government in some outlandish fashion, and the Navy was a winner for this episode. I met with Admiral Jim Holloway, III, CNO, another of my heroes and one of the Navy's most remarkable and well-liked officers.

"Sir," I said, "You don't have thirty-two C-9 trips to Las Vegas for training purposes. I think we should just stand up and say we believed the Tailhook Convention important enough to have our flyers there, and the C-9 was the way to do it."

The Vietnam War had ended, the Tailhook Convention has been a traditional morale builder, and the professional briefings that took place were valuable. This is even more true today than it was back then. Admiral Holloway agreed. I met with Senator Proxmire's staff, told them what I said to the CNO, and believe it or not, that was it. Proxmire got his publicity about the event, and he was already on another witch hunt, so the problem rather quietly went away.

I was responsible for overseeing all the air stations, target complexes, airspace training areas, maintenance and logistics programs, the overall inventory of aircraft, and even maintenance of the historical records of naval aviation. This was not a glamorous tasking, but I had plenty of autonomy to do what I thought was right, and Bill Houser didn't demand a plethora of reports of my activities. It turned out to be a most enjoyable, educational job, one which taught me much on how to play the game of Washington, D.C. This was essential in today's military, particularly in dealing with the U.S. Congress, which enacts the annual defense bill.

Diane; her son, Fritz; Wendy; and I bought a home in the Villa May area of Alexandria. Diane was close to her business again, Wendy attended Fort Hunt High School in Alexandria, Virginia, a prelude to her acceptance to the Naval Academy a couple of years later, and I was working in the heart of top naval aviation management. I had an idea of how the Navy did business in the place often referred to as the "Puzzle Palace," but I gained new insights in a hurry, particularly because I was dealing with large sums of money, for example, $800 million alone for the flight-hour program.

I became well steeped in what was called PPBS—the Planning, Programming, and Budgeting System. I won't go into cumbersome detail here, but I will mention I was involved in finding money to support development of the F-14 at a time when that new fighter's accident rate was uncomfortably high, especially with the occurrence of in-flight fires; VAST (the Versatile Avionics Systems Test); the transfer from Litchfield Park, Arizona, of "boneyard" aircraft—older aircraft wrapped mummy-like in anticorrosion material and parked securely in the desert air for potential use in the future; and introduction of the antisubmarine aircraft, the S-3 Viking. My plate was more than full, but I enjoyed the challenges despite the never-ending frustrations entailed in Pentagon duty. Working on problems with fellow officers dedicated to making things better for our aviators in the fleet was thankless work and rewarding only in the self-satisfaction we derived from programs that worked out well for naval aviation.

After two years as OP-51, I was moved up the chain to the post of assistant deputy CNO, OP-05B, in essence, the number two job in the air warfare organization. I worked closely with Vice Admiral Fred "Fox" Turner, who had relieved Vice Admiral Pete Peterson, a renowned test pilot, who had relieved Houser. But Peterson's tour was abbreviated, because he was reassigned as commander Naval Air Systems Command.

I greatly admired Fox Turner, as I had admired Bill Houser. When an issue came up, I'd lay it out before Bill or Fox, with recommendations, and, inevitably, with a request for money to carry out one program or another. They always backed me. This was especially significant, because these were leans years for the Department of Defense, in terms of funding.

I was involved in a study of aircraft carriers. There were some in the Jimmy Carter administration who advocated a reduction in the aircraft carrier force levels to eight. Others sought carriers of reduced size, an argument that continues today but that is usually set aside because the logic of using the big carrier wins the debate. We struggled against the option for eight carriers for obvious reasons, and Desert Storm and Operations Enduring Freedom and Iraqi Freedom have certainly proved the value not only of the big carrier concept but also of the numbers of carriers—twelve minimum, three more desirable—as the way to go. There was also a movement to acquire VSTOL—vertical, short takeoff and landing aircraft—but because of funding shortfalls, that program did not continue. Happily, today VSTOL is manifested in the Marine Corps' V-22 Osprey, a program with a troubled beginning but one that is doing especially well as this is being written.

I was in the Pentagon for three years, felt confident I knew how things got done, or undone, there, and learned much about dealing with Congress. I briefed various committees "on the Hill," primarily on subjects in the maintenance, logistics, and airspace-control areas. I learned the importance of lateral communications in the huge bureaucracies of the Defense Department and Congress.

Laboring with a cadre of naval officers and dedicated civil servants toward the singular goal of trying to sustain naval aviation as a key element in our nation's defense was a reward unto itself. The complexity of the duty was exhausting. Twelve-hour working days were the norm, not the exception, but mine was an enlightening and most satisfying tour of duty.

The major lesson I learned during that time was that the military, Congress, and the administration must work together as a cohesive team in order for our country to have an effective defense posture. This is a key factor in a strong democracy encountering today's dangerous world.

Chapter Twenty-Two

ON TO ANNAPOLIS

*"You're too early," she answered, "you're supposed to arrive two minutes
before 1100 and be seated before the procession of the choir
at the beginning of chapel. The choir's not ready, the chapel's not ready.
Please just go walk around the yard and come back."*

I HAD SERIOUS THOUGHTS about where I would go after the OP-05 tour. In
my heart I wanted to command a carrier group, but not having captained
an aircraft carrier, this was unlikely. It was the spring of 1978, and Adm.
Tom Hayward, a friend from test-flying days and a fellow astronaut aspirant
at Patuxent in the 1950s, was CNO. Rear Adm. Kinnard 'Kin' McKee, a
nuclear submarine officer, superintendent of the Naval Academy and a classmate of mine at Annapolis, had just been awarded his third star and was to
remain at the school for a third year. At the time, superintendents were two-
star rear admirals.

At a social event on the CNO's barge during a "cruise" on the Anacostia
River in Washington, D.C., Admiral Hayward pulled me aside. "Look," he
said, "I very much want to promote you to three stars, but I don't have
the available billets for that right now. However, I plan to send you over to
Annapolis to become superintendent of the Naval Academy."

"That's wonderful," I said, stunned and excited all at once over the prospect. I had not coveted this position, nor even thought about it, but I knew
I would love it. But McKee was supposed to stay another year.

Meanwhile, Adm. Jim Watkins, a nuclear trained officer, was chief of the
Bureau of Naval Personnel and lobbied vigorously to have an officer from the
nuclear power community—a "nuke"—get the job at the Academy. He felt
it would enhance the nuclear power program by attracting graduates into the
field.

It turned out that Admiral Hayward didn't want McKee, a newly crowned
vice admiral to stay at the Academy. "I need a three-star officer in the fleet
more than I need one heading the Naval Academy," he said.

The conflict over the assignment was elevated to the secretary of the Navy, Graham Claytor, who was vehemently opposed to a nuclear-trained officer taking the helm at Annapolis. "I refuse to do it," he told Hayward. He feared this would increase the influence of Adm. Hyman Rickover, the literal founder of the nuclear Navy and a powerful figure among the hierarchy of the Navy. Claytor had the last say, and that left a gap for me, into which I was happily inserted. McKee was ordered to command the Third Fleet, and Diane and I prepared to move into quarters at my alma mater.

The year before I became superintendent, women entered the Naval Academy for the first time in history. I shared the concerns of many as to whether this integration was going to work. It was clear that many in the senior leadership of the military were opposed to women attending the service academies. Even McKee spoke out against it, but after a time, he became an advocate for it. My wife, Diane, was very supportive of women in the military, while Wendy's grandfather, Anne's father, was vehemently against it, although he, too, changed once Wendy started school at Annapolis. Then he favored the integration.

One thing was certain. Wendy absolutely loved being a midshipman and from day one ate it up. She even thought her plebe year was a wonderful experience, which surprised me, because that first year at the Academy is not exactly a fun-and-games endeavor.

I met her at National Airport, now Reagan National Airport, on a commercial flight when she returned from England following a summer training deployment. She was aglow with excitement from the deployment. After she unwound a bit, I said, "I have something to tell you. I'm going to be superintendent of the Naval Academy." Her joyful expression was transformed to one of dismay.

"Oh, no," she said. "That's going to make things very difficult for me."

I supposed I shouldn't have been surprised at her reaction. She thought my being there was going to draw unusual attention to herself, and she didn't like that one bit. We talked about it, and I assured her she would not get any special treatment from me, and she didn't. She handled the situation very well. And for my part, I avoided any notion that I was more available to Wendy than to any other midshipman.

My first Sunday as superintendent was memorable. Wendy was assigned as head usher, and Diane and I walked to the chapel next door to the superintendent's residence. We arrived twenty minutes before the service was to begin at 1100. We were rather tired from the move and just wanted to sit and enjoy the organ music and the beauty of the chapel. I was in my dress blues, and as we started up the stone steps of the chapel, we saw Wendy at the door in her blues and white gloves.

"Stop," she said, "you can't come in."

"What do you mean?" I asked, a bit impatiently.

"You're too early," she answered, "you're supposed to arrive two minutes before 1100 and be seated before the procession of the choir at the beginning of chapel. The choir's not ready, the chapel's not ready. Please just go walk around the yard and come back."

The midshipmen functioning as ushers with Wendy didn't realize she was talking to her father and just about had apoplexy.

"Well, OK," I said reluctantly. Diane and I went on a delaying stroll and returned at the two-minute point as instructed. We were escorted down the center aisle and took our seats in the superintendent's pew, designated by small brass plaques honoring every superintendent from the beginning of the school in 1845. A few minutes later, I noticed a lady midshipman in blue uniform ducking under the railing that blocks the superintendent's section from the remainder of the pew. It was Wendy. She slid along the pew, moved next to Diane, and whispered in her ear for a moment. It appeared to me that Diane had asked her a question and Wendy withdrew to get an answer from another usher at the rear of the chapel. Wendy returned a couple of minutes later and said something to Diane, whereupon I said, "What's going on here?" This whispering was agitating to me.

Apparently the issue had to do with our egress from the chapel at the conclusion of the service. Wendy explained that two ushers would come to the end of our pew at the center aisle and lead Diane and me to the rear of the chapel, where we could offer greetings to the chaplain. Seemed like a lot of confusion over nothing to me. We returned to our quarters and had hardly entered the house when Wendy came in. "I can't believe it," she said. "You've been here a week and no one's briefed you on how to act in the chapel."

My back was up, as I said, "Wendy get this straight. Please tell the chaplain and anybody else that this superintendent is going to arrive at the chapel when he darn well pleases. Furthermore, I'm not going to lead processions up and down the aisle. You pass that on, OK?"

Consequently, that was the one and only Sunday during my tour at Annapolis that I led processions at the Naval Academy chapel. The incident is resurrected, with humor, at family gatherings.

About three months into my new assignment I started receiving fragmentary reports from the Naval Investigative Service (NIS) and other sources that some midshipmen were using drugs. At around this time, 48 percent of Navy enlisted men, primarily pay grade E-4 and below admitted on a confidential Department of Defense survey form that they used drugs in one form or another. If we had a problem with midshipmen using drugs, it certainly figured that young petty officers in the fleet likely were abusing them as well. We had no antidrug program at the time, and it would seem the type of individual who qualifies for the Academy would be disinclined to take drugs. So I encouraged NIS to dig further into the issue. A few months later, as the 1979 graduation week neared, it was reported to me that eighteen first classmen were suspected of being involved with drugs. I was suddenly confronted with a dilemma. Should the eighteen be withheld from the ceremony? I believed they should, but at the same time I ordered an Article 32 investigation.

I telephoned the vice CNO, Adm. Bill Small, and recounted the problem. I said, "I recommend you quickly pass this on to Secretary Claytor, because there may be serious repercussions over the matter."

Once the eighteen midshipmen were notified there would be a delay, or worse, in receiving their diplomas, their parents responded with angry calls to their congressional representatives. In turn, the legislators laid into Claytor. To his credit, Secretary Claytor told the lawmakers, "If the superintendent believes this is the right thing to do, I support him." He was steadfast in backing me despite all the flak.

We immediately commenced the investigation, and because our JAG staff was small—one active duty lawyer and an assistant—we sought supplemental support from JAG headquarters. A commander from the staff came over and was an enormous help. After a month of interviews and considering all the factors of the situation, we decided we did not have enough evidence to charge sixteen of the eighteen alleged offenders.

After making this determination, I directed our public affairs officer to prepare a press release announcing our actions and to distribute it to the media right away.

On an autumn Sunday in September 1978, a day after a Navy football game, the commandant of midshipmen, Capt. Jack Darby, called me. "I'd like to come over and talk to you," he said, a hint of trouble in his voice. It was not customary for the commandant to have a polite chitchat with the superintendent on a Sunday.

We convened in my study, and he got right to the point. "I'm afraid we might have a charge of rape on our hands."

There goes a relaxing Sunday.

He went on to explain that a plebe woman had gone to a company tailgate party and apparently consumed some beer or other spirits. This was before the twenty-one-year-old alcohol law which came into effect in 1984. Jack said the girl supposedly had never drunk much alcohol before and became inebriated. A "chivalrous" first classman offered to take her back to Bancroft Hall.

Once there, they ended up in bed together in the male midshipman's room. After a time, she returned to her quarters and told her roommates she had been raped. They reported this to the officer of the day, and the commandant was immediately alerted.

I shook my head in dismay. "Rape is really bad stuff, Jack," I said, wondering how we were going to get through this. "We must proceed on the basis this could be a court-martial offense."

I assigned the deputy commandant, Capt. (later Vice Adm.) Frank Donovan, to immediately contact the girl's family, to explain what allegedly happened, and to maintain a very close dialogue with the parents. I picked Frank, because he was a Catholic, and we knew the young woman was Catholic and had attended a Catholic girl's school, which could mean she had possibly led a relatively sheltered life, compared to public high school students. I also directed the public affairs officer to prepare a statement for the press. This was a reiteration of my philosophy that when something like this happens, it's best to bite the bullet and get the word out to the public.

Ironically, we sent the press release to the *Annapolis Capital,* and it didn't even print it. However, this set a pattern with that newspaper, at least, that meant we were completely open about what went on at the Academy regardless of the repercussions; that we weren't going to hide behind the walls and hope the story wouldn't get out. It did eventually—several months later—get into some newspapers.

We conducted an Article 32 investigation as a prelude to the court-martial. The astute handling of the situation by Frank Donovan was a huge factor in the outcome of the case. He established a special rapport with the family, and they developed a strong respect for him. He did not try to soft-pedal the male midshipman's potential guilt. In the end, the parents decided, "Our daughter does not want to testify, and we don't want her to either."

In effect we had no case for a court-martial. But we did impose a strong penalty on the young man—a lengthy restriction of privileges. We also assigned demerits to the young woman for her misconduct in becoming inebriated. She remained at the Academy. Thankfully, after a few weeks, the crisis subsided.

Interestingly, three years later, when I was commander Third Fleet, I rode a helicopter from Naval Air Station Barbers Point in Hawaii to visit the cruiser, USS *Fox*, commanded by Capt. Les Palmer (who later became commandant at the Academy), which was deployed off the California coast. Les met me as I disembarked from the helo on the fantail and led me up to the bridge.

There, he said, "I'd like to introduce you to my officer of the deck," which he did. The young officer looked at me rather strangely, and the wheels started spinning in my head. There was something familiar about him. I said nothing, and later in the visit I asked Les, "Tell me, what kind of an officer is your OOD?"

Les said, "He's the best officer on board and definitely the best officer of the deck I have." I did *not* tell Les that this particular individual was punished with severe restriction—no weekend liberty—during his entire first-class year for the incident involving the inebriated female midshipman. That was between me and the young officer. No one else needed to know. Apparently, Les's best officer took advantage of the time available as a midshipman in hack, hit the books, studied his trade, and turned a negative into a positive. Which goes to show you can make a serious mistake, rise above it, and still succeed.

Chapter Twenty-Three

CAMPUS LIFE

*"My God," I thought, "we've got a crew of seven midshipmen
on a yacht in that race, and we don't know what their status is."*

I'VE BEEN ASKED IF I EVER USED WENDY as a "spy" on student activities. The
answer is: never. However, I did discover a totally unexpected way to get a
finger on the pulse of midshipmen, thanks to Diane. The superintendent's
home at Annapolis is a huge, handsome structure, with four spacious floors,
sixteen hundred square feet of living space, and thirty-four rooms. Named
after Cdr. Franklin Buchanan, the Academy's first superintendent (from 1845
to 1847), it has been the superintendent's residence since 1909. The once-
open porches on the north and south sides of the house have been enclosed,
and the large open porch on the west face overlooks a beautifully landscaped
yard, with an abundance of flowers in season. During the annual commissioning week, garden parties are held here for the members of the graduating
class and their parents. The first two floors are used for official functions.
Guest bedrooms for distinguished visitors as well as the private quarters for
the superintendent and his family are located on the third floor. Additional
guest rooms are located on the fourth floor.

Over the years more guests have been entertained at the Buchanan
House than at any other official government residence except the White
House. Superintendents have hosted presidents, kings, queens, prime
ministers, admirals from many nations, and tens of thousands of other guests.
Obviously, with just Diane and me in the house, we certainly weren't crowded.

"We've got those three bedrooms upstairs on the fourth floor that we
don't use," Diane pointed out one day. "Why don't we let midshipmen have
their dates stay there for weekend social events?"

Initially, I hesitated. The notion of young ladies trooping about upstairs
didn't set right at first, but we tried it, and it turned out to be a wonderful
experience. We not only got to know the young ladies our midshipmen were

dating, but in the course of inevitable conversations because of our proximity, we learned about the midshipmen themselves—how they were doing, what their thought processes were like, were they pleased with their situations, that sort of thing.

When a female student asked if her date could stay at the house, Diane became concerned.

"I'm not sure we want a man up there with girls right next door," she worried.

"Let them work it out," I said. "It will take care of itself. They can post their own schedule for use of the bathroom."

We never had a problem hosting the dates (except when all the blow dryers blew the fuses, and I couldn't use my razor on the lower floor), and even developed some friendships that have continued over the years. Diane and I certainly weren't matchmakers, but we did comment now and then about the suitability of this or that young lady linking up with this or that midshipman.

Through the years, Navy football has engendered spirited support from the midshipmen, especially when Navy was winning. I have always believed participation in—and success whenever possible—on the athletic fields, whether it's at the varsity level or intramurals, is important. It enhances the image of the school and conveys the sense that we're turning out well-trained and physically fit Navy and Marine Corps officers. I had the benefit of three fine football seasons when I was superintendent: eight victories against three in 1978, and seven and four and eight and three in the succeeding two years. We won one bowl game in 1978 and lost one in 1980. George Welch was Navy coach until 1981, when he left to coach Virginia.

During my time at Annapolis, the key top executives who reported directly to the superintendent were the academic dean, the dean of admissions, the deputy for operations, the deputy for management, and the director of athletics. I wanted them to have direct access to me at virtually any time. Interestingly, Bo Coppedge, my athletic director, told me his counterpart at West Point needed two week's lead time to get an appointment with the superintendent. If Bo called me and I wasn't in conference or out of town, he could be in my office in ten or fifteen minutes. My purpose, of course, was to ensure these individuals knew I had an open-door policy, especially when problems occurred, in the hopes we could work them out swiftly, if at all possible.

Capt. Dick Stratton, a former POW and dear friend (a Georgetown graduate), set up a prototype family service center arrangement that was so heralded it became the model for similar organizations throughout the Navy. He was our director of operations and was ideally suited for the job. His wife, Alice, was also a huge plus, mainly because she had a degree in social work and lent her skills and knowledge to this project. Not only was he an effective manager, but he also gave exceptionally well-received lectures to the midshipmen.

In the summer of 1980, an Academy yacht was sailed across the Atlantic to participate in the Fast Net race taking place in the Irish Sea. A freak storm roared up and damaged a lot of boats in the race. We learned about this on television.

"My God," I thought, "we've got a crew of seven midshipmen on a yacht in that race, and we don't know what their status is."

I immediately called Dick and said, "Please set up a crisis management watch system, get in touch with all the parents, tell them we just learned about the storm and we're doing everything possible to find out the condition of our students."

Dick took rapid action and explained to the parents we were on the case. Fortunately, a classmate of mine, Charlie Hunter, was on the commander in chief U.S. Naval Forces Europe staff. I called Charlie and asked him to do what he could. He called the British Coast Guard, and in approximately two days, we received word that our midshipmen were OK and the yacht was undamaged.

I suppose this could be called overreacting, but I believed contacting the parents right away—even though it turned out their children were safe—was the way to go. I believe the parents appreciated the effort.

Women had been at the Academy for two years when I got there, and a third group was coming in. Our director of professional development, Capt. Dick Ustick, had purview over three departments—Leadership and Law, Seamanship and Navigation, and the Training Department. I added to his burden by designating him the dean of women, recognizing him as the principal authority on distaff matters at the Academy. In effect, he was the female midshipman's advocate. I did this for several reasons. Primarily, I wanted to send a signal that I felt strongly enough about women at the school that I made a Navy captain a point of contact. He became the cognizant official with respect to issues relating to integration of women in the student body. This worked out well, I thought. (In succeeding years, after I left, the designation was dropped.)

If the dean heard about a disciplinary offense involving women, he took immediate action to learn all the particulars so that we could take proper corrective action. This precluded certain problems from festering and, perhaps, from getting worse with the passage of time.

Still, a rather subtle form of harassment of the women manifested itself slowly and perhaps inevitably at the school. I began to hear about pranks played on the women. At lectures during question-and-answer sessions, a woman might ask a question, prompting derisive rejoinders from the men. There were instances of pies being pushed into the faces of females by men— just for fun, so it seemed. Regardless of the pranks, the subjects of such debasement felt helpless to respond. Generally, these occurrences were kept under wraps by the students themselves. Possibly the victims shared their experiences with classmates, but they were never reported formally.

Interestingly, Diane found out about the pie incidents when Midn. 1st Class Liz Belzer came to the quarters one Sunday afternoon to use an upstairs study room, which we kept as an informal retreat for Midshipmen to get away from Bancroft Hall. When the time came for Liz to return to the Hall, she appeared reluctant to leave. Diane approached Liz and asked if there was a problem she should know about. Hesitantly, Liz told Diane that several times when she returned to the company area, her company mates formed a gauntlet as she walked by and, one by one, threw pies in her face. As soon as Liz left, Diane reported this troublesome incident to me.

Liz had high visibility within the brigade: she had been plebe brigade commander during the summer of 1979 and, during her senior year, the first female brigade commander. It certainly could be that her stellar performance gave rise these chauvinistic attacks.

Yet, during my term at the Academy, no problems related to women I would describe as severe came to the surface. I'm very glad about that. But I didn't like the course the subtle harassment was taking in those early days of my tour.

The Naval Academy had not only been a men's school for 131 years, but it also was a domicile for type A, aggressive, and, yes, macho personalities. After all, the whole purpose of the Academy was to train warriors, people who would be willing and able to go in harm's way and put their life on the line for their country. The "intrusion" of the female sex into their midst and supposedly degrading the masculine image of the school simply didn't set well, even though the women were also supremely motivated, fit, and determined individuals.

Consequently, after about six months in the job, I decided to let everyone know where the "Supe" stood on such matters. At various classes and gatherings, I rendered a spiel on my policy.

I stated in the clearest terms I could muster: "I will not tolerate at this school any group or person being treated in an undignified manner. If infractions of this nature take place, I'll be very tough on the perpetrators."

To my staff I said, "There should be no doubt in anyone's mind that the chief public affairs officer (PAO) at the Naval Academy is the superintendent." This in no way denigrated the assigned staff PAO. But we had to be very media conscious at the time, and it was important that the superintendent be the chief spokesman when it came to situations that sparked negative potential beyond the borders of the campus.

In 1979, for example, the first women were on the threshold of becoming seniors (class of 1980) and would hold leadership positions, particularly with respect to the incoming plebe class. We knew this would draw lots of attention, and sure enough, a reporter from the *Washington Post* came over wanting to interview some of these ladies.

There happened to be three women in the class of 1980 who were standouts. Not only were they smart, self-confident, and enthusiastic (all were cheerleaders), with promising futures, but they also were also very photogenic. They were Sandy Irwin, Tina D'ercole, and Laurie Ramp, and I selected them to meet with the reporters. Beauty is vanity, I know, but I wanted the *Post*'s readers to know that competent women midshipmen could be strong leaders as well as being very feminine.

The mother of Ensign Carrie Jones called to tell me that Carrie's graduation diploma stated, "Having met all the requirements of the Academic program, *he* is awarded. . . ." I immediately ordered replacement diplomas for all the women of this class and had them mailed to their new duty stations. (Carrie Jones was later killed in a T-45 training accident in Corpus Christy, Texas.)

Nonetheless, when selected women from the class of 1980 were interviewed by the Naval Institute's top historian, Paul Stillwell, for his oral history archives, they were nearly unanimous in their belief that they felt unwelcome at the school.

The class of 1979 was the last all-male class at Annapolis. Their rings were inscribed with the phrase "All-Male." As graduation drew near, someone dreamed up the idea of filling their hats with ping-pong balls. This gesture would declare to the world the class's status as the final one anatomically equipped with you know what. I got wind of this and pondered what to do about it. I asked myself, "Should I hit this head on or be subtle?"

A graduation rehearsal, held one day before the actual exercise, is a must. It was designed primarily for the first classmen to ensure, among other matters, that they knew the procedure for lining up, moving forward to get their diplomas, and returning to their seats.

I was on the platform and practiced giving some of them their sheepskins. I took this opportunity to give the class a brief philosophical talk that would be totally separate from the speech I planned for the actual event.

In this talk I said, "Your class has a good reputation. You've done a good job here. But I can tell you that if you do something dumb at the ceremony, you will put a stigma on your class that will take years to overcome. So don't do something you would be ashamed of, something you would have to live with for a long time."

Clearly, they knew I knew what they were planning. But I never flat out told them not to stuff their hats with those ping-pong balls. So, it was with a measure of apprehension, at the conclusion of the graduation, that I waited for the traditional flinging of their covers into the air, a favorite spectacle for that time of year, recorded on national television and in the media at large. In other words, there would be an abundance of witnesses to ping-pong balls spilling out over the hoard of newly designated naval officers.

I actually held my breath when the moment came, hoping for the best. The hats went up, I watched with great intensity and concern, and waited for the balls to fall. They did not appear. I heaved a huge sigh of relief. Score one for the Supe.

Chapter Twenty-Four

WOMEN UNDER FIRE

For one thing, he described Bancroft Hall as a "horny woman's dream"
and that sex was rampart in the Hall.

THE MOST SERIOUS PROBLEM we experienced during my four years at
Annapolis had to do with a former graduate, Jim Webb, Naval Academy class
of 1968. He had an impressive portfolio: Marine officer, highly decorated
Vietnam veteran, and best-selling novelist. His *Fields of Fire* was a terrific
book, one that put him on the literary map. He was gifted with the written
word. He also would become secretary of the Navy for eleven months in
1987, well after our "collision" of differences at the Academy. All in all, Jim
Webb is a remarkable individual. But he created a serious problem for us that
lingered for years. Vestiges of it remain still, but with far less impact.

In December 1978 the director of the English and History Department,
Marine colonel Frank Zimolzac, came to see me with the chairman of the
English Department, Dr. Fred Fetrow.

"There's a Marine Corps graduate of the Academy who has an outstanding combat record, is a successful novelist, and has expressed interest in
becoming a writer in residence, teaching English here," he said. "We can
accommodate him with an eighteen-month contract in accordance with the
school's policy on such matters." We had the resources for such a contract,
and I was immediately attracted by the proposal.

"That's wonderful," I said. "With that background he ought to be a big
hit with the midshipmen." I'd never met Webb but recognized him as a well-
known author. Webb signed a contract in December 1978, agreeing to stay
for three semesters. His lectures were well received, and he was a popular
addition to our faculty. Then oddly, after only a couple of months, Webb
notified the department he wished to resign, that he wanted to leave in
June at the end of one semester. When I heard this, I thought, 'Well, OK,

everyone's plans change. So be it.' But in the subsequent discussions about his unexpected departure, I was told that during his abbreviated tenure, a sizeable number of students, male and female, were entering and leaving his office at an unusual rate.

When he was asked why he wanted to leave, Webb indicated he got so deeply involved with the midshipmen that he wasn't getting his writing done. That made sense, because he was an established and highly regarded author. So, Webb left the Academy, and life went on. A couple of months later he wrote me and said he had an article coming out in the *Washingtonian Magazine* and that it may appear to be a bit controversial. I wrote him back and said, "Don't worry about it, we can handle it."

The article was entitled, "Women Can't Fight," and no sooner had it hit the streets than it had an immediate and explosive impact on the Naval Academy. It garnered nationwide attention.

Webb's article was well written but, in my view, sensational in nature. I believed it contained inaccuracies and that he misrepresented some facts. For one thing he described Bancroft Hall as a "horny woman's dream" and that sex was rampart in the Hall. This was blatantly wrong. It would be possible, certainly, for occasions of sexual relations to take place but not to the excess implicated in the article. After all, there were three hundred women among the four thousand students in residence at Bancroft Hall. We weren't blind to the potential problems of sex on campus. We had our finger on the pulse of such things.

The article had an instantly demoralizing effect on the women not only at Annapolis but at West Point as well. More on this later. I admit I was furious about the article and had to seriously question Webb's ultimate purpose in becoming writer in residence in the first place, not to mention the extraordinary number of interviews that apparently took place and accounted for the often-intermittent parade of midshipmen in and out of his office. But that episode was over and done with. The article, as it turned out, gained notoriety, and I felt powerless to counteract it.

The English and History departments were housed in Sampson Hall. Colonel. Zimolzac notified Webb he was no longer welcome in that building. Webb let it be known he was banned from the entire Naval Academy. Learning this, I directed the staff to make damn well sure that Jim Webb was invited to every single event we had scheduled, every Forrestal Lecture, every parade, every social occasion. He accepted none of these and continued to claim he was banned from campus.

I made certain that copies of the article were made available in our library. It turned out to be one of the library's most popular documents, especially among the males.

A while later I received a call from former superintendent, Vice Adm. Charles Minter, who had been contacted by Gen. Wallace Green, former commandant of the Marine Corps and now retired. Greene had read the galleys of Webb's new book, *A Sense of Honor*, and said, "It depicts the Naval Academy in a manner with which I am not familiar. It's not the Academy I know."

Retired Navy captain Robert Bowler, executive director of the U.S Naval Institute, which is headquartered on the Academy grounds, called and said Webb had submitted the book to him to copublish along with a New York publishing company. Bowler and his editors read the manuscript and concluded that those portions relating to the Academy did not represent their views of it. So the institute declined the offer.

A novelist has every right to portray his subjects any way he chooses. The readers decide whether his or her story is credible or not. *A Sense of Honor* was a popular book, but it sure didn't do the Academy any good. It portrayed the Academy faculty in a negative way, it degraded nuclear officers, it depicted sexual activity between an officer and his former roommate's wife—the so-called stuff of life. Even so, it's a free society, and the book was available in our midshipmen's store.

A few months after the appearance of the book I received a call from the supply officer, who said the publishing company in New York had accused us of banning the book from the Naval Academy. He explained he ordered the book but, because of the subsequent decreasing demand for it, he reduced the number of books ordered, figuring it didn't have that much appeal to the students.

The publishing company issued a press release stating the Naval Academy had banned Webb's book. That ought to inspire sales, I thought. I directed the supply officer to draft a statement describing in detail what had really transpired. We released this to the public, adamantly denying we had banned the book. I wrote to the publishing company as well, stating our case.

Webb and I exchanged a number of letters over time regarding this and related issues, the focus of which was always the Academy, his beliefs regarding women in combat, and his criticism of the way we were doing business.

When he became secretary of the Navy, Webb remarked, "Now is the first time that I'm warmly received at the Naval Academy."

Permit me to jump ahead to April 1990 and my remarks to the Defense Advisory Committee on Women in the Service (DACOWITS), when I held a position as chairman of naval leadership at the Academy. The thrust of my testimony was two-fold: the adverse impact on acceptance of women at the Naval Academy as expressed in Webb's *Washingtonian Magazine* article and the detrimental effect on the admission of women to the service academies caused by the increased active duty obligation enacted by Congress in 1989.

I noted,

To understand why the "Women Can't Fight" article has such a serious and pervasive unfavorable influence, it might be well to discuss the major challenge to the acceptance of women at the academies. Because of the rigorous military and physical regimen at the service academies, these institutions attract a certain number of young men with a strong macho ethic. I define macho as the desire to be perceived as tough and virile. It is important to these young men that they be viewed by their civilian friends as undergoing a difficult rite of passage. In their eyes, the women degrade this macho, rite-of-passage-image of the academies; these young men resent their presence, and often make derisive comments and engage in cruel pranks on the women. Even though they daily see women successfully meeting all the requirements of the Academy program, their resentment is not diminished.

The Academy leaders must engage in a concerted effort to change the attitude of these young men over their four years at the school, and in most cases they are successful. But these young men look to the "Women Can't Fight" article written by a Vietnam hero, Naval Academy graduate, and now former Secretary of the Navy, as support for their position. These midshipmen still check out Webb's article from the library, and the library staff must keep a large supply of copies of the article on hand. Some midshipmen have formed a Webb cult at the Academy and have devised the acronym W.E.B.B.—Women Except Bancroft, Baby. When Webb became Secretary of the Navy, these young men were elated because they felt he would quickly remove women from the Academy.

What are some of the portions of Webb's article that are demoralizing to the women? First, Webb stated that the presence of women at the Academy "poisoned the preparation of men for combat" and that the Academies were "no longer turning out combat leaders." Next, Webb stated he never encountered a woman at the Academy whom he would trust to provide combat leadership to men. He further stated that "sex is common place in Bancroft Hall." The Hall, which houses 4,000 males and 300 females, "is a horny woman's dream." He stated that the appointment of Elizabeth Belzer, Naval Academy Class of 1980, the first woman graduate, to her high midshipman leadership position was politically inspired. Finally, he stated that the women would, in the long run, lose far more than they would gain from the Academy experience, that they would be permanently scarred.

To counter these statements and allegations, I will provide you the real facts. I have considerable combat experience, not including my six years as a POW, and while superintendent and in my present capacity, I can state categorically that the presence of women has not in any way degraded the quality of our program at the Academy and our ability to produce combat officers. In fact, it was my perception that women actually strengthened standards at the Academy because of their example of maturity, intelligence, professionalism, dedication and toughness. Their presence caused some of the immature, macho males, who are prone to walk around partially clad, to use excessive profanity, to refrain from these and other practices which contribute nothing to leadership development. By being closely associated with women, our male midshipmen are developing into leaders with greater breadth and human understanding.

The record of Academy graduates in Lebanon, Grenada, Persian Gulf, Libya, Panama, the *Achille Lauro* incident and other crises indicates no diminution of their capability to function effectively in combat. In addition to my own observations as Commander of the Third Fleet in the Pacific, I have talked to many military commanders, and they contend Academy graduates still have the "right stuff." I might add that Academy graduates are still being selected as astronauts, and that the Academy continues to be the prime supplier of personnel in the space program.

With regard to the allegation that women cannot lead men in a combat situation, in addition to the Captain Linda Bray incident in Panama. I can site numerable current examples of the superb leadership of women in arduous positions in the fleet operational environment.

Webb's statement that sex was rampant in Bancroft Hall was and is blatantly false. Our Academy officers are quite close to the situation in Bancroft Hall and though there have been isolated incidents of fraternization, they are relatively few. My daughter, who graduated from the Naval Academy in 1981, and many other midshipmen confirmed this for me.

Concerning the Liz Belzer political assignment allegation, I can assure everyone that her promotion was based purely on merit, because she was such a superb midshipman. She has continued to demonstrate her superior qualities as an officer. She qualified as a Surface Warfare Officer, served with great credit as a division officer on a destroyer tender on a deployment to the Indian Ocean, and she has obtained a Masters Degree from MIT and Woods Hole in Ocean Science.

I guess scar tissue must be stronger than normal tissue, because those "scarred" women are doing superbly in every field in our military services today. I could provide countless example of such performance, but time does not permit me to do so. I would add, as well, that those women graduates who have entered civilian life are performing extremely well, moving right up the corporate ladder in many cases.

I recommended to the panel that it would be a good idea if Jim Webb would make a public statement or write another article stating he had changed his views expressed in 1979, and further expressing his full support for women at the academies. From his statements at his confirmation hearings and the decisions he made as secretary of the Navy to place women in ammunition ships and fleet oilers, formerly combatant ships, I believed he had in fact changed his position. Indeed, as secretary of the Navy, in a Forrestal lecture to our midshipmen in September 1987, he stated, "I am not biased in any way to the issue of women here at the Academy or in the naval service, and in fact feel strongly that men and women should be treated equally in such matters." Furthermore, he did recommend opening surface, aviation, and seabee billets to females that were heretofore unavailable to them.

As to the second item on my agenda for the committee, I referred to the one-year extension, from five to six years, of the active-duty obligation of service academy graduates:

For the good of the country, the service academies must be able to attract the cream of American youth. High quality young people at age 17 or 18 simply are not sure what career field they wish to devote their lives to. Out of a spirit of patriotism they will enter the service academies and accept an active-duty obligation of four or even five years with the expectation they may decide to remain in the military for a full career. But active-duty obligations in excess of that amount will drive the fine young people away from the academies, to the great detriment of the country.

The situation is greatly exacerbated in the case of minorities and women for several reasons. First, minorities and women are well aware that our military services were previously white, male bastions. Although they are patriotic and wish to serve their country, they are still somewhat skeptical of entering a military career. A long obligation simply will turn them away out of fear they may encounter something they do not enjoy and be irrevocably committed for a large portion of their lives. Secondly, qualified women and minorities are strongly sought after by many universities in this country who require no post-graduation obligation. The service academies simply will lose their ability to compete in our recruiting when handicapped with a six-year active duty obligation. The situation is particularly critical because the 18-year-old population is in decline until 1994.

The previous obligation was not changed, so we didn't succeed on that score, but you can't win them all.

As to women in combat, my sense is that many still adhere to the belief it is wrong for females to be so engaged. That's a given. Does Jim Webb's article still reverberate through the halls of learning at Annapolis? Probably, a little bit. But with the passage of time, its impact has diminished considerably.

Chapter Twenty-Five

SUPERINTENDENT'S BUSINESS

I told Admiral Bob Long, then vice CNO, "Admiral Rickover's on record for being against sports and sex. Now he's after honor. How are we going to attract people to the school if honor is added to the list?"

THE ATTRITION RATE AT THE ACADEMY—and at other military schools—was 30 percent, which some attributed to the fallout of the Vietnam War. Regardless of the cause, this was unacceptable to me. One of our goals was to get that number down. When I arrived in the fall of 1978, one of the drivers of this problem was the rule that if a midshipman dropped out in the second year, he or she would incur a two-year active-duty obligation as an enlisted person. Were the person to wait until the third year, the obligation was for three years. Graduates were obligated for five years.

I developed a pitch that I gave early on to second-year students. It went something like this: "I'm not saying you should make the Navy your career. I'm basically telling you if you decide to stay after your third year and complete the Academy, and assume the five-year obligation, you're going to be better off seven years from now as compared to leaving school in that third year or before. Unless you have a specific desire to be a lawyer, a doctor, or something else, you'll only be twenty-seven years old or so and you will be a desirable candidate for work in the civilian field. Leaving the Naval Academy after the second year because you are concerned about a greater obligation, you're throwing away a lot."

I always cited my friend Ross Perot, who became phenomenally successful after leaving Annapolis and completing his active duty. There were many others who made their mark in the civilian world.

Concomitant with this attempt at persuasion, I urged the young officers of the staff to convey how they would improve matters at the school, including shoring up the relationships between students and officers, hoping this would be a plus in the struggle against high attrition. Capt. John Butterfield, director of U.S. international studies, was instrument in this effort, which, slowly but surely, led to an 8 percent decrease in the attrition rate.

Diane and I maintained as much visibility on campus as we could. (When I was a midshipman, we hardly ever saw the superintendent, much less his wife.) Our schedule was frantic, and we had commitments most evenings and weekends. But the experience was most rewarding, and we enjoyed it immensely. Naturally, as I've written, there were conflicts.

For example, I had the deepest respect for Adm. Hyman Rickover, but he was the proverbial thorn in my side when it came to his precious nuclear program. He deserved the title, "Father of the Nuclear Navy;" no doubt about that. But he went overboard when it came to recruiting youngsters for his program. In truth, there were far more midshipmen interested in aviation and surface navy duty as compared to submarines. That was trouble enough, but Rickover's standards were so high and so concentrated on academic achievement that he literally discarded any other accomplishments or skills a midshipman might possess, be it athletics or cut-above leadership characteristics.

Among others, I consulted the then-vice chief of naval operations (and later CNO), Adm. Jim Watkins, himself a "nuke," on numerous occasions to try and resolve conflicts. He supported our position, thankfully, which was not easy for him.

Rickover was actually turning down volunteers who sought nuclear submarine duty and selecting nonvolunteers, particularly those who opted for assignment to aviation.

"I think you should trade off academic standing in the case of a motivated volunteer," I once pleaded with him as the situation worsened.

"No, that's immature," he countered adamantly.

An All-American lacrosse player and aeronautical engineering student who wanted aviation was selected by Rickover but flat out declared to the admiral that he would refuse a nuclear assignment. Rickover was so furious that he wanted the midshipman court-martialed.

I told Admiral Watkins, "If that happens, we're going to destroy the relationship between the Academy and the nuclear power community and greatly exacerbate the ability of midshipmen to go into that community."

A "shoot-out" with Rickover followed, but he finally backed off in this case and agreed to deselect the lacrosse player after he wrote a letter of apology to the admiral. Happily, the lacrosse player went on to a successful career as a naval aviator.

At another point later on, Rickover tried to persuade the midshipman honor chairman to quit that position so that he could improve his grades and go nuclear. I told Adm. Bob Long, then vice CNO, "Admiral Rickover's on record for being against sports and sex. Now he's after honor. How are we going to attract people to the school if honor is added to the list?"

Admiral Long, who probably had more influence with Rickover than anyone else, got him to back off that. So, there were some victories in this ongoing dilemma, but I fear some outstanding midshipmen who might have gone on to stellar careers in the nuclear navy never got the opportunity to do so.

One goal I failed to achieve was improving the relationship between the Marine Corps community and the school. Only 14 percent of each class were "going Marine," when the goal was 16 percent. I tried various measures: assigning a Marine officer as my flag lieutenant (then Capt. Gordon Jackson, class of 1970); helping to persuade the hierarchy to designate a new sports facility, "Lejeune Hall," in honor of the renowned USMC hero, John Lejeune (a move much opposed by vintage admirals, who couldn't see their way to naming a Naval Academy building after a Marine); and inviting senior Marine Corps leaders to virtually all the major events, including parades and football games. In truth, their attendance was minimal.

To my regret, I never got the Marines to come around. Indeed, I sensed there was an anti-Naval Academy bias ingrained in the Marine Corps. I even had graduates who went into the Marine Corps tell me they perceived resentment toward Academy graduates. Some even got to the point of removing their U.S. Naval Academy class rings before attending Marine Corps social events. However, I believe the situation has improved with time.

With respect to African-Americans at the Academy, I never witnessed any overt racial discrimination. There were some indications that bothered me, such as the black football players sitting together at the annual banquet, while the white players sat separately. But I think this largely stemmed from the perceived comfort level of each group, particularly as to cultural background, during a rather formal occasion.

On the gridiron there certainly were no problems. I don't believe racial discrimination is a problem at Annapolis now.

The Academy has always had a solid reputation as an outstanding engineering school—we had eight engineering majors when I became superintendent. That makes sense, considering the line of work its graduates are destined for. But having had an acute interest in history and the value of the knowledge that preceded our current state of existence, I opted to have at least one history course as a requirement for all students added to the curriculum. The under secretary of the Navy during my tour was James Woolsey, a lawyer and a Rhodes scholar. He avidly approved having the history requirement. Not surprisingly, this met opposition from some on the faculty, but only because they believed there was already plenty on each midshipman's academic plate. We worked it out by modifying the required electives options.

When I arrived as superintendent, midshipmen were allowed to drink beer in Dahlgren Hall after the end of their daily military obligations, a practice that had been in force several years before. I was very anxious about this and didn't like it, but I wasn't about to rock the boat by terminating it. The eighteen year-old drinking law was in effect, and my fears were realized in the spring of 1979, when two first classmen drove off the seawall by the library and plunged into the Severn River. The inebriated driver survived. His passenger drowned. I separated him through the administrative conduct system, although he fought dismissal through the federal courts. The federal judge supported the Academy's decision to dismiss the student. Two years later another midshipman under the influence plowed into a tree on the parade grounds, again killing a passenger. I authorized a court-martial for him, a proceeding that precluded redress through the federal courts. The court sentenced him to dismissal.

Subsequently, much pressure was brought to bear on me in behalf of this student, who otherwise was highly regarded. I received calls from some old-timers, who said, "There, but for the grace of God, go I."

I realized that teenage drinking was perceived to be rampant in those days and reminded myself that midshipmen are in that age group and that, although they were considered a cut above the average, they were still human. So, we reduced the punishment to a one-year probation in working on a drug and alcohol abuse program. Happily, the young man preformed well during that year and went on to graduate with the class of 1981.

Mine was a gratifying tour at Annapolis. I was pumped up every time I participated in a parade of midshipmen when a student and felt the excitement even more so as the head of the Academy. A combination of pride, beautiful precision, love of country, and a pervasive sense of accomplishment embedded in the student body illuminate those parades as unforgettable events. I experienced the same emotions when I witnessed those young men and women marching by.

Chapter Twenty-Six

THIRD FLEET

The Russians were enmeshed in Afghanistan at the time,
and I'm sure they realized we weren't trying to provoke them.

DESPITE MY SIX-YEAR HIATUS IN HANOI and resultant lack of operational experience, I was assigned a major command. I was genuinely surprised and flattered when I received orders to command the Third Fleet, based at Pearl Harbor, Hawaii. Adm. Tom Hayward was CNO and was instrumental in approving the assignment. John Lehman had been secretary of the Navy for about six months and had visited the Naval Academy a couple of times in that period, but we did not have the opportunity to sit down, get to know each other, or discuss any school matters at length. I surmised he didn't oppose my selection as a fleet commander.

The primary mission of the Third Fleet was to assist those battle groups destined for duty in the far eastern parts of the Pacific in honing their operational skills. In essence, we evaluated their performance through various exercises, pointing out shortcomings and helping them correct any deficiencies before heading further west for duty.

As a prelude to the new job, I took some time off before transferring from Annapolis, traveled west, and talked with the commanders of the aviation and surface forces of the Pacific Fleet, officials at the Tactical Warfare Training Center at Point Loma. I also met with officials at the Naval Intelligence Center in Suitland, Maryland. I wanted to acquire an up-to-date picture of Soviet capabilities and related matters. I also was updated on the latest technology and activities in the field of ASW—antisubmarine warfare—knowing my knowledge was weak in this area.

Diane and I were delightfully situated in flag quarters on Ford Island, and although she commuted periodically to the mainland to tend to her therapy business, we had a wonderful time in Hawaii, fully appreciating the balmy breezes, the brilliant seascapes, and the cobalt sky, which was frequented by a parade of white tufted clouds. We also experienced a not-unexpected influx of visitors—friends who thought it would be a nice time to visit the Lawrence family at its new duty station. This was fine with us, because we had room, and the guests, for the most part, preferred touring the scenic highlights of Hawaii to spending time with us.

Diane and I seemed to have social commitments several evenings a week. This wasn't too distracting, because it was customary in Hawaii to terminate socializing at 9:30 PM. I'm not sure why this was so. Perhaps people wanted to retire early so they could meet the dawn and take full advantage of the spectacular weather and the romantic tropical setting.

One of my new key responsibilities was serving the Pacific Fleet commander as the agent for tactical doctrine development, a duty I shared with my counterpart in Norfolk, Virginia, who commanded the Second Fleet. One of our early projects, for example, involved the Tomahawk cruise missile—the Tactical Land Attack Missile (TLAM). This was a complex undertaking because of the multiple project offices involved, ranging from those in the Pentagon to battle group commanders and plenty of points in between. Integrating the command and control process of the Tomahawk into the whole structure of the Navy task force was the challenge.

Initially, I had the sense that our sailors and officers were so busy conducting routine operations that there was a noticeable reluctance to actively engage in Tomahawk development. Staff people weren't traveling to Washington for Pentagon meetings regarding the missile, claiming the travel was too costly. I appreciated that concern, but, conversely, we envisioned the Tomahawk as a vital addition to the Navy's arsenal of weapons. To make it effective operationally, we had to evaluate it carefully and thoroughly, starting right now. I made that clear shortly after arrival, and I was pleased the staff and all hands in the Third Fleet turned to and made the Tomahawk a priority venture.

At the time, the Tomahawk was primarily an antiship missile, but at this writing, it has proved most successful as a land-attack missile, as evidenced in both Desert Storm and the Iraqi War. Its accuracy was a boon to combat operations, especially because of its over-the-horizon targeting ability.

The U.S. Navy had shown very little "presence" in the northern Pacific since World War II. Our deployment patterns had been pretty much stereotyped, focusing on the waters off Japan and the sea around the Philippines. I was curious as to how the Russians would react if we sent a carrier group into the Northern Pacific up by the Kuril Islands, which stretched northward from the northernmost tip of Japan. It was 1982 and the Cold War was still on. I certainly had no intention of provoking the Soviets. But I did believe it would give our personnel valuable experience to operate in a place they hadn't been before.

I called Adm. Jim Watkins, commander in chief of the Pacific Fleet at the time, and asked, "Would you object if I made a proposal to run a battle group up toward the Kuril Islands?" I explained my motivation, and he asked a few questions before agreeing to seek clearance from the CNO.

"Work up the plans," he said, "and we'll see."

I wished that I had a flagship, because I would have liked to accompany the fleet on this journey, which, with minimum reservations, was approved. We sent a three-carrier battle group into the region, and even though I remained at Pearl Harbor, I was in constant contact with the battle group through our state-of-the-art communications system on base. The battle group kept its distance from the Okhotsk Sea as it traveled along the length of the Kuril chain. The ships' crews and air wings learned to operate in an area totally unfamiliar to them, and one that was significantly colder than they were used to.

Interestingly, we prompted very little response from the Russians. We knew the Russian Navy, apart from its ballistic missile submarines, conducted very few blue water operations, staying in port a lot, preserving, it seemed, their new ships. At one point a Backfire bomber sortied from the Soviet mainland and headed in the direction of our fleet, but it never went beyond the Kurils.

We went back a year later with a three-carrier battle group headed by Rear Adm. Tom Brown, an outstanding and aggressive naval aviator and skipper. We purposely planned the track of the carrier to proceed toward the approaches to Petropavlovsk, a key seaport on the southern end of the Kamchatka Peninsula. Tom did just that, although at one point I radioed him and said, "Better back off a little, Tom, and not get any closer."

Again, there was minimum response from the Russians. As best we could tell, only one Victor submarine was dispatched to "look us over."

I came away from these exercises with the belief the Soviets were really very benign in this period. It was as if they had no desire to enter into any kind of a naval conflict with us. Conversely, there was the shoot-down of the Korean 747 that year (1983), but I believe that was an anomaly, a huge and terrible mistake. Russia was enmeshed in Afghanistan at the time, and I'm sure they realized we weren't trying to provoke them. Plus, they were embroiled in serious economic problems.

Another Third Fleet highlight was the biennial RIMPAC—Rim of the Pacific—exercise, wherein the allied navies of Australia, New Zealand, Japan, Britain, Canada, and other nations participated. RIMPACs were excellent training exercises for all the participants, but there were difficulties stemming from the Japanese role in RIMPAC events. I found myself playing with a political football that I had to toss around with circumspection.

Following World War II, the Japanese were allowed to develop a Maritime Self-Defense Force (it was not called a navy), the key word being "Defense." Thus, during the RIMPAC exercise, the Japanese had to be used in an exclusively nonoffensive manner. So, we assigned them escort responsibilities for the amphibious task force scheduled to make a landing on Kahoolawe in the Hawaiian chain, an island, one end of which was used for bombing and gunnery training. This was fine with the Japanese officers, but the Japanese press disagreed. One article published in a homeland newspaper declared, "Yes, the Maritime Self-Defense Force is set to play a defensive role, but for an offensive mission."

The Japanese officers had an intense distaste for the media. They contrived to lie whenever they could to deceive the press. Exacerbating the issue was the presence of the media personnel on the ships of the amphibious force who fired off inflammatory articles to the Japanese newspapers, charging the Maritime Self-Defense Force with participating in nondefensive maneuvers, a violation of the laws of that country.

At one point, I was designated the point man at a press conference with the Japanese media to put the exercise in perspective. The Japanese CNO called me numerous times before the conference, advising me what to say to the media. Had I complied, I would have made blatantly false statements. In other words, they wanted me to lie.

I explained to the Japanese CNO, "We don't lie to the media in America. They deserve the facts whether we like to present them or not. There's no way of getting around that."

He was very angry, not so much with me personally, but more with the situation itself. So I reiterated that the Japanese units in the exercise were playing a purely defensive role when they escorted the amphibious group. I stuck with this assertion, and neither the media nor the Japanese CNO were satisfied. Thankfully, the ruckus eventually blew over. There was certainly no love lost between the leaders of the Japanese Maritime Self-Defense Force and the scribes representing the home country.

The USS *Ohio* was the Navy's first *Trident* submarine. Strategic deterrence has been the sole mission of the fleet ballistic missile submarine (SSBN) since its inception in 1960. The SSBN provides the nation's most survivable and enduring nuclear strike capability. The *Ohio* class submarine replaced aging fleet ballistic missile submarines built in the 1960s and is far more capable. *Ohio* class/*Trident* ballistic missile submarines provide the sea-based "leg" of the triad of U.S. strategic deterrent forces. The eighteen *Trident* SSBNs (each carrying twenty-four missiles), carry 50 percent of the total U.S. strategic warheads. Although the missiles have no preset targets when the submarine goes on patrol, the SSBNs are capable of rapidly targeting their missiles should the need arise, using secure and constant at-sea communications links. It was to be home-ported at the Navy's Bangor, Washington, sub base, although it came under my cognizance as a Third Fleet ship.

Greenpeace, an organization that advocates preservation of the environment, and other activist groups were sharply opposed to allowing a nuclear-powered ship to be based in Bangor. Exacerbating matters, the Catholic bishop of Seattle had a strong, antimilitary bias and was very vocal about it. How to handle the anticipated protests was the question. I traveled to Seattle for the Seattle Sea Fair, where some of our cruisers and destroyers would appear for public display. This coincided with the planned arrival of the *Ohio*. There was notable unrest about the sub's arrival, and as a result, a Seattle newspaper asked to interview me. I said sure, and the first question the reporter asked was, "How are you going to handle all the protests you're going to have here? Are you going to bring the submarine in in the middle of the night? Are you going to have it come through Puget Sound submerged?"

"Of course not," I responded. "*Ohio* will arrive in broad daylight for all to see, and we're going to announce its arrival in advance." The reporter was openly surprised at my reply. "For one thing," I continued, "there are families of the crew and many other friends and supporters who will be on the pier to greet their loved ones. For another, we would never consider bringing the submarine submerged through Puget Sound."

"What about the dissenters?" asked the reporter?

"We'll respect the dissenters," I said. "We'll do our best in the interests of public safety to accommodate them, but we'll have Coast Guard vessels in the area to remove boat-borne protestors who might impede *Ohio* on the way in."

In an even voice, I went on, "I respect the right of people to protest. That's fundamental to democracy. I served in two wars and spent six years as a POW preserving the freedom of speech in this country. I'm not going to be the one who advocates restricting the dissent of protesters."

I wasn't sure what to expect in the newspaper the next day, but when it came out, I was relieved and pleased. There was a strong editorial praising me. The reporter had written, "Finally, we have a military officer who is open minded. One who is not trying to conceal things and one who respects those who are exercising their right to protest."

In the end, Greenpeace was there, but their armada consisted of just a few people and several row boats, which the Coast Guard easily prevented from getting in the *Ohio's* way.

Of more concern was a Soviet Trawler that loitered off shore and tracked the submarine when the *Ohio* went to sea for exercises. The Russians dispersed an unknown type of sonobuoy, which prompted me to order minesweepers into the area. We found nothing, although one of the sonobuoys washed ashore and was discovered a few days after the *Ohio* was well out to sea. We didn't learn much from it, but there was a sense at the time that we were dealing with some highly classified activities, and we didn't take them lightly.

The trawler and the submarine played a kind of tag as they worked their way north toward the Aleutians. The Russians were obviously anxious to learn everything they could about the *Trident* sub, and we were anxious to counter their probes. This went on for many days, but in the end neither got the best of the other.

Back in warmer climes, we had an unexpected clash with a small and mostly Hawaiian sect called the Ohana. They believed religious artifacts were on Kahoolawe and issued a series of protests against our use of part of the island as a bombing range. We gave the Ohana escorted tours of the island, so they could seek out the artifacts without crossing into the bombing area. But they never seemed satisfied. When they demonstrated in front of the main gate at Ford Island at the outset of the RIMPAC exercise, I finally decided we had to get some closure on this problem.

I summoned the public affairs staff, and we discussed what action we could take. It turned out the editor of the *Honolulu Star Bulletin* had been a World War II naval officer, and he was amenable to a question-and-answer type interview focusing on the Ohana problem.

I'm sure it angered the Ohana, because our exchange was forthright and honest. I explained that for safety purposes we had to escort the Ohanas when they were on the island. We wouldn't impede their desire to continue seeking artifacts—as long as we escorted them when a couple of times a month they arrived from the main island of Maui, which was only six miles away.

As luck would have it, their protests grew less and less frequent to the point that the Ohana were no longer a negative issue. This probably resulted more from the small size of their organization and their lack of support from a larger segment of the Hawaiian population than from our interview in the *Honolulu Star Bulletin*.

Then there was the problem with the goats. When Capt. James Cook, the British explorer, traveled the Pacific, he placed goats on the various islands along his journey. Reason: to provide a source of meat during return visits to the islands. Goats are not popular in Hawaii, because they eat plants and shrubbery, causing severe erosion of the soil. Indeed, there was a sizeable goat population on Kahoolawe, which had decimated the foliage, and there was pressure to reduce the goat population on the island.

This brought joy to the Marines in our command, many of whom volunteered for goat duty on Kahoolawe. Equipped with their rifles, they were sent to the island to shoot the helpless goats. Since there no inhabitants on the island to use the goat meat, the carcasses were left.

I thought, here in Hawaii we're getting criticized because we're not killing the goats fast enough, while on San Clement Island, another training range off the California coast, we were taken to task because we weren't sufficiently sustaining the goats there. In fact, it cost the Navy a couple of million dollars to remove the goats from San Clemente and place them in sanctuaries elsewhere.

Conclusion: special interest groups could tie us in knots.

"Don't worry, Admiral," Lt. Cdr. Moe Gibbs, who headed our meteorology department, told me one day in November 1982, "there hasn't been a typhoon is history in this part of the Pacific that, when it was on a northeast track, didn't turn to the northwest once past the 19 degree parallel. "There is very little chance it will come to Oahu."

I wanted to believe him. Nobody likes messing with a typhoon. But something in the back of my mind told me to be cautious with this one. I remembered my history and Adm. William F. Halsey's dilemma when the Third Fleet, under his command, got caught in a typhoon in 1944 that cost the lives of 790 people and three ships. On December 17, 1944, the ships of Task Force 38, seven fleet and six light carriers, eight battleships, fifteen cruisers, and about fifty destroyers were operating about three hundred miles east of Luzon in the Philippine Sea. The carriers had just completed three days of heavy raids against Japanese airfields, suppressing enemy aircraft during the American amphibious operations against Mindoro in the Philippines.

Although the sea had been becoming rougher all day, the nearby cyclonic disturbance gave relatively little warning of its approach. On December 18th, the small but violent typhoon overtook the task force while many of the ships were attempting to refuel. Many of the ships were caught near the center of the storm and buffeted by extreme seas and hurricane-force winds. Three destroyers, USS *Hull*, USS *Spence*, and USS *Monaghan*, capsized and went down with practically all hands, while a cruiser, five aircraft carriers, and three destroyers suffered serious damage.

Approximately 740 officers and men were lost or killed, with another 80 injured. Fires occurred on three carriers when planes broke loose in their hangars, and some 146 planes on various ships were lost or damaged beyond economical repair by fires, by impact damage, or by being swept overboard. This storm inflicted more damage on the Navy than any storm since the hurricane at Apia, Samoa, in 1889. In the aftermath of this deadly storm, the Pacific Fleet established new weather stations in the Caroline Islands and, as they were secured, Manila, Iwo Jima, and Okinawa. In addition, new weather central offices (for coordinating data) were established at Guam and Leyte.

We began a succession of meetings to track the progress of the storm. In each of these, the meteorologist insisted there was nothing to fear. "Don't worry, Admiral," he said, "no sweat."

Finally, at another meeting with the staff as the typhoon kept on coming, I said, "If I order all the ships in Pearl Harbor to sortie and go to sea, it's going to take twenty-four hours. As you know, only one ship at a time can get through the mouth of the harbor. We would have ships queued up for some time. The aircraft can pull out much quicker. But my concern is the ships and the submarines."

I paused and let this sink in.

"Therefore," I said, "sortie the ships."

One officer said, "Admiral, you don't have to do that. The typhoon will turn away. It always has. Think of the impact on morale if we sortie the ships. For one thing you're going to have to recall people from liberty, and that won't set well."

I suppose it was kind of an inexplicable sixth sense, but in my heart and mind I had a notion this typhoon was going to be different, and nothing was going to change my mind.

"Sortie the ships," I ordered with a bit of a bite in my voice. "That's my decision."

The staff was not happy, and there followed a collective, though unenthusiastic, "Aye, aye, Sir." We sortied the ships.

As it turned out, the last ship passing the mouth of Pearl Harbor to escape the storm was the USS *Goldsborough* (DDG-20*)*. It was struck by a huge freak wave driven by the increasing force of the winds—prelude to the oncoming typhoon—and an officer on the bridge was slammed against a bulkhead and severely injured.

The typhoon roared directly over Pearl Harbor, tore off the roofs from buildings at Schofield Barracks, and battered downtown Honolulu. One hundred knot winds pulled huge trees from the ground throughout the area, and many houses on Ford Island were damaged. But all of our ships and aircraft were able to evade the devastating winds and turbulent seas, and none suffered any damage.

Tragically, the officer injured on the *Goldsborough* perished, even though a courageous helicopter crew and a very brave young doctor hurried out to the ship to help. The doctor, Lt. (later Capt.) John Wilkens, was lowered by cable to the ship in the increasingly strong winds and did his best to save the officer's life. I felt guilty about this tragedy. Had we sortied twelve hours earlier, the winds wouldn't have been that strong and the *Goldsborough* wouldn't have experienced that enormous wave.

At a subsequent staff meeting, there were sheepish expressions on the faces of the people. One of them asked, "Do you have some special powers we don't know about, Admiral?"

"I wish I did have," I responded, "but I don't. Frankly, I'd rather face the consequences of being wrong and sending the ships away unnecessarily than play it close to the chest and leave it to chance in a situation like this." Perhaps I should have proclaimed the importance of knowing history—meaning the Halsey episode—but I didn't feel it right to get into that.

Chapter Twenty-Seven

BUPERS

*Basically, on a day-to-day basis, we maintained a "slate" depicting jobs
that were coming open, who was appropriate and available to fill them,
who was retiring, who had been promoted, and so forth.
It was a relentlessly active and often complex operation.*

I WAS CAUGHT COMPLETELY OFF GUARD when I was ordered to command
the Bureau of Naval Personnel in Washington. I had no prior service in the
bureau, not that this was a criteria for the assignment, but it would be like
entering a new world for me. I had developed a reputation as a people-ori-
ented officer, but that did not necessarily translate to qualification for the top
job in the Navy dealing directly with those issues that affect personal lives.
Nevertheless, Adm. Jim Watkins, with the concurrence of Sec. John Lehman,
selected me for the job.

We moved back to Washington and to quarters located on Nebraska Avenue,
directly across from American University. My office was in the Arlington Annex
up a hill from the Pentagon, a distance of several long forward passes, and adjacent to the southeastern edge of Arlington National Cemetery.

I don't know any person, officer, enlisted, or civilian, who isn't concerned
about what kind of a job he or she is assigned, where they are to be geograph-
ically stationed, or what their chances for promotion are. In retrospect, I had
good luck with each set of orders I had received over the years. Yet, I had
talked to my detailer in the BUPERS only one time. I believed it important
that every young officer in the Navy hold no inhibition about getting on the
phone and communicating with his detailer. So, we set procedures in motion
to do this.

Obviously, I was putting a load on BUPERS personnel. The detailers already were on the phone a lot. This would increase their burden of
work, to be sure, but I tried to instill in our people the notion that it was an
integral part of their duties to talk personally to officers, especially the
younger ones.

My staff and I had barnstormed this concept. I was ably assisted in this critical endeavor by Captain Mike Boorda, my executive assistant. Boorda had been an enlisted man and ultimately became the first individual to rise from seaman all the way up through the ranks to the top office in the Navy as chief of naval operations. He had previous experience in the bureau before joining my staff, which was a huge bonus. Mike was smart as a whip, possessed a great deal of common sense, and had wonderful compassion for the troops.

Before World War II, the Navy was divided into a number of bureaus. The Bureau of Navigation, for example, was not only in charge of navigation matters, it also handled personnel issues and was actually the predecessor to the Bureau of Naval Personnel. Other bureaus included aeronautics, ordnance, engineering, construction and repair, supply and accounts, medicine and surgery, and yards and docks. After World War II, they were placed under the control of the CNO and the chief of naval personnel (CNP) with the Naval Academy falling under the CNP.

We decided to call ours a "never say no" policy. We promulgated this to our people and emphasized that when contacted by an individual, the first inclination in any discussion was to say "yes," meaning we'll do all we can to satisfy an individual's preferences for a duty assignment. We wanted everyone to prove to themselves they were totally justified in those cases where you had to say no to a request.

Admittedly, there was a lingering attitude among some detailers to the effect, "Why are you bothering me?" in response to incoming calls. That began to erode over time, fortunately.

Clearly, mine was a very demanding job. One responsibility increased the degree of difficulty dramatically compared to other duties. That was detailing all flag officers below the three-star rank. I worked with the CNO on the detailing of three-star officers but had to personally handle the one and two-stars, which numbered around five hundred individuals. There were laws to abide, so I had to be very familiar with them. Additionally, we had to be sure we understood each of the categories of officers in the restricted line: medical corps, supply corps, and so forth. Obviously, we relied heavily on inputs from the heads of these groups. The chief of the Medical Corps would have significant inputs for flag selection among his or her cadre of personnel. The unrestricted line was composed of the vast bulk of flag officers, and we were responsible for the management of their careers. This was an exceptionally time-consuming task.

Basically, on a day-to-day basis, we maintained a "slate" depicting jobs that were coming open, who was appropriate and available to fill them, who was retiring, who had been promoted, and so forth. It was a relentlessly active and often complex operation.

I met two or three days a week with the vice chief and the CNO to brief them on individuals and offer recommendations.

Unfortunately, our tasks were made more difficult because of the tendency of the secretary of Navy, John Lehman, to intervene not only in the detailing of certain officers but in the promotion process. Lehman, himself a naval flight officer in the reserves, was a forceful individual and a great advocate for naval aviation who became the head of the naval service in early 1981. Adm. Tom Hayward was CNO at the time, and the relationship between the two men was contentious. They hardly spoke to each other. Their respective executive assistants handled most of the communications between these two top offices. Hayward's successor was Adm. James D. Watkins, who took over in June 1982.

One of my responsibilities was running the promotion boards, which are composed of carefully selected individuals, led by a senior officer, designated the president of the board, who reviewed the records of candidates eligible for promotion and voted on which individuals would be advanced in rank. During the first flag board during my tour as CNP, it became apparent to me that the president of the board had received direction from Lehman to select Lehman's executive assistant for promotion to flag rank. This individual was a very bright officer with an outstanding record but had only been in the Navy nineteen years and been a captain for a comparatively brief period of time. I believed that others in line for promotion had more experience and were better qualified. The executive assistant was promoted.

In subsequent boards it became apparent that the secretary had his druthers. For example, if a board did not select enough naval flight officers, there was fear that the president of the board might be dressed down by Lehman or that the secretary might order the board back in session to reconsider the selections.

In one case the results of a board convened to select officers for promotion to the rank of captain did not please the secretary. However, the rear admiral who was the president of that board stood fast, and a testy situation developed that got the attention of the Senate Armed Services Committee.

I believed the secretary's actions were in violation of at least the spirit of the law. I talked to Admiral Watkins about this problem. He was very sympathetic to my feelings about this matter, but he was in a tough position. He believed we had to try do what we could to get along with the secretary.

Fortunately, Congress eventually passed a law specifically restricting the service secretaries from intervening in the case of promotion board actions. This was obviously prompted, in large part, by the actions of Secretary Lehman.

I attended meetings at the secretary's office but, in general, my dealings with him took the form of communications relayed from him to me via lower-echelon officers. In other words, I did not have a lot of face-to-face time with John Lehman.

There was one action he took that I thought was inexcusable. It had nothing to do with promotion boards. A press report revealed that ashtrays installed in E-2C Hawkeye aircraft at Naval Air Station Miramar in California cost over one hundred dollars each. Allegedly, someone in the supply department at Miramar reported this on the fraud, waste, and abuse hotline. The secretary became aware of the matter, which got some national attention. He called a press conference and announced that he was relieving the cognizant flag officer at Mirarmar, the commanding officer of the air station, and the supply officer.

It turned out, however, that these three men didn't deserve the blame. The basic price of the ashtrays had been set by the Navy supply system via agreement with the contractor. Lehman's actions were unjust. The affected officers never had a chance to present their side of the issue or to appeal the decision handed down by the secretary.

Chapter Twenty-Eight

MISSION COMPLETE

With these events, coupled with my inclination—some call it drive—to give 100 percent to the Navy, I had entered into the terrible danger zone of burnout.

IN FEBRUARY 1985 I FLEW TO PENSACOLA for my annual "ex-POW" physical. Those of us who had been incarcerated were part of a research program led by Capt. Bob Mitchell, a wonderful doctor who really worried about and took care of us with respect to what happened to our minds and bodies in prison. I'd been "BuPers" for two years at the time. I got high marks on my physical, and I felt really good despite the frustrations I was encountering in my job.

A month later, however, I started feeling ill. My energy was sapped, I had difficulty concentrating, and I was bewildered by what the cause was. I figured time would take care of it and pressed on with the multitude of my responsibilities.

This was the wrong decision. I got progressively worse. I made a huge mistake in not going back to Pensacola to see Doc Mitchell. I felt I could "gut this situation out." Months went by, my energy level never improved, and it became more and more difficult to concentrate. One thing driving me was that Adm. Jim Watkins, then CNO, told me I was to become the next vice CNO, the number two post in the Navy and a four-star assignment. Furthermore, he said I would be his first choice to succeed him as CNO.

I checked in at the National Naval Medical Center in Bethesda, Maryland, for evaluation. I stayed at Bethesda for two weeks and was described as in a state of depression, but no one could specifically identify the cause for this. I later learned that I had suffered what is call clinical depression and psycho motor shutdown. Admiral Watkins, the CNO, visited me several times at the hospital. I knew everyone was pulling for me to make a complete recovery. I also realized my recovery might take a long time. The CNO's executive assistant, my friend and former executive assistant Mike Boorda, kept track of how I was progressing via communications with my aide, Lt. (later Capt.)

Ray Donahue. It became apparent that a new chief of naval personnel was going to have to be brought in.

Admiral Watkins telephoned me at the hospital and explained that because of my medical condition and the pressing matters at hand, he really had no choice but to bring in a replacement for me. This was incredibly difficult for him to do because we had had such a great relationship and were solid friends who deeply respected each other. This decision was as devastating as it was necessary. I told the CNO that I understood completely and it was time for me to retire.

Diane was waiting in the hall outside my room at Bethesda with my aide, Ray Donahue. Both were obviously shaken by the event and did their very best to console me. Diane stayed with me for many hours before driving back to our home.

Exacerbating this reality was the supreme disappointment—and embarrassment—of not being able to do what the Navy wanted me to do. I believed I let down many who had supported me all these years, Adm. Tom Moorer in particular.

Rear Adm. David Harlow, commander Naval Personnel Command, ably held the fort at the Bureau of Personnel in my absence, with help from my deputy, Rear Adm. Larry Burkhart. My eventual relief was Vice Adm. Dudley Carlson.

I thus retired from the Navy in February 1986, and we settled into the home we had purchased while I was superintendent at the Naval Academy, a large, lovely, two-story house overlooking the Severn River in Crownsville, Maryland. Some remodeling was needed, so Diane and I sequestered ourselves in a couple of rooms upstairs, even doing some cooking in a bathroom, as the carpenters did their thing. The pressures of the job had dissipated, but in my morose condition, I was operating at no better than 50 percent efficiency. My loyal friend, Ross Perot, an American patriot of unparalleled devotion to our country and particularly to all POWs, took an intense interest in my well-being. He arranged and endowed a "Chair of Leadership and Ethics" at the Naval Academy, and I was installed to fill it. It primarily entailed giving lectures to members of the senior class on aspects of leadership and ethics. This was a godsend, because it gave me something to do and kept me close to the school that I loved. Frankly, I wasn't capable of doing much else.

I continued medical treatment, with mixed results. I thought I was getting better in the summer of 1988. But Ross felt I needed even more help and insisted I visit the Menninger Clinic in Topeka, Kansas, renowned as the top mental health facility in the country. It was not a short visit. I was there for nearly a year and seemed to get better. I developed better control of my mind, enough so that I tried to analyze what triggered the breakdown.

I recognized that my difficulties with John Lehman may have been a contributing factor to my illness. Conversely, frustrations are part of any job, at any level in the chain of command. I worked up a tabulation of the number of "days off" I had throughout my Navy career. There was a paucity of them. Of course in the POW camp there is no day off, and when I returned to the United States, I was fortunate to be assigned great jobs with challenging responsibilities that precluded taking much time off. Indeed, from the early 1960s to 1985, I don't think I took more than week or so leave, total. In retrospect, I considered what had happened to me—the incarceration, the divorce, having to take charge of the kids, and the Navy's generosity in putting me on the fast track toward great and challenging duty assignments that entailed favorable possibilities of promotion despite my six-year hiatus. With these events, coupled with my inclination—some call it drive—to give 100 percent to the Navy, I had entered into the terrible danger zone of burnout.

In retrospect, I accepted the fact that I always worked harder than was necessary, a costly deficiency.

My depression was more difficult to handle than those years in Hanoi. I was subject to various medications, some of which did more harm than good, but eventually my mental health improved. Still, no cause could be found for what ignited my illness, and I still wasn't up to full battery. Back home after the Menninger experience, I had a cyst cut off my tongue at the National Naval Medical Center in Bethesda, Maryland. Unfortunately, this led to a condition called subacute bacterial endocarditis, exacerbated by a lack of antibiotics. This led to intravenous antibiotic treatment at Bethesda for five long weeks, which didn't do my depression any good.

I thank God for Diane, who has stood by me with what she calls her "Pennsylvania girl toughness" through this whole ordeal. Her strength is amazing. Her patience endless. Which brings up a philosophical matter that in recent years has held special meaning for me. I've given many speeches and done considerable writing during my retirement. I've had numerous occasions to address midshipmen at the Academy. I believe love of country and love of God are critical. In those talks I also presented four components for happiness. The first is a proud, close-knit family. The second is solid friendships. The third is a good reputation fortified by self-esteem—and you can only acquire a good reputation and self-esteem by doing worthwhile things. The fourth is good health. Easily said, not so easily achieved. Please note; money didn't make the list.

I feel immensely lucky in that I have struggled against and defeated severe bitterness born of a divorce while in captivity and a professional career cut short as I was approaching its zenith. Had I remained sullen and angry over these setbacks, I would consider myself a loser. We live near my beloved alma mater and root for all of Navy's athletic teams, particularly the football squad, with a fervor as great now as when I played many years ago. I couldn't ask for better, more loving, and more accomplished children. Diane is at my side as the greatest partner anyone could hope for. I look back on my Navy experience with undying pride. And I am convinced I did the very best I could to serve my country.

EPILOGUE

By Diane Wilcox Lawrence

MY LOVE STORY WITH BILL LAWRENCE really began in the spring of 1973, when our Vietnam POWs returned home to their families. Some knew they had lost their wives and children because of divorce, remarriage, or alienation. Others did not know their marriages had ended until they were officially told the devastating news when they reached the Philippines, the first stop on the way home. Bill Lawrence was one of these men.

I volunteered my services as a physical therapist to help John McCain, a well-known returning POW, restore movement in his severely injured and essentially immobile knee, shattered during bailout of his aircraft when he was shot down over Hanoi. John was a wonderful, witty patient, who withstood unrelenting, aggressive treatment during two-hour sessions twice a week. We became close friends, even though John delighted in telling all who would listen that I was his "physical terrorist."

In May 1974 John took his physical exam in Pensacola, demonstrating to the flight surgeons that after nine months of rehab, his formerly frozen knee now had the mobility required for him to fly. He passed, and I cried.

A few months after repatriation, John and Bill received orders to the National War College in Washington, D.C. Although the two had been cellmates for a time in Hanoi, they became even closer friends while at the college. John knew about Bill's divorce and was hell-bent on becoming a matchmaker. He thought Bill and I would be perfect for each other.

"My physical therapist is just the lady," John told Bill.

To me he coaxed, "Hey, Honey, you've got to meet Bill Lawrence. What more could anyone want than intelligence and Boy Scout character?"

Because of professional commitments, both Bill and I resisted meeting. In addition to working at the National War College and pursuing a master's degree at George Washington University, Bill was traveling to Nashville every other weekend to supervise his children's school performance and to continue to reestablish his bond with them, which had been interrupted during his six years in captivity. My business partner and I were expanding our physical rehabilitation business in Northern Virginia.

Bill and I finally agreed to meet at an evening dinner party on December 19, 1973, at John and Carol McCain's home. Several other POWs and their wives were guests. Not a chatty guy, Bill expressed his thoughts intelligently and succinctly. I was impressed that whenever he did speak, his friends seemed to want to listen. In return, Bill showed a special kindness toward his comrades—most of them younger than he.

The evening went wonderfully, and as we walked to our cars during the heavy snowstorm, I demonstrated to this Tennessee boy some Yankee know-how by extricating his blocked car from a snowdrift. Romance and love blossomed and led to our marriage in August of that year in Lemoore, California. John McCain knew what he was doing. Bill and I *were* right for each other.

When, not by choice, my husband had to step down from duty in the naval service he loved for more than forty years, he nevertheless kept active. He was a part-time senior consultant for the Carlyle Group. He became president of the Association of Naval Aviation (ANA), and he served in that capacity from 1991 to 1994, boosting ANA's membership by persuading a large number of active-duty officers to join this organization. ANA (the title of the organization was changed in 2005 to the Naval Aviation Foundation) educates the public, Department of Defense, and Congress on the value and importance of Bill's beloved naval aviation.

In the mid-1990s, Bill and journalist Frank Aukofer wrote a well-received book titled *The Relationship between the Military and the Media.* Since the coauthors were a journalist and a military officer, they were dubbed "The Odd Couple." Frank later wrote, "Among other things, it recommended the embedding of reporters with military units which is practiced to this day."

Bill did a lot of work in support of the U.S. Naval Academy (USNA). For the USNA Alumni Association he traveled the country briefing alumni chapters on the status of affairs at the school. For four years he wrote "Capitol Hill," a column on congressional matters, for *Shipmate* magazine, the association's monthly publication. When Ross Perot established a "Leadership Chair" at the Academy, Bill became its principal lecturer for several years. He was an official with the National Football Foundation and College Hall of Fame, Inc., and also a consultant to the President's Council on Physical

Fitness and Sports. He served on the boards of directors of several corporations. The list could go on.

In 1995 Bill suffered a massive stroke as a result of heart surgery to replace a slightly leaking aortic valve. Paralyzed in his left arm and left leg, half of him was gone. One of his shipmates told me, "Fifty percent of Bill Lawrence is better than 100 percent of any other man I've ever known." Yet, even the medical staff gave little hope of survival. Bill's good friend Ross Perot even flew to the Naval Hospital in Bethesda to make sure his longtime friend was receiving all possible care.

Bill Lawrence's life hung in the balance, and we were advised to prepare for a funeral. Selfishly, I suppose, I asked myself, "What in the world will I do without Bill Lawrence?"

I began thinking about pallbearers, cremation, and the ultimate dark side of human existence. But after four weeks of tubes, monitors, and twenty-four-hour medical supervision, Bill, who had survived being a prisoner of war, didn't die. His strong spirit and body beat the incredible odds. Although in a wheelchair and enfeebled, he was allowed to return home, his left side still almost useless. Ironically, and thankfully, his speech and intelligence were fully intact. We no longer talked about a funeral.

We set up our large kitchen like a well-equipped rehab department. A trusted therapist and friend helped, and we put Bill through an intensive program of therapy six hours a day, seven days a week, for four months. Bill cooperated. "Just get me so I can walk again," he said, "and I'm not going to use a cane." Later he admitted, "A lot of it was exhausting and I hated doing it all day after day, but I knew I had to give it my best shot if I was going to get better." He never complained. He was a perfect patient.

Bill eventually became well enough to travel with a companion, and in his last years made a number of trips to functions that were dear to him, like the National Football Hall of Fame meetings in New York, the National Museum of Naval Aviation Symposia in Pensacola, Golden Eagles meetings, and Navy football and basketball games. Capt. Ed Wallace, executive director of the Naval Academy Foundation, told me, "We all know Bill Lawrence's blood runs blue and gold."

The writing of this autobiography was also a tonic. Putting his memoirs in order gave him a strong sense of accomplishment and satisfaction. It's amazing how, despite all his stroke-related travail, he continued to have vivid and accurate recall of all aspects and interests of his life. He was a walking repository of facts about history, political issues, presidencies, world geography, football scores and plays—all fixed indelibly in his mind.

Bill especially remained current on matters that had an impact on the Navy. He was a regular at Navy football and basketball games, attended professional symposia, sat in on biweekly lectures at the Naval Academy given by his friend and former chairman of the Joint Chiefs of Staff, Adm. William J. Crowe Jr., and participated in various Academy luncheons and dinners, particularly those related to athletics and professional ethics. Bill maintained contact with a multitude of friends and classmates. One, Pete Hill, wrote to our son, "There were few like him in industry—and fewer in government. He was a cut above the rest of us."

Noontime on December 2, 2005, his clothes laid out in preparation for the bus trip he would take to the Army-Navy football game the next day, Bill died in his bed. He had said only that he had a headache and just wanted to rest a bit.

His funeral at the U.S. Naval Academy chapel was held on December 14, the altar aglow with candles, two magnificent Christmas trees, and an abundance of glorious poinsettias. The Naval District Washington, D.C., Honor Guard carried Bill's ashes, contained in a polished wooden box, to the altar. Sixteen honorary pallbearers of family and close friends followed them. More than twenty-five hundred people came to honor Bill Lawrence, including twenty-five former Vietnam POWs, classmates, loyal friends, and bereaved family.

Capt. Alan Baker, senior chaplain at the Academy, gave the opening blessing and invocation. Then we stood to sing "A Mighty Fortress."

In respect, the guests stood as Ross Perot read a letter addressed to me from the president of the United States, and then Ross gave his own personal words of tribute to his beloved friend. Chaplain Baker spoke the prayer for comfort and illumination. Our children, nieces, and nephews read from scripture, and the Naval Academy Glee Club sang from the antiphonal choir loft "There Is a Balm in Gilead" and the Welch hymn, "God Who Mad'st Earth and Heaven."

Bill's physicians, as well as former POW Capt. Edwin A. "Ned" Shuman III, USN (Ret.), and Adm. Michael G. Mullen, the current chief of naval operations, gave words of tribute and remembrance. Then, up to the lectern marched Mrs. Lipscomb Davis, Bill's ninety-three-year-old fourth grade teacher. She recited a poem Bill had written in her class and read from "Oh Tennessee, My Tennessee," composed by Bill while in solitary confinement in the Hanoi Hilton. This poem was designated the State Poem of Tennessee by Act of State Legislature in 1973, and it concludes with heart-wrenching words:

And o'er the world as I may roam,
No place exceeds my boyhood home.
And, oh how much I long to see
My Native land, my Tennessee.

The chaplain noted that at the end of World War II, the nation knew America needed more than superior military might and advanced military technology in order to thrive. "We needed men and women of exceptional character and uncommon integrity. Bill Lawrence had those qualities in abundance; they were the cornerstones of his life and his performance as a military leader."

"Admiral Lawrence," he went on, "never retired, he never turned away from teaching through his words, and more importantly, he lived the most vital principle of leadership: Be first a person of honor."

The Honorable John S. McCain remembered with faltering voice Bill's leadership as a fellow POW. "We witnessed a thousand acts of courage, compassion, and love, and the best of us was Billy Lawrence. He seemed to know that some of us weren't as strong as he was, particularly when times were tough. He inspired us to do things we weren't capable of doing, to go one more round with our captors, and he always led us with love."

On a bitter winter day we buried Bill on a gentle slope overlooking his beloved school. His journalist-friend, Frank Aukofer, wrote of the event: "On the hillside the throng prayed with the academy chaplain, listened to the mournful playing of Taps, heard the crack of honor guard rifles, and trembled to the crashes of a 15-gun cannon salute. Four Navy warplanes roared overhead in missing-man formation as tribute to a fallen warrior."

Dr. Seuss wrote, "Don't cry because it's over. Smile because it happened." Now that I've lost Bill Lawrence after thirty-one years of marriage, those words are difficult for me to accept, but I know there's value in the message. It will never be over between my husband and me. Our fair share of the golden years may have ended earlier than for many, but at least we had them. I am privileged to have shared the life of this treasured American patriot and undeniably wonderful man.

May 2006

INDEX

McNamara, Robert, 90, 93, 96–97
Medal of Honor winners among POWs, 132
Med Moor, 62
Mehl, Jim, 119
Menninger Clinic, 210–11
Mercury program, 59
Middle East: command authority in, 90, 97; travels in, as aid to Gen. Adams, 94
Midway, 35
Miller, Ed, 127–28
Miller, Jerry, 89
Miller, Joe, 93
Miller, Rip, 8–9
Minter, Charles, 186
Miramar Naval Air Station, 70, 98–99, 101
Missouri, 13
Mitchell, Bob, 209
Mitchell, John, 37, 39, 45–46
Mobutu, Sese Seko, 94
Moffett Field, 31
Monaghan, 203
Moore, Bill, 134
Moorer, Joe, 60
Moorer, Tom: Adams' Strike Command and, 94–95, 97; career of, 60; character of, 105; and flag lieutenant duty, 60–61, 63–68; and POW career paths, 164; support from, 91, 210
Mount Fujiyama, 39–41
Mullen, Michael G., 216
Mulligan, Jim, 131

Nam Dinh, bomb run on, 104, 109–10
Nance, Bud, 85
Napoleon, 6
NASA (National Aeronautics and Space Administration), astronaut search, 59–60
Nashville, childhood in, 1–7
National Aeronautics and Space Administration. *See* NASA
national defense, political unity and, 171

National Football Foundation, 214
National Museum of Naval Aviation, 215
National War College, 163–64, 211
NATO (North Atlantic Treaty Organization): exercises, 64, 79; Standing Group meeting, 61
NATOPs. *See* Naval Air Training and Operating Procedures program
Naval Academy: and active-duty obligation, 189–91; appointment to, 8–9; attrition rate, 191; aviation courses, 15; Chair of Leadership and Ethics, 210, 214; cheating at, 16–18; curriculum, 10, 16, 194; decision to attend, 5–6, 8; drinking at, 194; family service center at, 179–80; first-classmen liberties, 12, 19; food at, 11; Honor Concept established at, viii, 17–22; midshipman days at, viii, 9–23; plebe year, 9–10, 173; post-retirement involvement with, 214, 216; racial attitudes at, 193; social activities at, 11–13; sports at, 11–12 (*See also* Navy football); summer "temporary-duty" assignments, 13, 22; Wendy Lawrence at, 170, 173–74, 178, 188. *See also* superintendent of Naval Academy; women at Naval Academy
Naval Air Training and Operating Procedures (NATOPs) program, 75
naval aviation: Association of Naval Aviation, 214; attraction to, 13; and Cold War, 65; departure from, 72; hazards of, 31, 70, 75; Naval Academy courses in, 15; and paper work, 86; return to, 79, 81; in VF-14, 81–90; in VF-101, 69–72, 81, 86; in VF-193, 31–46; in Vietnam War, 99–110; wing-pinning ceremony, 29. *See also* flight training; test pilot duty
Naval Aviation Foundation. *See* Association of Naval Aviation

ABOUT THE AUTHOR

VICE ADMIRAL WILLIAM P. LAWRENCE excelled in the classroom and on the athletic fields of his native Tennessee, and at the United States Naval Academy. He became an outstanding naval aviator, a test pilot, a squadron commander, and an esteemed leader. He was shot down and captured during the Vietnam War and was credited by fellow POWs for his unwavering bravery and leadership in the prison camp during six years of incarceration. After repatriation, he picked up the pieces of his life and put them together in a way that demonstrated his tireless will to overcome obstacles and to succeed in his beloved U.S. Navy.

Admiral Lawrence rose to flag rank, was Superintendent of the Naval Academy, commanded the Third Fleet, and was on the threshold of achieving four-star rank when illness forced his retirement after thirty-seven years in uniform. In the succeeding years he wrote extensively, held a chair at the Naval Academy, fought the miseries of a stroke and various other maladies, but endured—largely through the love of his wife, Diane, his own driving will to live, and the support of his intimate friend, fellow midshipman, and supreme patriot, H. Ross Perot. Admiral Lawrence passed away in December 2005.

ROSARIO RAUSA, a retired U.S. Navy captain and naval aviator, is the editor of *Wings of Gold* magazine, the voice of the Naval Aviation Foundation. He has written or coauthored seven nonfiction books on aviation subjects.

THE NAVAL INSTITUTE PRESS is the book-publishing arm of the U.S. Naval Institute, a private, nonprofit, membership society for sea service professionals and others who share an interest in naval and maritime affairs. Established in 1873 at the U.S. Naval Academy in Annapolis, Maryland, where its offices remain today, the Naval Institute has members worldwide.

Members of the Naval Institute support the education programs of the society and receive the influential monthly magazine *Proceedings* and discounts on fine nautical prints and on ship and aircraft photos. They also have access to the transcripts of the Institute's Oral History Program and get discounted admission to any of the Institute-sponsored seminars offered around the country. Discounts are also available to the colorful bimonthly magazine *Naval History*.

The Naval Institute's book-publishing program, begun in 1898 with basic guides to naval practices, has broadened its scope to include books of more general interest. Now the Naval Institute Press publishes about seventy titles each year, ranging from how-to books on boating and navigation to battle histories, biographies, ship and aircraft guides, and novels. Institute members receive significant discounts on the Press's more than eight hundred books in print.

Full-time students are eligible for special half-price membership rates. Life memberships are also available.

For a free catalog describing Naval Institute Press books currently available, and for further information about subscribing to *Naval History* magazine or about joining the U.S. Naval Institute, please write to:

Member Services
U.S. Naval Institute
291 Wood Road
Annapolis, MD 21402-5034
Telephone: (800) 233-8764
Fax: (410) 571-1703
Web address: www.navalinstitute.org